Mastering MCP Servers

The Ultimate Guide to Building Context-Aware AI Systems with Model Context Protocol

Written By

Camila Jones

Copyright

Mastering MCP Servers: The Ultimate Guide to Building Context-Aware AI Systems with Model Context Protocol

© 2025 Camila Jones

Table of Content

Introduction

1.1 What is Model Context Protocol (MCP)?

1.1.1 Overview of MCP and Its Relevance to AI

The **Model Context Protocol (MCP)** is an open standard that defines how AI models and external tools (databases, APIs, file systems, etc.) communicate in a structured, reliable way. Rather than embedding custom integration logic inside each AI application, MCP provides:

- **Decoupling**
  Separates the AI "brain" from the data-access tools, so each can evolve independently.
- **Consistency**
  Enforces a uniform request/response format (using JSON-RPC 2.0), reducing errors and simplifying debugging.
- **Reusability**
  Lets you register and reuse the same tool implementations across multiple AI projects.
- **Scalability**
  Standardizes integration patterns, making it easier to scale your system horizontally or swap out services without rewriting AI code.

Why Context Matters in AI

Traditional AI pipelines focus solely on model inference: "given text X, produce output Y." But many real-world applications require **context**—additional information that the model didn't see during training:

- **User history** (past interactions, preferences)
- **External data** (real-time stock prices, sensor readings, customer records)
- **System state** (current workflow step, authenticated user roles)

Without a clear protocol for fetching and updating this context, systems become brittle—ad hoc API calls are scattered throughout your code, and each change risks breaking multiple integrations.

How MCP Works

At its core, MCP sits between your AI model and your external services:

pgsql

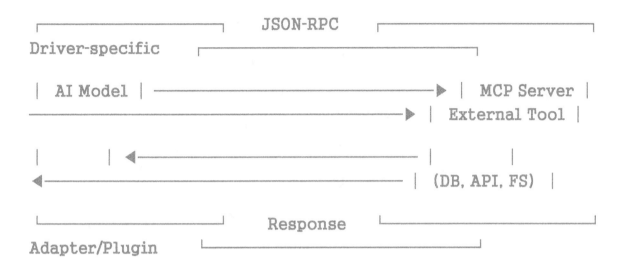

1. **AI Model** issues a standardized MCP "tool call" (JSON-RPC request) asking for data or action.
2. **MCP Server** routes that call to the appropriate adapter or plugin.
3. **External Tool** executes the operation (e.g., database query, HTTP request) and returns results.
4. **MCP Server** packages the result into a JSON-RPC response and passes it back to the AI Model.

Real-World Example

Customer Support Chatbot
A chatbot needs to fetch a user's order history:

1. **Without MCP:**
   - The bot's code directly calls the e-commerce API, handles authentication, parses responses, and formats the data—all inside its own logic.
   - If the API changes, every bot implementation must be updated.

2. **With MCP:**
   - The chatbot sends an MCP tool call named getOrderHistory(userId).
   - The MCP server has a single ecommerce_api_adapter plugin that knows how to talk to the shop's REST API.
   - Any chatbot (or other AI agent) using MCP can call getOrderHistory without reimplementing authentication or parsing logic.

Key Benefits of MCP for AI Systems

Benefit	Description
Modularity	AI logic and data-access tools live in separate, replaceable components.
Reliability	Uniform error handling and retries managed by MCP, not ad hoc code paths.
Maintainability	Updates to external integrations happen in one place (the adapter/plugin).
Collaboration	Teams can independently build AI models and tool adapters in parallel.
Future-proofing	As new data sources or services emerge, you only add a new MCP adapter.

By providing this **standardized bridge** between AI models and the external world, MCP makes it dramatically easier to build, maintain, and scale **context-aware AI systems**—and sets the foundation for all the practical, hands-on implementations you'll explore in the chapters ahead.

1.1.2 History and Evolution of the Protocol

The Model Context Protocol (MCP) emerged from a growing need in the AI community to standardize how models interact with external services. Its evolution can be traced through several key milestones:

Origins and Early Motivations

- **Pre-2022**: AI applications hard-coded integrations to databases, REST APIs, and other tools. This led to fragmented codebases, duplicated logic, and brittle systems.
- **Early 2022**: As "function calling" features appeared in major LLM APIs, developers began to see the value of a unified integration layer. Community discussions started around using JSON-RPC 2.0 as a common messaging format.

Version 1: Formal Specification (August 2022)

- A working group of AI practitioners published the first MCP v1 draft on GitHub.
- Defined core concepts: tool registrations, standardized JSON-RPC requests/responses, and error schemas.
- Early adopters built adapter prototypes for simple data sources (SQL, filesystem, HTTP).

Version 1.1: Plugin Patterns (December 2022)

- Introduced the notion of "capability plugins" to encapsulate authentication, retries, and data parsing.
- Documented best practices for registering multiple adapters on a single server.
- Sparked the first third-party implementations in LangChain and custom internal frameworks.

Version 2: Dynamic Loading & Streaming (March 2023)

- Added support for dynamic capability discovery: clients could query available tools at runtime.
- Introduced streaming responses for long-running or chunked data (e.g., real-time sensor feeds).
- Standardized rate-limiting headers and back-off signaling in the protocol.

Version 2.1: Security and Extensibility (February 2024)

- Enhanced authentication schemes, including OAuth2 flows and API key rotation.
- Defined extension points for custom error codes and metadata fields.
- Improved schema validation using JSON Schema drafts.

Version 3: Manifest Introspection & Versioning (June 2024)

- Introduced tool manifests: self-describing JSON documents listing method names, parameter types, and usage examples.
- Added a formal versioning scheme, allowing clients and servers to negotiate protocol versions.
- Aligned MCP more closely with emerging open standards in AI tool integration.

Wider Adoption and Ecosystem Growth

- **Late 2023–2024**: Frameworks like n8n, CrewAI, and Flowise built first-class MCP support, embedding adapter libraries and out-of-the-box templates.
- **Early 2025**: MCP became the de facto standard for AI workflows in many enterprises, driving plug-and-play pipelines that can swap out data sources without code changes.

Timeline of Key MCP Releases

Date	Version	Highlights
Apr 2022	–	Community discussions around unifying AI tool integrations
Aug 2022	v1.0	First formal MCP spec: JSON-RPC 2.0, tool calls, error formats
Dec 2022	v1.1	Plugin/adapter patterns, registration best practices
Mar 2023	v2.0	Dynamic capability discovery, streaming support

| Feb 2024 | v2.1 | Advanced security (OAuth2, key rotation), extensibility points |
| Jun 2024 | v3.0 | Tool manifests, protocol versioning, introspection |

By tracing MCP's history, you can see how each iteration addressed real-world challenges—moving from ad hoc integrations toward a robust, extensible standard that underpins modern context-aware AI systems. This evolution ensures that MCP remains aligned with both developer needs and broader industry trends.

1.1.3 How MCP Fits into the AI Development Landscape

As AI systems grow more sophisticated, they increasingly rely on external data sources, microservices, and dynamic workflows. The **Model Context Protocol (MCP)** occupies a unique position in this evolving ecosystem, serving as a **standardized bridge** between AI models and the tools they invoke.

Key Trends in AI Development

- **Ad Hoc Integrations**
  Early AI projects embedded API calls and database queries directly in model code, leading to tangled logic and maintenance headaches.
- **LLM Function Calling**
  Modern LLMs (e.g., GPT-4's function-call support) introduced structured calls but remain tied to a specific model provider's interface.
- **Retrieval-Augmented Generation (RAG)**
  RAG pipelines fetch external documents at inference time, yet each retrieval mechanism is often custom-built.
- **Microservices & Orchestration**
  Enterprises adopt microservice architectures and orchestration frameworks (e.g., Kubernetes, Airflow), but AI-to-service communication still lacks a unified protocol.

Where MCP Sits

MCP unifies and extends these trends by offering:

- **Protocol-Level Standardization**
  A vendor-agnostic, JSON-RPC–based format that any AI model or agent can use.
- **Dynamic Tool Discovery**
  Clients can query available capabilities at runtime, enabling truly plug-and-play workflows.
- **Context Management**
  Built-in support for carrying state (user data, session variables, streaming inputs) across multiple tool calls.
- **Separation of Concerns**
  AI logic focuses on "what" to do, while MCP adapters handle "how" to do it.

Comparative Overview

Aspect	Traditional API	LLM Function Calling	MCP
Standardization	None, ad hoc	Vendor-specific	Universal JSON-RPC–based protocol
Tool Discovery	Hard-coded	Static (at model definition)	Dynamic (runtime introspection)
Context Handling	Manual state management	Limited to function inputs	Native support for session and streaming context
Reusability	Low (duplicated code)	Medium (model-specific)	High (cross-project adapters)
Scalability	Difficult	Improved by LLM providers	Optimized for distributed, load-balanced setups

Practical Implications

1. **Rapid Prototyping**
   Experiment with new AI agents by swapping MCP adapters (e.g., from a test database to production APIs) without touching model code.
2. **Production-Ready Workflows**
   Leverage dynamic discovery and rate-limiting to manage hundreds of tool calls per second in a resilient, monitored MCP server.
3. **Cross-Team Collaboration**
   Model developers, backend engineers, and DevOps teams work in parallel: AI teams define tool interfaces, while ops teams build and secure adapters.

By fitting neatly between **model inference** and **service orchestration**, MCP transforms how AI applications are **designed**, **built**, and **maintained**, enabling a **modular, future-proof** approach to context-aware AI development.

1.2 The Importance of Context-Aware AI Systems

1.2.1 What Makes AI "Context-Aware"?

An AI system is **context-aware** when it can sense, interpret, and adapt its behavior based on information beyond the immediate input. Rather than treating each request in isolation, a context-aware AI incorporates additional data—such as user history, environmental factors, or system state—to produce more relevant, personalized, and accurate outputs.

Key Elements of Context-Aware AI

1. Context Sensing
   - The ability to collect or receive external data (e.g., user profiles, sensor readings, time of day).
   - May involve explicit data retrieval (API calls, database queries) or implicit signals (session variables, device metadata).
2. Context Representation
   - Standardized formats (JSON objects, vectors, metadata fields) that describe the contextual information.
   - Ensures the AI model and downstream components interpret context consistently.
3. Context Processing

- Logic or model layers that incorporate context into decision-making (e.g., concatenating context vectors with prompts, rule-based adjustments).
- Often implemented via middleware (such as an MCP server) that manages context separately from core inference code.
4. Adaptive Response
   - Outputs that dynamically change based on context (e.g., personalized recommendations, location-aware instructions, or session-specific dialogues).
   - May include proactive behaviors, such as anticipating user needs or caching likely data requests.

Types of Context

Context Type	Description	Example
User History	Past interactions or preferences	Previous purchases, saved settings
Environmental	Physical or temporal conditions	Geolocation, local time, weather data
System State	Internal application status	Current workflow step, authentication token
Real-Time Data	Live streams or sensor inputs	Stock prices, IoT sensor readings

Why Context Matters

- **Relevance**: By factoring in user history or environmental data, AI can tailor its responses—reducing irrelevant or generic outputs.
- **Continuity**: Systems that "remember" prior steps (session context) avoid redundant questions and create smoother user experiences.
- **Accuracy**: Incorporating up-to-date external data (e.g., live sensor feeds) helps models make more informed decisions.

- **Efficiency**: Proactively fetching or caching context can reduce latency and API usage by anticipating likely data needs.

Practical Illustration

A customer support agent using context-awareness will:

1. Retrieve the user's past orders (user history) via an MCP tool call.
2. Check the current support ticket status (system state).
3. Incorporate real-time system metrics (API response times) to decide whether to escalate.
4. Personalize the conversation flow based on the customer's region and language (environmental context).

Without context-awareness, each of these steps would require ad hoc code within the model logic. By treating context as a first-class concern—managed by a protocol like MCP—developers create modular, maintainable, and scalable AI systems that truly understand "where," "when," and "for whom" they're operating.

1.2.2 Real-World Examples of Context-Aware Systems

In practice, context-aware AI systems power many of today's intelligent applications. Below are several industry-leading implementations that illustrate how context boosts relevance, efficiency, and user satisfaction.

Customer Support Chatbots

- **Context Used**: User profile, past interactions, current ticket status
- **Behavior**:
  - Automatically fetches a customer's order history and open tickets.
  - Adapts the conversation flow (e.g., skipping verification steps for returning users).
  - Proactively suggests solutions based on similar past issues.
- **Benefit**: Reduced resolution time and fewer hand-offs to human agents.

Smart Home Automation

- **Context Used**: Time of day, occupancy sensors, weather forecast

- **Behavior:**
  - Adjusts lighting and thermostat settings when the homeowner returns.
  - Closes windows or retracts shades if rain is imminent.
  - Arms security systems only when the house is unoccupied.
- **Benefit:** Improved energy efficiency, comfort, and safety.

Healthcare Monitoring Systems

- **Context Used:** Patient vitals (heart rate, blood pressure), medication schedule, activity levels
- **Behavior:**
  - Triggers alerts when readings deviate from personalized baselines.
  - Reminds patients to take medication if a dose is missed.
  - Escalates critical events (e.g., abnormal ECG) to medical staff in real time.
- **Benefit:** Early detection of health issues and better adherence to treatment plans.

Autonomous Vehicles

- **Context Used:** GPS location, traffic data, weather conditions, sensor inputs (LIDAR, cameras)
- **Behavior:**
  - Dynamically adjusts speed and route based on congestion and road closures.
  - Modifies braking distance in rain or fog.
  - Selects parking maneuvers according to curbside availability.
- **Benefit:** Safer navigation and optimized travel times.

Context-Aware Retail & E-Commerce

- **Context Used:** Browsing history, real-time inventory, location
- **Behavior:**
  - Recommends products in stock at the nearest store or warehouse.
  - Sends push notifications about nearby in-store promotions.
  - Personalizes homepage banners based on seasonal or local trends.
- **Benefit:** Higher conversion rates and more relevant promotions.

Industrial IoT & Predictive Maintenance

- **Context Used:** Machine vibration, temperature, operating hours, environmental factors
- **Behavior:**

- Predicts equipment failures by comparing live sensor data to historical norms.
- Schedules maintenance tasks during low-production windows.
- Issues safety warnings if thresholds are exceeded.
- **Benefit**: Reduced downtime and lower maintenance costs.

Each of these systems relies on a **structured approach** to gathering, representing, and processing context—exactly the capabilities that MCP standardizes. In the following chapters, you'll learn how to build similarly powerful, context-aware applications by leveraging MCP servers to manage state, fetch external data, and coordinate dynamic workflows.

1.2.3 The Role of MCP in Enhancing AI Capabilities

The Model Context Protocol (MCP) acts as a **catalyst** that elevates AI systems from isolated inference engines to fully integrated, adaptive solutions. By standardizing how models request and consume contextual information, MCP enables several key enhancements:

1. Rich, Dynamic Context Feeding
   - **On-Demand Data Retrieval**: Models can fetch the precise data they need—user profiles, live metrics, or workflow state—only when they need it.
   - **Streaming & Updates**: Long-running tasks (e.g., monitoring a sensor feed) receive incremental data updates, allowing AI to react in real time.
2. Separation of Concerns
   - **AI Logic vs. Tool Logic**: Core inference code remains focused on "what" to compute; MCP adapters handle "how" to connect, authenticate, and parse external services.
   - **Cleaner Codebases**: Less tangled integration code translates to fewer bugs and faster feature development.
3. Modularity & Reusability
   - **Shared Adapters**: Once you build an MCP adapter for, say, a CRM API, every model or agent in your organization can reuse it without duplication.
   - **Plug-and-Play Workflows**: Swap data sources or enrichers by pointing MCP at a new adapter—no AI-side rewrites required.
4. Reliability & Resilience
   - **Uniform Error Handling**: MCP's JSON-RPC layer standardizes retries, timeouts, and error codes, so models can gracefully handle failures.
   - **Rate Limiting & Throttling**: Built-in support for usage quotas protects both your AI and downstream services from overload.

5. Scalability & Performance
   - **Load Distribution**: Horizontal scaling of MCP servers behind a load balancer allows hundreds of concurrent tool calls without saturating any single instance.
   - **Caching & Batching**: MCP can cache frequent requests or batch multiple calls into a single external API request, reducing latency.
6. Collaborative Development
   - **Clear Contracts**: Tool manifests define method signatures, parameter types, and return schemas—AI engineers and backend teams can work in parallel.
   - **Version Negotiation**: Clients and servers agree on protocol versions at runtime, enabling safe upgrades and backward compatibility.

Example: Enhancing a Personalization Engine

Without MCP	With MCP
Personalization logic embeds raw HTTP calls to each API.	Model issues getUserPreferences(userId) via MCP; adapter handles HTTP.
Each service change requires AI-code edits.	Service updates only touch the MCP adapter—models remain untouched.
Error handling scattered throughout model code.	MCP standardizes retries and propagates meaningful JSON-RPC errors.
No built-in rate limiting; services get overwhelmed.	MCP adapter enforces per-user and global rate limits before calling API.

By providing this **robust integration layer**, MCP amplifies the practical power of AI models—making them more context-aware, maintainable, and enterprise-ready. In the coming chapters, you'll see how these enhancements translate into hands-on solutions for real-world AI challenges.

1.3 The Purpose and Scope of This Book

1.3.1 What You Will Learn in This Book

In this book, you'll gain both a **deep theoretical understanding** and **hands-on practical skills** to design, build, deploy, and maintain context-aware AI systems using the Model Context Protocol (MCP). By the end, you will be able to:

1. Master MCP Fundamentals
   - Grasp the core architecture of MCP servers and clients
   - Write and interpret JSON-RPC 2.0 requests and responses
   - Understand how MCP decouples AI logic from integration code
2. Set Up and Configure Production-Grade MCP Servers
   - Prepare development environments on local machines and cloud platforms
   - Implement basic and advanced server configurations (scalability, load balancing, fault tolerance)
   - Secure your servers with authentication, rate-limiting, and encryption
3. Build Context-Aware AI Workflows
   - Define, capture, and represent contextual information (user history, system state, real-time data)
   - Integrate context into model prompts and decision logic
   - Manage session state and streaming updates via MCP
4. Integrate with External Systems and Data Sources
   - Connect to SQL/NoSQL databases and file systems
   - Consume REST, GraphQL, and WebSocket APIs through standardized MCP adapters
   - Extend MCP to IoT devices, sensors, and custom data pipelines
5. Develop Advanced MCP Server Capabilities
   - Create and register dynamic capability plugins for custom tools
   - Handle streaming data and event-driven architectures
   - Implement best-practice security, error handling, and performance optimizations
6. Troubleshoot, Debug, and Optimize
   - Diagnose common MCP server errors and JSON-RPC issues
   - Leverage logging, monitoring, and load testing to benchmark performance
   - Apply caching and batching strategies to reduce latency and resource usage
7. Apply Real-World Case Studies
   - Design an MCP-powered healthcare monitoring system

- o Build context-aware robotics integrations for autonomous control
- o Deploy a smart-city data orchestration platform connecting IoT, APIs, and AI

8. Scale and Deploy in Production
   - o Containerize MCP servers with Docker and Docker Compose
   - o Implement CI/CD pipelines for automated testing and rollout
   - o Configure horizontal scaling and high-availability clusters on AWS, GCP, or Azure

9. Adopt Best Practices for Maintenance and Security
   - o Establish monitoring, health checks, and automated alerts
   - o Manage protocol versioning, backward compatibility, and migrations
   - o Enforce security hardening and compliance in enterprise environments

10. Look Ahead to Future Trends
    - o Explore emerging standards and extensions in MCP and AI tool integration
    - o Learn how to contribute new adapters, plugins, and protocol improvements
    - o Identify resources and communities for continuous learning and collaboration

Throughout each chapter, you'll encounter **interactive Q&A prompts** to reinforce your learning and **industry-specific discussion points** that tie concepts to real challenges in healthcare, robotics, finance, and smart infrastructure. A companion GitHub repository provides all code samples, templates, and project starters so you can immediately apply what you learn and adapt it to your own AI initiatives.

1.3.2 Target Audience and Prerequisites

Target Audience
This book is designed for technical professionals who build, integrate, and operate AI systems that rely on external data and services. In particular, it will benefit:

- **AI Developers & ML Engineers**
  Those writing model-driving code (e.g., prompt engineering, inference pipelines) who need a reliable way to fetch and update context at runtime.
- **Backend & Integration Engineers**
  Developers responsible for building APIs, microservices, and adapters that expose data to AI applications.
- **System Architects & DevOps Professionals**
  Engineers who design scalable, fault-tolerant AI infrastructure and deployment pipelines.

- **Automation & Workflow Engineers**
  Practitioners automating business processes with AI agents and orchestrated tool chains.

Even if you're new to MCP, as long as you fall into one of these roles and need to bridge AI models and external systems, this book will guide you from fundamentals to production-ready implementations.

Prerequisites

To get the most out of this book, you should have:

1. Programming Skills
   - Proficiency in **Python 3** (writing functions, handling exceptions, managing virtual environments).
   - Comfort with reading and writing **JSON** data structures.
2. Web & API Basics
   - Experience calling and consuming **RESTful APIs** (GET, POST, authentication headers).
   - Familiarity with **HTTP** concepts (status codes, headers, query parameters).
3. Command-Line & DevOps Fundamentals
   - Basic Linux/macOS command-line usage (navigating directories, running scripts).
   - Understanding of containerization (e.g., **Docker**) and simple CI/CD workflows.
4. AI/ML Concepts
   - A working knowledge of **large language models (LLMs)** or AI inference frameworks.
   - Awareness of common AI patterns (prompting, retrieval-augmented generation).
5. Optional—but Helpful
   - Prior exposure to **JSON-RPC 2.0** or other RPC mechanisms (you'll learn the MCP specifics here).
   - Experience with a microservices framework (e.g., Flask, FastAPI, Express) for quick adapter development.

With these skills and tools in place, you'll be ready to follow the code examples, set up MCP servers, and integrate them into real-world AI workflows with confidence.

1.3.3 How to Approach This Book for Maximum Benefit

To get the most out of **Mastering MCP Servers**, follow these guidelines as you work through each chapter:

1. **Read Sequentially, But Leverage Modularity**
   The chapters are arranged to build your knowledge progressively—from fundamentals to advanced topics—so it's best to read them in order on your first pass. However, once you've grasped the basics (Chapters 1–3), you can jump directly to specific areas (e.g., troubleshooting in Chapter 6 or deployment in Chapter 8) as your projects demand.

2. **Engage with Interactive Q&A Prompts**
   At the end of each section you'll find **Discussion Points** and **Review Questions**. Pause to answer these in writing or in conversation with peers. They're designed to reinforce key concepts and spark ideas about applying MCP in your own environment.

3. **Run, Modify, and Experiment with Code Samples**
   Every code snippet in this book is meant to be **runnable**. Clone the companion GitHub repository, execute the examples locally, and then tweak parameters or adapters to see how different configurations behave. Hands-on experimentation will solidify your understanding far more than passive reading.

4. **Complete the End-of-Chapter Projects**
   Each chapter ends with a **mini-project** or **case study exercise**. Treat these as real assignments: set aside uninterrupted time, follow the instructions step by step, and verify your results. If you run into issues, refer back to the troubleshooting tips in Chapter 6.

5. **Use the Companion Resources**
   In addition to code samples, the GitHub repo includes Docker files, CI/CD templates, and environment-setup scripts. Bookmark the MCP Quick Reference (Appendix A) and JSON-RPC Cheat Sheet (Appendix B) for fast lookup. These resources are updated regularly, so pull the latest changes before you begin each chapter.

6. **Apply to Your Own Projects Immediately**
   As you learn new patterns—whether it's dynamic capability loading (Chapter 5) or streaming data handling—identify a small slice of your own workflow where you can implement that pattern. Real-world application accelerates retention and uncovers nuances that purely contrived examples can't reveal.

7. **Engage with the Community**
   Join the MCP discussion forum or GitHub Issues for questions, feature requests, and community-contributed adapters. Sharing your experiences and reading others' solutions will expose you to best practices and innovative uses you might not discover on your own.

By combining **step-by-step reading**, **active experimentation**, and **community engagement**, you'll transform the concepts in this book into practical skills—enabling you to design, deploy, and maintain robust, context-aware AI systems powered by MCP.

1.4 Interactive Q&A

1.4.1 Discussion Points to Explore After Reading This Chapter

1. Assessing Context Needs in Your Projects
   - Which types of context (user history, system state, real-time data) are most critical for your current AI workflows?
   - How would adding that context improve model accuracy or user experience?
2. Evaluating Integration Challenges
   - In your existing applications, where do you see brittle or duplicated integration code?
   - What pain points might MCP solve by centralizing those integrations?
3. Comparing Protocol Approaches
   - How does JSON-RPC (as used by MCP) differ from REST, gRPC, or direct SDK calls in terms of flexibility, performance, and standardization?
   - In what scenarios might an alternative protocol be preferable?
4. Organizational Impact of Decoupling
   - What changes would your team need to make to separate AI logic from data-access logic?
   - How might roles and responsibilities shift between AI developers and backend engineers?
5. Designing for Future Growth
   - Which parts of your AI stack are likely to change in the next 6–12 months (e.g., new data sources, third-party services)?
   - How would adopting MCP today prepare you for those changes?
6. Security and Governance Considerations
   - What authentication and authorization mechanisms does your organization require for tool access?
   - How could MCP's standardized error and rate-limit handling help enforce governance policies?
7. Measuring Success
   - What metrics or KPIs would you track to evaluate the impact of moving to an MCP-based architecture (e.g., development speed, error rates, scalability)?
   - How would you benchmark before and after MCP adoption?
8. Community and Ecosystem Engagement

- What existing MCP adapters or plugins could you leverage, and where might you need to build custom implementations?
- How can you contribute back to the MCP community (e.g., open-source adapters, best practices)?

Reflect on these points individually or discuss them with your team to deepen your understanding of MCP's role and to identify practical next steps for integrating context-aware capabilities into your AI systems.

1.4.2 Key Takeaways and Review Questions

Key Takeaways

- **MCP Defined**: MCP is a JSON-RPC–based protocol that decouples AI inference logic from data-access tools, enabling modular, maintainable integrations.
- **Protocol Evolution**: Since its v1 launch in August 2022, MCP has matured through plugin patterns, streaming support, security enhancements, and manifest versioning to become a robust standard.
- **AI Landscape Fit**: MCP sits between model inference and service orchestration, unifying ad hoc API calls, LLM function-calling, and RAG pipelines under a vendor-agnostic interface.
- **Context-Aware AI**: Context—user history, system state, real-time data—is essential for relevance, continuity, and accuracy; MCP streamlines context sensing, representation, and processing.
- **Book Structure & Usage**: Read the book sequentially for foundational concepts, use interactive Q&As and end-of-chapter projects to reinforce learning, and apply examples immediately in your own workflows.

Review Questions

1. **Define MCP.** What problem does it solve in AI system integrations?
2. **List three core benefits** that MCP provides over traditional, ad hoc API calls.
3. **Explain JSON-RPC's role** in MCP. How does it standardize communication?
4. **Describe "context-aware" AI.** What types of context can an AI system use?
5. **Give two real-world examples** of context-aware systems and identify the context types they leverage.
6. **Compare MCP to LLM function calling.** What capabilities does MCP add beyond static function definitions?
7. **Identify the prerequisites** needed before working through this book's examples.

8. **Outline your personal approach** plan: how will you engage with the interactive Q&As and hands-on exercises to maximize your learning?

Chapter 1: Fundamentals of MCP

1.1 The Architecture of MCP

1.1.1 Core Components of MCP Servers and Clients

An MCP system separates **AI clients** (models or agents) from **MCP servers** (the integration layer), enabling each to evolve independently. The primary components are:

MCP Client

- **Role:** Issues tool calls to request data or actions from external services.
- Key Responsibilities:
    - Construct JSON-RPC 2.0 requests with a unique id, method name, and a params object containing both a context block (session IDs, user metadata, timestamps) and an args block (tool-specific inputs).
    - Handle responses by matching on id, processing the returned result or reacting to standardized errorobjects.
    - Integrate returned data into model prompts or downstream logic.

MCP Server

- **Role:** Acts as the central broker, receiving client requests and routing them to the appropriate adapter.
- Key Responsibilities:
    - **Request Routing:** Inspect each request's method field and dispatch to the matching adapter/plugin.
    - **Error Handling & Retries:** Enforce timeouts, retry policies, and surface uniform JSON-RPC error codes.
    - **Rate-Limiting:** Throttle per-client or per-method traffic to protect downstream services.
    - **Manifest Exposure:** Serve a tool registry (manifest) so clients can discover available methods and parameter schemas at runtime.

Adapter / Plugin

- **Role:** Encapsulates the logic for a specific external resource (database, API, file system, etc.).
- Key Responsibilities:

- Translate MCP calls into driver-specific operations (e.g., SQL queries or HTTP requests).
- Manage authentication and authorization flows (API keys, OAuth2).
- Parse and normalize external responses into the JSON structure expected by MCP (result or error).

Tool Manifest (Registry)

- **Role:** A self-describing list of supported methods, their parameter schemas, and return types.
- Key Responsibilities:
  - Enable clients to dynamically call listMethods and retrieve method definitions.
  - Provide method names, argument types, descriptions, and example payloads.
  - Support versioning to allow clients and servers to negotiate compatible protocol versions.

JSON-RPC Transport Layer

- **Role:** Defines the standardized envelope for all MCP communication.
- Key Features:
  - **Uniform Envelope:** Fields jsonrpc, id, method, params; responses use result or error.
  - **Notifications:** Support "fire-and-forget" calls without an id.
  - **Batching:** Group multiple requests into a single array to optimize throughput.

Component	Responsibility
Client	Issues JSON-RPC requests; integrates returned result or error into AI logic
Server	Routes requests, enforces retries/limits, exposes the tool manifest
Adapter	Implements the actual external call (DB, API, file I/O), handles auth & parsing

Tool Manifest	Describes available methods, parameters, return schemas
JSON-RPC Layer	Standardizes messaging format, supports notifications & batch calls

By clearly delineating these components, MCP ensures that **AI clients** stay focused on inference and decision logic while **MCP servers** and **adapters** manage all aspects of external integration—resulting in a modular, maintainable, and scalable architecture.

1.1.2 The MCP Message Flow and Data Structure

MCP relies on a **JSON-RPC 2.0**-based request–response pattern. This section breaks down the end-to-end flow, the structure of each message, and best practices for defining your payloads.

1.1.2.1 End-to-End Message Flow

plaintext

```
AI Client          MCP Server          Adapter          External Service
_____  _____
_____  _____

   |                   |                   |                        |

   | —— JSON-RPC Request ———————————▶ |                        |
   |

   |  {                |                   |                        |

   |    "jsonrpc":"2.0",    |              |                        |

   |    "id": 1,       |                   |                        |
```

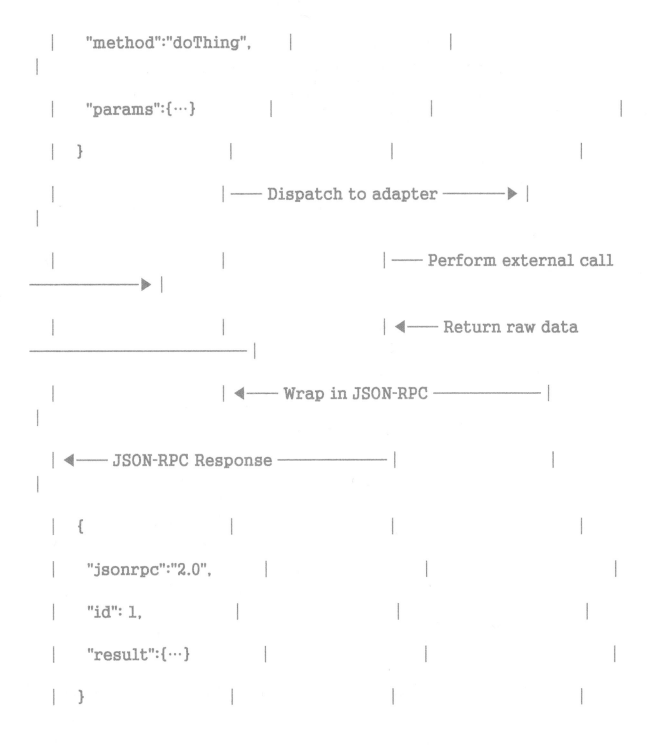

```
|     "method":"doThing",     |                    |
|                                                  |
|     "params":{...}          |                    |                 |
|   }                 |                 |                    |
|                 | —— Dispatch to adapter ——▶ |
|                                                  |
|                 |                 |  —— Perform external call
—————————▶ |                 |                    |
|                 |                 |  ◀—— Return raw data
——————————————— |                 |                    |
|                 | ◀—— Wrap in JSON-RPC ——————— |
|                                                  |
| ◀—— JSON-RPC Response ——————— |                 |
|                                                  |
|   {                 |                 |                    |
|     "jsonrpc":"2.0",        |                    |                 |
|     "id": 1,            |                 |                    |
|     "result":{...}          |                 |                 |
|   }                 |                 |                    |
```

1. **Client → Server**: AI client sends a JSON-RPC **request** (with id, method, params).
2. **Server → Adapter**: MCP server routes by method to the correct adapter.
3. **Adapter → Service**: Adapter executes the external operation (DB query, HTTP request, file read).

4. **Service → Adapter:** Service returns raw data.
5. **Adapter → Server:** Adapter returns data in MCP's expected JSON structure.
6. **Server → Client:** MCP server wraps it in a JSON-RPC **response** with the same id.

1.1.2.2 JSON-RPC Request Structure

Field	Type	Description
jsonrpc	string	Protocol version, always "2.0".
id	number/string	Unique identifier for correlating request and response.
method	string	Name of the tool or action (e.g., "fetchData").
params	object	Encapsulates both context metadata and method arguments:
└── context	object	Metadata such as sessionId, userId, timestamp.
└── args	object	Tool-specific parameters (e.g., { "recordId": 123 }).

<details> <summary><strong>Example Request</strong></summary>

json

{

```
  "jsonrpc": "2.0",

  "id": 42,

  "method": "getOrderDetails",

  "params": {

   "context": {

    "sessionId": "abc123",

    "userId": "user789",

    "timestamp": "2025-04-17T11:00:00Z"

   },

   "args": {

    "orderId": 5678

   }

  }

}
```

</details>

1.1.2.3 JSON-RPC Response Structure

Field	Type	Description
jsonrpc	string	Protocol version, always "2.0".
id	number/string	Matches the request's id.

result	object	Present on success, contains method-specific output.
or		
error	object	Present on failure, with code, message, data.

<details> <summary>Example Success Response</summary>

json

```json
{
  "jsonrpc": "2.0",
  "id": 42,
  "result": {
    "order": {
      "id": 5678,
      "status": "shipped",
      "items": [ ... ]
    }
  }
}
```

</details> <details> <summary>Example Error Response</summary>

json

```json
{

  "jsonrpc": "2.0",

  "id": 42,

  "error": {

    "code": -32001,

    "message": "Order not found",

    "data": { "orderId": 5678 }

  }

}
```

</details>

1.1.2.4 Notifications & Batch Calls

Notifications (no id): Fire-and-forget operations (e.g., logging).
json

```json
{

  "jsonrpc": "2.0",

  "method": "logEvent",

  "params": {

    "context": { "sessionId": "abc123" },
```

```json
    "args": { "level": "info", "message": "User login" }

  }

}
```

Batch Calls: Send an array of requests/notifications to reduce latency.
json

```json
[

  { "jsonrpc":"2.0","id":1,"method":"a","params":{...} },

  { "jsonrpc":"2.0","id":2,"method":"b","params":{...} }

]
```

1.1.2.5 Best Practices for Data Structure

1. **Minimal Context**: Include only essential metadata (sessionId, userId, timestamp).
2. **Schema Definitions**: Declare parameter/result schemas in your manifest so clients validate before sending.
3. **Clear Error Codes**: Reserve -32000 to -32099 for server errors; use distinct values for authentication, validation, and rate limits.
4. **Streaming Support**: For long tasks, use notifications or partial responses in sequence.
5. **Payload Size Management**: Avoid embedding large blobs; instead, store and fetch via reference (e.g., object key or URL).

By following this structured flow and payload design, MCP ensures **predictable**, **debuggable**, and **extensible**communication between AI clients and external systems.

1.1.3 How MCP Facilitates Seamless Communication Between AI Tools and External Systems

MCP provides a **uniform integration layer** that abstracts away the complexities of connecting AI clients to diverse external services. It achieves this through several core mechanisms:

1. Standardized Messaging via JSON-RPC

- Every tool invocation uses the same JSON-RPC envelope (jsonrpc, id, method, params), ensuring clients and servers "speak" a common language.
- Clients don't need custom serializers or parsing logic—any MCP-compliant server understands the same format.

2. Adapter Abstraction Layer
- **Adapters** encapsulate service-specific details (authentication, API quirks, data parsing).
- AI code simply calls invokeTool("methodName", params), and the adapter handles the actual HTTP, SQL, or file I/O operations.
- When a service changes, only its adapter needs updating—AI clients remain untouched.

3. Dynamic Tool Discovery
- Clients can call a built-in listMethods endpoint to retrieve the server's **tool manifest** at runtime.
- New tools become immediately available without redeploying clients, enabling plug-and-play extensibility.

4. Context Propagation
- Each request carries a context block (e.g., sessionId, userId, timestamp) that adapters use for logging, authorization, or custom logic.
- Consistent context handling lets AI workflows maintain state across multiple calls without bespoke session management.

5. Uniform Error Handling and Retries
- MCP defines standard error codes and messages, so clients can implement generic retry, fallback, or escalation strategies.
- Servers centralize timeout and back-off policies, preventing every integration from reinventing error logic.

6. Built-In Rate Limiting and Throttling
- Servers enforce per-method or per-client quotas before dispatching to adapters, safeguarding downstream services.
- Clients receive explicit "Rate limit exceeded" errors and can adjust their invocation patterns accordingly.

7. Batching and Streaming Support
- **Batch Calls** let clients group multiple requests into one payload, reducing network overhead.
- **Notifications** and **partial responses** support streaming or fire-and-forget use cases, such as telemetry or event logging.

Example Flow

plaintext

```
AI Client              MCP Server            CRM Adapter              CRM
Service

_____                    _____
_____                    _____

    |                      |                    |                        |

    |— invokeTool("getProfile", params) —▶ |                        |
    |

    |                      |— dispatch to "getProfile" ———▶ |
    |

    |                      |                    |— HTTP GET
/profiles/{userId} ——▶ |

    |                      |                    | ◀—— { ...profile data }
————————— |

    |                      | ◀— wrap in JSON-RPC response ——— |
    |

    | ◀— receive standard response ————— |                        |
    |
```

Benefits at a Glance

Feature	Impact
Protocol Uniformity	Eliminates custom integration code; simplifies client implementations.

Adapter Abstraction	Localizes service-specific logic; eases maintenance.
Dynamic Discovery	Enables runtime extensibility without client changes.
Context Propagation	Maintains state across calls; supports multi-turn workflows.
Error & Retry Semantics	Standardizes failure handling; improves resilience.
Rate Limiting	Protects downstream systems; enforces organizational policies.
Batching & Streaming	Optimizes performance for bulk and real-time data flows.

By combining these mechanisms, MCP turns a fragmented set of point-to-point integrations into a **cohesive, extensible ecosystem**, letting AI tools focus on inference while the protocol manages all aspects of communication and orchestration.

1.2 JSON-RPC 2.0 Integration

1.2.1 Understanding JSON-RPC and Its Role in MCP

JSON-RPC 2.0 is a minimal, transport-agnostic Remote Procedure Call protocol that uses JSON as its data format. MCP builds on JSON-RPC to provide a **uniform**, **extensible**, and **lightweight** mechanism for AI clients to invoke external tools.

Key Features of JSON-RPC 2.0

1. Standardized Envelope

Every message—request, response, notification—shares the same structure:
json

{

```
"jsonrpc": "2.0",

"id": 1,          // omitted for notifications

"method": "toolName",  // for requests

"params": { ... }      // arguments and context

}
```

- Responses mirror the request id and include either a result or an error block.
2. Notifications & Batch Calls
   - **Notifications** (no id) allow fire-and-forget operations (e.g., logging).
   - **Batch calls** pack multiple requests into one array, reducing round-trips.
3. Error Objects
   - Standard fields (code, message, optional data) let servers convey precise failure reasons and clients handle retries or fallbacks generically.
4. Versioning
   - The jsonrpc field (always "2.0") ensures clients and servers agree on the protocol version.

Why MCP Chooses JSON-RPC

Criterion	Benefit for MCP
Uniformity	All tool calls share the same format—clients need only one parser.
Extensibility	MCP can add a context sub-object without altering the core spec.
Lightweight	Minimal overhead ideal for high-throughput AI workflows.
Transport-Agnostic	Works over HTTP, WebSocket, or any message bus.

Role in the MCP Workflow

1. Client Side
   - AI code packages each tool call into a JSON-RPC request, embedding both context (session IDs, auth tokens, timestamps) and args (method parameters).
2. Server Side
   - The MCP server parses the JSON envelope, validates the jsonrpc version, and routes the call based on method.
3. Adapter Layer
   - Adapters receive the raw params, perform the external operation (database query, HTTP call, file read), then wrap the response or any error into the JSON-RPC format.
4. Back to Client
   - The AI client matches responses by id, handles the result data or processes standardized error objects, and continues its inference or workflow.

Example Request & Response

Request

json

```
{

 "jsonrpc": "2.0",

 "id": 101,

 "method": "getUserPreferences",

 "params": {

  "context": {

   "sessionId": "abc123",

   "userId": "user789",
```

```json
    "timestamp": "2025-04-17T11:00:00Z"
  },
  "args": {
    "language": "en"
  }
}
}
```

Success Response

json

```json
{
  "jsonrpc": "2.0",
  "id": 101,
  "result": {
    "preferences": { "theme": "dark", "notifications": true }
  }
}
```

Error Response

json

```json
{

  "jsonrpc": "2.0",

  "id": 101,

  "error": {

    "code": -32004,

    "message": "Preferences service unavailable",

    "data": { "retryAfter": 30 }

  }

}
```

By leveraging JSON-RPC 2.0, MCP ensures that **all tool interactions**—from simple data fetches to long-running, streamed operations—adhere to a **predictable, self-describing** format. This uniformity underpins MCP's ability to deliver **modular, maintainable**, and **scalable** context-aware AI systems.

1.2.2 Structuring Requests and Responses Using JSON-RPC

MCP uses JSON-RPC 2.0 envelopes to carry every tool call and response. Below is the recommended structure for **requests**, **responses**, **notifications**, and **batch calls**.

JSON-RPC Request Envelope

Each request must include the following top-level fields:

Field	Type	Description
jsonrpc	string	Protocol version, always "2.0".

id	number|string	Unique identifier to match the response; omit for notifications.
method	string	Name of the tool/action (e.g., "fetchUserProfile").
params	object	Contains two sub-objects:
└─ context	object	Metadata such as sessionId, userId, timestamp.
└─ args	object	Method-specific parameters (e.g., { "userId": "u123" }).

json

```json
{

  "jsonrpc": "2.0",

  "id": 7,

  "method": "fetchUserProfile",

  "params": {

    "context": {

      "sessionId": "xyz789",

      "userId": "u123",

      "timestamp": "2025-04-17T13:00:00Z"
```

```
    },
    "args": {
      "includePreferences": true
    }
  }
}
```

JSON-RPC Success Response

On success, the server returns the same id and a result object:

Field	Type	Description
jsonrpc	string	Always "2.0".
id	number|string	Matches the request's id.
result	object	Tool-specific output data.

json

```
{
  "jsonrpc": "2.0",
  "id": 7,
  "result": {
    "profile": {
```

```json
      "name": "Alice",

      "preferences": { "theme": "dark" }

    }

  }

}
```

JSON-RPC Error Response

If an error occurs, the response contains an error object instead of result:

Field	Type	Description
jsonrpc	string	Always "2.0".
id	number|null	Matches the request's id, or null if unrecognized.
error	object	Contains code, message, and optional data.

json

```json
{

  "jsonrpc": "2.0",

  "id": 7,

  "error": {

    "code": -32004,

    "message": "Profile service unavailable",
```

```
    "data": { "retryAfter": 30 }

  }

}
```

Notifications

For **fire-and-forget** operations (e.g., logging), omit the id field. No response is returned.

json

```
{

  "jsonrpc": "2.0",

  "method": "logEvent",

  "params": {

    "context": { "sessionId": "xyz789" },

    "args": { "level": "info", "message": "User logged in" }

  }

}
```

Batch Calls

Combine multiple requests into a single array to reduce round-trips:

json

```
[

  {

    "jsonrpc": "2.0",
```

```json
    "id": 8,

    "method": "getInventory",

    "params": { /* ... */ }

  },

  {

    "jsonrpc": "2.0",

    "id": 9,

    "method": "getPricing",

    "params": { /* ... */ }

  }

]
```

The server responds with an array of matching responses (order may vary):

json

```json
[

  { "jsonrpc": "2.0", "id": 9, "result": { /* ... */ } },

  { "jsonrpc": "2.0", "id": 8, "result": { /* ... */ } }

]
```

Best Practices

- **Unique IDs**: Use sequential or UUID-based id values to prevent collisions.
- **Schema Validation**: Declare parameter and result schemas in your manifest so clients can validate before sending.

- **Minimal Context**: Include only essential metadata in context to keep payloads lean.
- **Distinct Error Codes**: Reserve ranges (e.g., -32000 to -32099) for server errors; use custom codes sparingly.
- **Manage Payload Size**: Avoid embedding large data blobs; reference external storage when necessary.

By adhering to this structured approach, MCP ensures every interaction is **predictable**, **self-documented**, and **easy to debug**, building a solid foundation for scalable, context-aware AI integrations.

1.2.3 Error Handling and Debugging JSON-RPC Calls

Robust error handling and effective debugging are critical for maintaining reliable MCP integrations. This section covers the standard JSON-RPC error schema, best practices for handling errors in your client and server code, and techniques for tracing and diagnosing issues.

Standard JSON-RPC Error Object

Every error response uses a uniform structure:

Field	Type	Description
code	integer	Numeric error code. Standard range: • -32700–-32799: JSON-RPC parse/format errors • -32000–-32099: Server errors • -32029: Rate limit exceeded • Application-specific codes (>= 1000)

message	string	Human-readable description of the error.
data	object	Optional additional info (e.g. validation failures, retry hints).

<details><summary>Example Error Response</summary>

json

```json
{
  "jsonrpc": "2.0",
  "id": 13,
  "error": {
    "code": -32002,
    "message": "Database connection failed",
    "data": { "host": "db.prod.local", "retryAfter": 5 }
  }
}
```

</details>

Common Error Categories

Category	Code Range	Typical Causes

Parse Error	-32700	Malformed JSON in request.
Invalid Request	-32600	Missing required fields (method, params).
Method Not Found	-32601	Unknown method name.
Invalid Params	-32602	Parameter types or schemas do not match.
Internal Error	-32603	Unexpected server failure.
Server Error	-32000--32099	Adapter or downstream service errors.
Rate Limit Exceed	-32029	Client has exceeded configured request quotas.
Application Errors	1000+	Domain-specific issues (e.g., "Order not found").

Client-Side Error Handling Best Practices

1. Validate Before Sending
   - Use your tool manifest's JSON Schema to validate params locally.
   - Catch schema violations and raise client-side errors rather than sending bad requests.
2. Retry and Back-Off
   - For transient server errors (-32000--32019), implement exponential back-off with a capped retry count.
   - Honor retryAfter hints in the data field when provided.
3. Graceful Degradation

- Provide fallback behavior (e.g., cached data, partial functionality) when non-critical tool calls fail.
- Surface meaningful feedback to end users or downstream services.
4. Logging and Metrics
   - Log every request and response, including id, method, code, and message.
   - Emit metrics (error counts, latency, retry rates) to your observability system.

Server-Side Error Handling and Logging

1. Centralized Error Mapping
   - Map exceptions from adapters and downstream services to appropriate JSON-RPC codes.
   - Ensure that message is concise and data provides actionable details (e.g., stack trace in dev mode).
2. Request Validation
   - Reject malformed requests early with -32600 Invalid Request or -32602 Invalid Params.
   - Return detailed validation errors in the data field for developer insight.
3. Rate-Limiting and Throttling
   - Enforce per-client and per-method limits.
   - Return -32029 Rate limit exceeded with data.retryAfter set to the number of seconds until the next allowed request.
4. Structured Logging
   - Use structured logs (JSON format) including fields: requestId, method, code, durationMs.
   - Correlate logs with client-side id and sessionId for end-to-end tracing.

Debugging Techniques

1. Request/Response Tracing
   - Capture full JSON-RPC envelopes on both client and server.
   - Compare payloads to ensure id, method, and params align.
2. Enable Verbose Adapter Logs
   - In development mode, log HTTP requests, SQL statements, or file paths invoked by adapters.
   - Record upstream response codes and bodies before translation.
3. Step-Through Debugger
   - Attach a debugger to your MCP server process.
   - Set breakpoints in request routing and adapter invocation to inspect live data.

4. Simulate Edge Cases
    - Write unit tests that intentionally send invalid JSON, missing fields, or malformed params.
    - Verify that your server returns the correct JSON-RPC error code and message.
5. Monitoring and Alerts
    - Configure alerts for spikes in error-rate metrics or specific error codes (e.g., authentication failures).
    - Use dashboards to visualize trends and identify systemic issues early.

Sample Python Client Wrapper

python

```python
import requests, json


class MCPClientError(Exception):

  pass


class MCPClient:

  def __init__(self, endpoint):

    self.endpoint = endpoint

    self.next_id = 1


  def call(self, method, context, args):

    payload = {

      "jsonrpc": "2.0",

      "id": self.next_id,
```

```python
            "method": method,
            "params": {"context": context, "args": args}
        }
        self.next_id += 1

        resp = requests.post(self.endpoint, json=payload, timeout=5)
        data = resp.json()

        if "error" in data:
            err = data["error"]
            raise MCPClientError(f"{err['code']}: {err['message']} ({err.get('data')})")

        return data["result"]


# Usage example
client = MCPClient("http://localhost:8000/mcp")
try:
    result = client.call("getOrderDetails", {"sessionId": "s1"}, {"orderId": 123})
    print("Order:", result)
except MCPClientError as e:
    print("MCP Error:", e)
```

By following these guidelines and leveraging structured logging, retries, and detailed validation, you'll ensure your MCP-based systems handle errors gracefully and remain maintainable—even as integrations grow in complexity.

1.3 How MCP Enhances AI Tool Integration

1.3.1 Simplifying Integrations with Databases, File Systems, and APIs

MCP abstracts away the repetitive, error-prone work of wiring AI clients to external data sources. By encapsulating each integration behind a **uniform JSON-RPC "tool" interface**, you gain:

- **Consistency**: Every data source—whether it's a SQL database, a local file store, or a REST API—uses the same call pattern.
- **Reusability**: Write each adapter/plugin once and reuse it across multiple AI agents and projects.
- **Maintainability**: Changes to connection details, authentication, or query logic live in a single adapter, not scattered throughout your AI code.

A. Database Integrations

1. Adapter Responsibilities
   - Manage connection pooling and credentials (e.g., via environment variables or secrets vault).
   - Translate MCP tool calls into parameterized SQL (or ORM) queries.
   - Map result rows into JSON structures under result.

Client Call Example
json

```json
{

  "jsonrpc": "2.0",

  "id": 21,

  "method": "queryUserOrders",

  "params": {

   "context": { "sessionId": "sess42" },

   "args": { "userId": "u100", "limit": 10 }
```

```
}

}
```

Adapter Pseudocode
python

```python
def handle_queryUserOrders(params):

    conn = get_db_connection()

    rows = conn.execute(

        "SELECT * FROM orders WHERE user_id = %s ORDER BY created_at
        DESC LIMIT %s",

        (params["args"]["userId"], params["args"]["limit"])

    )

    return {"orders": [dict(r) for r in rows]}
```

B. File System Integrations

1. Adapter Responsibilities
   ○ Resolve and sanitize file paths.
   ○ Read/write in a controlled directory (prevent traversal attacks).
   ○ Stream large files in chunks via JSON-RPC notifications if needed.

Client Call Example
json

```json
{

  "jsonrpc": "2.0",

  "id": 22,

  "method": "readConfigFile",

  "params": {
```

      "context": { "sessionId": "sess42" },

      "args": { "path": "configs/app.yaml" }

  }

}

Adapter Pseudocode
python

```python
def handle_readConfigFile(params):

    base = Path("/safe/configs")

    target = (base / params["args"]["path"]).resolve()

    if not str(target).startswith(str(base)):

        raise MCPError(-32001, "Invalid file path")

    content = target.read_text()

    return {"content": content}
```

C. REST API Integrations

1. Adapter Responsibilities
    ○ Handle HTTP methods, headers, query strings, and body serialization.
    ○ Support OAuth2 or API-key authentication.
    ○ Parse JSON or XML responses and map them to MCP's result.

Client Call Example
json

{

  "jsonrpc": "2.0",

  "id": 23,

```json
  "method": "fetchWeather",

  "params": {

    "context": { "sessionId": "sess42" },

    "args": { "location": "London,UK" }

  }

}
```

Adapter Pseudocode
python

```python
def handle_fetchWeather(params):

    resp = requests.get(

        "https://api.weather.com/v3/wx/conditions/current",

        params={"apiKey": WEATHER_KEY, "format": "json", "language": "en-US", "location": params["args"]["location"]}

    )

    resp.raise_for_status()

    data = resp.json()

    return {"temperature": data["temperature"], "condition": data["narrative"]}
```

D. Best Practices Across All Adapters

Practice	Benefit
Validate args via schema	Catch errors before invoking external services

Centralize credentials	Simplify rotation and secure storage
Enforce timeouts & retries	Improve resilience against transient failures
Log requests & responses	Enable end-to-end tracing and auditing
Version your adapters	Safely roll out protocol or API changes

By defining each integration as an MCP "tool," you free your AI clients from low-level details and ensure a **scalable**, **secure**, and **consistent** approach to consuming any external data source.

1.3.2 Use Cases in AI Systems and Automation Pipelines

MCP's standardized "tool" abstraction unlocks a wide range of real-world scenarios where AI agents and automation pipelines need reliable, context-aware integrations. Below are several representative use cases.

1.3.2.1 Intelligent Chatbot Context Management

Scenario: A customer-support chatbot that must fetch user profiles, order histories, and live ticket statuses to personalize each interaction.
MCP Role:

- The chatbot issues JSON-RPC calls like getUserProfile(userId) and getOpenTickets(userId) via MCP.
- Adapters handle authentication and API calls to the CRM, returning structured data without bloating the bot's code.
  Example Request:

json

```
{

"jsonrpc":"2.0","id":101,"method":"getOpenTickets",
```

```
"params":{

  "context":{"sessionId":"s1","userId":"u123"},

  "args":{}

 }

}
```

1.3.2.2 Retrieval-Augmented Generation (RAG) Pipelines

Scenario: An LLM-based document assistant that retrieves relevant passages from a knowledge base before answering user queries.
MCP Role:

- The model calls searchDocuments(query, topK) through MCP.
- The RAG adapter queries Elasticsearch (or a vector DB), formats the top hits, and returns them for prompt enrichment.
  Benefit: Decouples your LLM orchestration code from search-engine specifics, letting you swap engines without rewriting search logic.

1.3.2.3 Multi-Agent Automation Workflows

Scenario: An orchestrated workflow where one AI agent gathers sales figures, another analyzes trends, and a third generates a summary report.
MCP Role:

- Each agent uses MCP to call shared tools—getSalesData(period) and generateReport(data).
- The MCP server ensures consistent context (e.g., period, authentication tokens) flows between steps.
  Advantage: You can add or reorder agents without touching adapter logic, since each agent simply invokes standardized tool methods.

1.3.2.4 IoT and Real-Time Monitoring

Scenario: A predictive-maintenance system that streams sensor readings from factory equipment and triggers alerts when anomalies appear.
MCP Role:

- Use JSON-RPC **notifications** (streamSensorData(sensorId)) for continuous data feeds.
- An anomaly-detection adapter processes each reading and, upon detecting issues, invokes sendAlert(machineId, details).
  Benefit: Handles high-velocity data smoothly by separating streaming logic in adapters from core model processing.

1.3.2.5 Batch Data Processing & Orchestration

Scenario: Nightly ETL jobs that extract records from multiple databases, transform them, and load them into a data warehouse.
MCP Role:

- Scripts issue **batch calls** (arrays of JSON-RPC requests) such as extractTable(tableName) for each source.
- The MCP server dispatches in parallel, collects results, and feeds them into transformation agents.
  Outcome: Simplifies your scheduling code—just package multiple tool calls into one batch request and let MCP handle parallelism and error aggregation.

These use cases demonstrate how MCP turns diverse integration challenges into consistent, maintainable workflows. By defining each external interaction as a "tool" call, you keep your AI logic clean and focused, while adapters encapsulate all the complexity of connecting to databases, APIs, file systems, or streaming services.

1.3.3 MCP's Role in Creating a Universal Framework for Tool Integrations

MCP establishes a **consistent, extensible foundation** that all AI clients and external tools can share—transforming a patchwork of bespoke integrations into a cohesive ecosystem. Its universality stems from several key design principles:

1. Single Invocation Pattern
   o **Uniform Tool Calls**: Every integration—be it a database query, an HTTP API request, or a file operation—is invoked using the same JSON-RPC envelope (method, params, id).
   o **Centralized Client API**: AI clients need implement only one call interface (e.g., invokeTool(name, params)), regardless of the underlying service type.
2. Self-Describing Manifests
   o **Tool Registry**: The MCP server exposes a manifest listing every available method, its parameter schema, and return types.

- ○ **Runtime Discovery**: Clients can query listMethods() dynamically, making it trivial to add, remove, or update tools without client redeployment.
3. Adapter Plug-Ins
   - ○ **Encapsulated Logic**: Service-specific details (authentication, data serialization, retries) live entirely within adapters, not scattered across AI code.
   - ○ **Reusable Libraries**: Adapters become shareable modules that any project in the organization can drop into its MCP server.
4. Protocol-Driven Extensibility
   - ○ **Context Block**: A reserved context object carries metadata (session, user, timestamp) uniformly to every tool, enabling cross-cutting concerns (audit logging, RBAC).
   - ○ **Error and Rate-Limit Semantics**: Standard JSON-RPC error codes and built-in throttling ensure consistent handling of failures and capacity constraints across all integrations.
5. Transport Agnosticism
   - ○ **Any Transport Layer**: MCP's reliance on JSON-RPC makes it compatible with HTTP, WebSocket, message queues, or gRPC tunnels—allowing teams to choose the best infrastructure without changing tool definitions.

Principle	Benefit
Single Invocation Pattern	Simplifies client code; one interface for all tools
Self-Describing Manifests	Enables runtime discovery; decouples clients from server updates
Adapter Plug-Ins	Localizes complexity; fosters reuse and consistency
Protocol-Driven Extensibility	Standardizes context, errors, and routing across every integration

| Transport Agnosticism | Allows flexible deployment architectures without protocol changes |

By codifying these principles into a **universal framework**, MCP frees AI developers from writing—and constantly maintaining—custom integration glue code. Instead, they focus on core inference logic, while the MCP ecosystem handles discovery, routing, security, and error management in a uniform, scalable manner. This universality is what makes MCP a powerful backbone for **any** tool integration in context-aware AI systems.

1.4 Interactive Q&A

1.4.1 Review Questions to Test Comprehension of MCP Fundamentals

1. Core Components
   - What are the primary roles of the MCP **client**, **server**, and **adapter/plugin** in the MCP architecture?
2. Message Flow
   - Describe the six steps of the end-to-end MCP message flow, from the client's JSON-RPC request to the final response.
3. JSON-RPC Envelope
   - What top-level fields must appear in every JSON-RPC 2.0 request? What fields differentiate success responses from error responses?
4. Context Block
   - Why does MCP include a context sub-object in each request? Name three examples of context metadata you might carry.
5. Tool Manifest
   - What information does the MCP tool manifest expose, and how do clients use it at runtime?
6. Adapter Abstraction
   - How do adapters simplify integrations with databases, file systems, or REST APIs? Give one concrete example.
7. Error Handling
   - What JSON-RPC error code ranges are reserved for server errors, and how can clients use the optional data field in error responses?
8. Batching & Notifications
   - How do MCP batch calls improve throughput? When would you use a "notification" instead of a standard request?
9. Rate Limiting

- Which component enforces rate limits, and what standard JSON-RPC error code indicates a quota has been exceeded?

10. Separation of Concerns
    - In what ways does MCP decouple AI inference logic from integration logic, and why is this separation beneficial for maintainability and scalability?

1.4.2 Discussion Points on How MCP Can Be Applied to Various Industries

1. Healthcare & Telemedicine
   - How could MCP manage patient context (medical history, real-time vitals) across multiple tools (EHR, monitoring devices, decision-support models)?
   - What adapters would you build for common healthcare systems (HL7, FHIR, PACS), and how would you secure PHI in transit?

2. Finance & Trading
   - In algorithmic trading, how might MCP fetch live market data, risk metrics, and portfolio positions to feed into an AI strategy engine?
   - Which rate-limiting or retry policies are critical when connecting to high-stakes financial APIs?

3. Retail & E-Commerce
   - How can MCP integrate customer profiles, inventory systems, and recommendation engines to deliver personalized shopping experiences?
   - What challenges arise when coordinating context (cart contents, geolocation, loyalty tiers) across web, mobile, and in-store channels?

4. Manufacturing & Industry 4.0
   - How would you use MCP to orchestrate data from PLCs, SCADA systems, and predictive-maintenance ML models?
   - What streaming patterns (notifications vs. batch calls) suit high-frequency sensor feeds on the factory floor?

5. Automotive & Autonomous Vehicles
   - In a self-driving car, how could MCP handle context from GPS, LIDAR/camera sensors, and traffic-management services?
   - How would you design adapters to ensure low-latency responses and fail-safe behavior under network disruptions?

6. Smart Cities & Infrastructure
   - Which tools (traffic cameras, utility meters, weather APIs) would you expose via MCP to power adaptive traffic control or energy-management agents?

- How do you ensure secure, multi-tenant context separation across different city services?

7. Robotics & Automation
   - For a multi-robot coordination system, how could MCP standardize commands (navigation, manipulation) and state reports (battery levels, sensor readings)?
   - What patterns support real-time streaming of telemetry while still allowing high-level task orchestration?

8. Media & Entertainment
   - How might MCP fetch dynamic content (news feeds, social-media trends, user preferences) to drive an AI-powered content recommendation engine?
   - What adapter strategies help manage rate-limits and batching when aggregating from multiple public APIs?

9. Education & EdTech
   - In adaptive learning platforms, how could MCP integrate student profiles, curriculum content, and real-time assessment models?
   - How would you handle sensitive context (grades, behavioral data) and ensure compliance with privacy regulations (e.g., FERPA, GDPR)?

Reflect on these points to identify industry-specific tools, context requirements, and adapter designs that will make MCP a powerful enabler of context-aware AI in your domain.

Chapter 2: Setting Up and Configuring MCP Servers

2.1 Preparing the Development Environment

2.1.1 Software Requirements: Tools, Frameworks, and Dependencies

Before building your first MCP server, ensure you have the following software stack in place. This section covers the essential tools, frameworks, and libraries needed for a robust development environment.

1. Operating System & Command-Line Tools

- **Supported Platforms**: Linux (Ubuntu, Debian), macOS; Windows (WSL recommended)
- **Shell & Utilities**:
  - bash or zsh for scripting
  - git for version control
  - curl or httpie for testing HTTP/JSON-RPC endpoints

2. Language Runtime & Package Management

- Python 3.8+
  - MCP examples and adapters are written in Python—ensure you're on 3.8 or newer for full async/awaitsupport.
- Virtual Environments
  - **venv** (built-in): python -m venv venv
  - Or **pipenv** / **poetry** for dependency and environment management
- Package Installer
  - pip (upgrade to latest: pip install --upgrade pip setuptools)

3. Web Framework & ASGI/WSGI Server

- **FastAPI** (recommended)
  - Lightweight, async-friendly, automatic OpenAPI generation
  - Install: pip install fastapi
- **Uvicorn** (ASGI server)
  - High-performance server for FastAPI
  - Install: pip install uvicorn[standard]
- *Alternative*: **Flask** + **gunicorn** for WSGI-based setups

4. JSON-RPC Library

- **jsonrpcserver / jsonrpcs / aio-jsonrpc**
  - ○ Parses and validates JSON-RPC 2.0 requests/responses
  - ○ Example: pip install jsonrpcserver jsonrpcclient
- *Or* implement a minimal handler yourself using built-in json module and FastAPI's request body parsing

5. HTTP Client & Utilities

- **httpx** (async HTTP requests)
  - ○ Install: pip install httpx
- *Or* **requests** for synchronous calls: pip install requests
- **python-dotenv** for loading .env configuration files: pip install python-dotenv

6. **Database & Cache Drivers (Optional)**
Depending on your adapters, you may need one or more of:

- **psycopg2** or **asyncpg** for PostgreSQL
- **pymysql** or **aiomysql** for MySQL
- **motor** for MongoDB
- **redis / aioredis** for caching and pub/sub
- **sqlalchemy** (ORM) for unified database access

7. Logging, Monitoring & Metrics

- **structlog** or built-in logging module for structured logs:
  - ○ pip install structlog
- **Prometheus client** for instrumenting metrics (optional):
  - ○ pip install prometheus-client

8. Containerization & Orchestration

- **Docker** & **Docker Compose**
  - ○ Dockerfile templates for building your MCP server image
  - ○ docker-compose.yml for multi-service setups (e.g., server + Redis + database)
- *Optional*: Kubernetes manifests or Helm charts for production deployment

9. Development & CI/CD Tooling

- **Pre-commit** hooks for linting and formatting:
  - ○ pip install pre-commit plus .pre-commit-config.yaml

- **GitHub Actions, GitLab CI**, or **Jenkins** for automated testing and deployment pipelines
- **pytest / tox** for unit and integration testing:
  - pip install pytest tox

10. Code Quality & Formatting

- **Black** for code formatting: pip install black
- **Flake8** for linting: pip install flake8
- **MyPy** for optional static type checking: pip install mypy

Tip: Capture all dependencies in a requirements.txt or pyproject.toml so teammates can reproduce your environment with a single command (pip install -r requirements.txt or poetry install).

With these tools and frameworks installed and configured, you're ready to build, test, and deploy production-grade MCP servers that integrate seamlessly with any external data source.

2.1.2 Setting Up Your Local Environment for MCP Development

Follow these steps to prepare a clean, reproducible local workspace before you start building MCP servers.

1. Create a Project Directory

bash

```
mkdir mcp-server

cd mcp-server
```

2. Initialize Version Control

bash

git init

3. Choose and Activate a Virtual Environment

Use one of the following methods:

venv (built-in)
bash

```
python3 -m venv .venv

source .venv/bin/activate
```

pipenv
bash

```
pip install pipenv

pipenv shell
```

poetry
bash

```
pip install poetry

poetry init --name "mcp-server" --dependency fastapi --dependency uvicorn

poetry shell
```

4. Pin Your Dependencies

Create a requirements.txt (for venv/pipenv) or update pyproject.toml (for Poetry). At minimum include:

css

```
fastapi
```

uvicorn[standard]

jsonrpcserver

jsonrpcclient

httpx

python-dotenv

Then install:

bash

```
pip install -r requirements.txt
# or
pipenv install
# or
poetry install
```

5. Configure Environment Variables

Create a .env file in the project root:
env

```
MCP_SERVER_HOST=127.0.0.1

MCP_SERVER_PORT=8000

DATABASE_URL=postgresql://user:pass@localhost:5432/mcp
```

Load it in your application using python-dotenv:

python

```python
from dotenv import load_dotenv

load_dotenv()  # must be at top of main.py
```

6. Scaffold a Basic MCP Server

Create main.py with a minimal FastAPI + JSON-RPC setup:

python

```python
from fastapi import FastAPI, Request

from jsonrpcserver import method, async_dispatch


app = FastAPI()


@method
async def ping(context: dict, args: dict):
    return {"message": "pong", "context": context}


@app.post("/rpc")
async def rpc_endpoint(request: Request):
    request_text = await request.body()
    response = await async_dispatch(request_text.decode())
```

```
    return response
```

7. Run and Test Your Server

Start the server:
bash

```
uvicorn main:app --reload --host $MCP_SERVER_HOST --port $MCP_SERVER_PORT
```

In another terminal, send a test request:
bash

```
curl -X POST http://127.0.0.1:8000/rpc \

  -H "Content-Type: application/json" \

  -d '{"jsonrpc":"2.0","id":1,"method":"ping","params":{"context":{"sessionId":"s1"},"args":{}}}'
```

Expect a response similar to:
json

```
{"jsonrpc":"2.0","id":1,"result":{"message":"pong","context":{"sessionId":"s1"}}}
```

8. Set Up Code Quality Tools

Black (formatter):
bash

```
pip install black

black .
```

Flake8 (linter):
bash

```bash
pip install flake8

flake8 .
```

Pre-commit (hooks):
bash

```bash
pip install pre-commit

pre-commit install
```

Include a .pre-commit-config.yaml:

yaml

```yaml
repos:
  - repo: https://github.com/psf/black
    rev: stable
    hooks:
      - id: black
  - repo: https://gitlab.com/pycqa/flake8
    rev: 6.0.0
    hooks:
      - id: flake8
```

9. Write Your First Test

Create tests/test_ping.py:

python

```python
from starlette.testclient import TestClient
from main import app

client = TestClient(app)

def test_ping():
    response = client.post("/rpc", json={
        "jsonrpc":"2.0","id":1,"method":"ping",
        "params":{"context":{"sessionId":"s1"},"args":{}}
    })
    data = response.json()
    assert data["result"]["message"] == "pong"
```

Run tests:

bash

```bash
pytest
```

With these steps, your local environment is primed for MCP server development. You can now proceed to build adapters, define manifests, and implement advanced features covered in the next chapters.

2.1.3 Configuring Your First MCP Server

After scaffolding a minimal MCP server, the next step is to configure it for real-world use. You'll externalize settings, register your first adapter, and expose the RPC endpoint on a configurable host/port.

A. Define Configuration Settings

Use a Pydantic settings class (or environment variables + python-dotenv) to centralize your server configuration:

python

```python
# config.py

from pydantic import BaseSettings, Field


class MCPSettings(BaseSettings):

    host: str = Field("127.0.0.1", env="MCP_SERVER_HOST")

    port: int = Field(8000, env="MCP_SERVER_PORT")

    log_level: str = Field("info", env="LOG_LEVEL")

    rpc_path: str = Field("/rpc", env="MCP_RPC_PATH")


    class Config:

        env_file = ".env"

        env_file_encoding = "utf-8"
```

```python
settings = MCPSettings()
```

Tip: Keep sensitive values (API keys, database URLs) in your .env and out of version control.

B. Load Configuration in Your Application

Modify main.py to use these settings:

python

```python
# main.py

from fastapi import FastAPI, Request

from jsonrpcserver import method, async_dispatch

from config import settings

import logging


# Initialize logging

logging.basicConfig(level=getattr(logging, settings.log_level.upper()))


app = FastAPI()


@method

async def ping(context: dict, args: dict):

    return {"message": "pong", "context": context}
```

```python
@app.post(settings.rpc_path)
async def rpc_endpoint(request: Request):

    request_text = await request.body()

    response = await async_dispatch(request_text.decode())

    return response


if __name__ == "__main__":

    import uvicorn

    uvicorn.run(

        "main:app",

        host=settings.host,

        port=settings.port,

        log_level=settings.log_level,

        reload=True

    )
```

- **settings.rpc_path** lets you change the RPC endpoint without touching routes.
- **logging.basicConfig** ensures your log level respects the configuration.

C. Register Your First Adapter

Typically you'll organize adapters in a dedicated module. For example:

bash

```
mcp-server/

├── adapters/

│       └── hello_adapter.py

├── config.py

├── main.py

└── .env
```

python

```python
# adapters/hello_adapter.py

from jsonrpcserver import method


@method
def sayHello(context: dict, args: dict):
    name = args.get("name", "world")
    return {"greeting": f"Hello, {name}!"}
```

Then import the adapter so its methods are registered:

python

```python
# main.py (add near the top)
```

```python
import adapters.hello_adapter
```

Now the server understands "sayHello" calls.

D. Test Your Configured Server

Start the server:
bash

```bash
uvicorn main:app --host $MCP_SERVER_HOST --port $MCP_SERVER_PORT --reload
```

Invoke the adapter:
bash

```bash
curl -X POST http://127.0.0.1:8000/rpc \

  -H "Content-Type: application/json" \

  -d '{

    "jsonrpc":"2.0",

    "id":10,

    "method":"sayHello",

    "params":{"context":{},"args":{"name":"Alice"}}

  }'
```

Expected response:
json

```json
{

  "jsonrpc": "2.0",
```

```
  "id": 10,

  "result": { "greeting": "Hello, Alice!" }

}
```

E. Additional Configuration Considerations

CORS: If your AI clients run in browsers, add:
python

```python
from fastapi.middleware.cors import CORSMiddleware


app.add_middleware(

    CORSMiddleware,

    allow_origins=["*"],

    allow_methods=["POST"],

    allow_headers=["*"],

)
```

- **TLS**: For production, terminate TLS at a reverse proxy (NGINX, Traefik) or use Uvicorn's --ssl-keyfile/--ssl-certfile.
- **Health Check Endpoint**: Add a simple GET /health that returns {"status":"ok"} for load balancer probes.

Monitoring: Mount Prometheus metrics:
python

```python
from prometheus_client import start_http_server


start_http_server(8001)  # Exposes /metrics
```

With this configuration in place, your MCP server is ready for iterative development—new adapters, improved logging, and secure deployment—while keeping settings centralized and easily adjustable.

2.2 Creating a Basic MCP Server

2.2.1 Step-by-Step Guide to Building a Simple MCP Server

Follow these steps to build and verify a minimal, working MCP server using **FastAPI** and **JSON-RPC 2.0**. You'll end up with a server that can register methods ("tools") and respond to JSON-RPC calls.

Step 1: Create and Enter a Project Directory

bash

```
mkdir mcp-basic
cd mcp-basic
```

Step 2: Initialize Git and a Virtual Environment

bash

```
git init
python3 -m venv .venv
source .venv/bin/activate
```

Tip: Keeping your environment isolated prevents dependency conflicts.

Step 3: Install Core Dependencies

bash

```bash
pip install fastapi uvicorn[standard] jsonrpcserver python-dotenv
```

fastapi: Web framework

uvicorn: ASGI server

jsonrpcserver: JSON-RPC dispatcher

python-dotenv: Load .env variables

Step 4: Add Configuration File

Create a file named .env:

env

```env
MCP_SERVER_HOST=127.0.0.1
MCP_SERVER_PORT=8000
MCP_RPC_PATH=/rpc
LOG_LEVEL=info
```

Step 5: Define Settings with Pydantic

Create config.py:

python

```python
# config.py

from pydantic import BaseSettings, Field


class Settings(BaseSettings):

    host: str = Field("127.0.0.1", env="MCP_SERVER_HOST")

    port: int = Field(8000, env="MCP_SERVER_PORT")

    rpc_path: str = Field("/rpc", env="MCP_RPC_PATH")

    log_level: str = Field("info", env="LOG_LEVEL")


    class Config:

        env_file = ".env"


settings = Settings()
```

Why? Centralizing your configuration makes the server easy to adjust for different environments.

Step 6: Scaffold the Main Application

Create main.py:

python

```python
# main.py

import logging
```

```python
from fastapi import FastAPI, Request

from jsonrpcserver import method, async_dispatch

from config import settings

from dotenv import load_dotenv


# Load .env settings

load_dotenv()


# Configure logging

logging.basicConfig(level=getattr(logging, settings.log_level.upper()))


app = FastAPI()


# 1. Define a sample MCP method
@method
async def ping(context: dict, args: dict):
    """
    A simple health-check tool.
    Returns "pong" along with any passed context.
    """
    return {"message": "pong", "context": context}


# 2. Register JSON-RPC endpoint
```

```python
@app.post(settings.rpc_path)
async def rpc_endpoint(request: Request):
    request_text = await request.body()
    response = await async_dispatch(request_text.decode())
    # FastAPI will set content-type automatically
    return response


# 3. Health check (optional)
@app.get("/health")
async def health():
    return {"status": "ok"}


# 4. Start the server if run directly
if __name__ == "__main__":
    import uvicorn
    uvicorn.run(
        "main:app",
        host=settings.host,
        port=settings.port,
        log_level=settings.log_level,
        reload=True
    )
```

Step 7: Run the Server

bash

```bash
uvicorn main:app --reload
```

--reload: auto-restarts on code changes

Verify the logs show the server listening on 127.0.0.1:8000.

Step 8: Test Your MCP Method

Use curl (or any HTTP client) to invoke the ping tool:

bash

```bash
curl -X POST http://127.0.0.1:8000/rpc \
 -H "Content-Type: application/json" \
 -d '{
   "jsonrpc":"2.0",
   "id":1,
   "method":"ping",
   "params":{
     "context":{"sessionId":"test-session"},
     "args":{}
   }
 }'
```

Expected Response:

json

```json
{
  "jsonrpc": "2.0",
  "id": 1,
  "result": {
    "message": "pong",
    "context": {
      "sessionId": "test-session"
    }
  }
}
```

Step 9: Verify Health Endpoint

bash

```bash
curl http://127.0.0.1:8000/health
```

Response:

json

```json
{ "status": "ok" }
```

Step 10: Commit Your Initial Code

bash

```
git add .

git commit -m "Initial MCP server scaffold with ping method"
```

You now have a working MCP server that:

- Loads configuration from .env
- Exposes a JSON-RPC endpoint at /rpc
- Registers a basic ping tool
- Provides a health check

2.2.2 Connecting Your Server to External Data Sources (APIs, Databases)

A key benefit of MCP is that your server can treat any external system—whether a REST API or a database—as a "tool" simply by writing an adapter. This section shows you how to connect to two common data sources.

A. Consuming a REST API

Install HTTP Client
bash

```
pip install httpx
```

Adapter Structure
Create adapters/weather_api.py:
python

```
# adapters/weather_api.py

import os
```

```python
from jsonrpcserver import method

import httpx


API_KEY = os.getenv("WEATHER_API_KEY")

BASE_URL = "https://api.openweathermap.org/data/2.5"


@method
async def fetchWeather(context: dict, args: dict):
    """

    Fetches current weather for a given city.

    Params:

        args["city"]: city name (e.g., "London,UK")

    """

    city = args.get("city")

    if not city:

        raise ValueError("Missing required argument: city")


    url = f"{BASE_URL}/weather"

    params = {"q": city, "appid": API_KEY, "units": "metric"}


    async with httpx.AsyncClient(timeout=5.0) as client:

        resp = await client.get(url, params=params)
```

```python
    resp.raise_for_status()

    data = resp.json()


    return {

        "city": data["name"],

        "temperature": data["main"]["temp"],

        "description": data["weather"][0]["description"]

    }
```

Environment Variable
In your .env:
env

```
WEATHER_API_KEY=your_openweathermap_key
```

Register the Adapter
In main.py, add:
python

```python
import adapters.weather_api  # noqa: F401
```

Test the API Tool
bash

```bash
curl -X POST http://127.0.0.1:8000/rpc \

 -H "Content-Type: application/json" \

 -d '{
```

```
  "jsonrpc":"2.0","id":2,"method":"fetchWeather",

  "params":{"context":{},"args":{"city":"New York,US"}}

 }'
```

Expected result:
json

```json
{

 "jsonrpc":"2.0",

 "id":2,

 "result":{

  "city":"New York",

  "temperature":15.3,

  "description":"clear sky"

 }

}
```

B. Connecting to a PostgreSQL Database

Install Database Driver
bash

```bash
pip install asyncpg
```

Configure Database URL
In .env:
env

```env
DATABASE_URL=postgresql://user:password@localhost:5432/mydb
```

Adapter Structure

Create adapters/user_db.py:

python

```python
# adapters/user_db.py

import os

from jsonrpcserver import method

import asyncpg


DATABASE_URL = os.getenv("DATABASE_URL")


@method
async def getUserOrders(context: dict, args: dict):
    """
    Retrieves the latest N orders for a user.
    Params:
      args["user_id"]: string
      args["limit"]: int (optional)
    """
    user_id = args.get("user_id")
    limit = args.get("limit", 5)

    if not user_id:
        raise ValueError("Missing required argument: user_id")
```

```python
    conn = await asyncpg.connect(DATABASE_URL)
    try:
        rows = await conn.fetch(
            """
            SELECT order_id, total_amount, status, created_at
            FROM orders
            WHERE user_id = $1
            ORDER BY created_at DESC
            LIMIT $2
            """,
            user_id, limit
        )
    finally:
        await conn.close()

    # Convert records to dictionaries
    orders = [dict(row) for row in rows]
    return {"orders": orders}
```

Register the Adapter

In main.py, add:

python

```python
import adapters.user_db  # noqa: F401
```

Test the Database Tool
bash

```bash
curl -X POST http://127.0.0.1:8000/rpc \
  -H "Content-Type: application/json" \
  -d '{
    "jsonrpc":"2.0","id":3,"method":"getUserOrders",
    "params":{"context":{},"args":{"user_id":"u42","limit":3}}
  }'
```

Expected result:
json

```json
{
  "jsonrpc":"2.0",
  "id":3,
  "result":{
    "orders":[

{"order_id":101,"total_amount":50.0,"status":"shipped","created_at":"2025-04-10T09:00:00Z"},

{"order_id":98,"total_amount":75.5,"status":"processing","created_at":"2025-04-08T15:30:00Z"},
```

{"order_id":90,"total_amount":20.0,"status":"delivered","created_at":"2025-04-05T11:45:00Z"}

```
    ]

  }

}
```

C. Best Practices for External Integrations

Practice	Description
Connection Pooling	For high throughput, reuse database connections (e.g., via asyncpg.create_pool).
Timeouts	Set sensible HTTP and DB timeouts to prevent hung requests.
Retries with Back-off	Use exponential back-off for transient failures (network glitches, rate limits).
Credential Management	Store secrets in a vault or environment variables; never hard-code them.
Logging & Monitoring	Instrument adapters to log request durations, errors, and status codes.
Schema Validation	Validate args against JSON Schema in your manifest to reject bad data early.

By following these patterns, you'll turn any API or database into an MCP "tool" that your AI clients can invoke seamlessly—cleanly separating integration logic from your core inference workflows.

2.2.3 Testing and Validating the Server Setup

Ensuring your MCP server works correctly before production is crucial. This section shows you how to perform **manual smoke tests**, write **automated tests** with **pytest**, and validate both **happy paths** and **error handling**.

2.2.3.1 Manual Smoke Tests with curl

Ping Method
bash

```
curl -s -X POST http://127.0.0.1:8000/rpc \

 -H "Content-Type: application/json" \

 -d
'{"jsonrpc":"2.0","id":1,"method":"ping","params":{"context":{"sessionId"
:"test"},"args":{}}}'
```

Expected:
json

```
{"jsonrpc":"2.0","id":1,"result":{"message":"pong","context":{"sessionId":
"test"}}}
```

Weather API Adapter
bash

```
curl -s -X POST http://127.0.0.1:8000/rpc \

 -H "Content-Type: application/json" \

 -d
'{"jsonrpc":"2.0","id":2,"method":"fetchWeather","params":{"context":{},"
args":{"city":"London,UK"}}}'
```

   o **Check:** temperature is numeric and description is non-empty.

Database Adapter
bash

```bash
curl -s -X POST http://127.0.0.1:8000/rpc \
 -H "Content-Type: application/json" \
 -d '{"jsonrpc":"2.0","id":3,"method":"getUserOrders","params":{"context":{},"args":{"user_id":"u42","limit":1}}}'
```

- **Verify**: orders `is an array of length ≤ 1, each element has keys` order_id, status.
2. Error Handling

Missing required param:
bash

```bash
curl -s -X POST http://127.0.0.1:8000/rpc \
 -H "Content-Type: application/json" \
 -d '{"jsonrpc":"2.0","id":4,"method":"getUserOrders","params":{"context":{},"args":{}}}'
```

- **Expected error**: Code -32602 or adapter's ValueError mapped to -32001, with message indicating missing user_id.

2.2.3.2 Automated Tests with pytest

Install Test Dependencies
bash

```bash
pip install pytest httpx pytest-asyncio
```

Create tests/conftest.py to provide a FastAPI TestClient:
python

```python
import pytest

from fastapi.testclient import TestClient

from main import app


@pytest.fixture(scope="module")

def client():

    return TestClient(app)
```

Write RPC Endpoint Tests
python

```python
# tests/test_rpc.py

import pytest


@pytest.mark.parametrize("method, params, expected", [

    ("ping", {"context": {"sessionId": "x"}, "args": {}}, {"message": "pong",
"context": {"sessionId": "x"}}),

    ("sayHello", {"context": {}, "args": {"name": "Alice"}}, {"greeting":
"Hello, Alice!"}),

])

def test_rpc_methods(client, method, params, expected):

    payload = {"jsonrpc": "2.0", "id": 1, "method": method, "params":
params}
```

```python
    response = client.post("/rpc", json=payload)

    data = response.json()

    assert response.status_code == 200

    assert data["result"] == expected


def test_invalid_method(client):

    payload = {"jsonrpc": "2.0", "id": 2, "method": "noSuchTool", "params": {"context": {}, "args": {}}}

    response = client.post("/rpc", json=payload)

    data = response.json()

    assert "error" in data

    assert data["error"]["code"] == -32601  # Method not found
```

Test External Adapters with Mocking

For adapters making HTTP requests, use **pytest-monkeypatch** or **respx** to simulate API responses without real network calls.

python

```python
# tests/test_weather.py

import pytest

import httpx

from adapters.weather_api import fetchWeather


@pytest.mark.asyncio

async def test_fetch_weather(monkeypatch):
```

```python
class FakeResponse:

    def __init__(self): self.status_code = 200

    def raise_for_status(self): pass

    def json(self): return
{"name":"TestCity","main":{"temp":20},"weather":[{"description":"sunny"
}]}

async def fake_get(*args, **kwargs): return FakeResponse()


monkeypatch.setattr(httpx.AsyncClient, "get", fake_get)


result = await fetchWeather({}, {"city": "TestCity"})

assert result["city"] == "TestCity"

assert isinstance(result["temperature"], (int, float))
```

Run All Tests
bash

```bash
pytest --maxfail=1 --disable-warnings -q
```

2.2.3.3 Validating JSON-RPC Schema

Schema Enforcement: Use your tool manifest's JSON Schema definitions and a
library like **jsonschema** to validate incoming params in each adapter.
python

```python
from jsonschema import validate, ValidationError
```

```python
schema = {
    "type": "object",
    "properties": {
        "context": {"type": "object"},
        "args": {
            "type": "object",
            "properties": {"user_id": {"type": "string"}, "limit": {"type": "integer"}},
            "required": ["user_id"]
        }
    },
    "required": ["context", "args"]
}


@method
async def getUserOrders(context, args):
    try:
        validate({"context": context, "args": args}, schema)
    except ValidationError as e:
        raise JsonRpcError(-32602, f"Invalid params: {e.message}")
    # ... proceed with DB logic ...
```

2.2.3.4 Observability and Health Checks

1. Health Endpoint
   ○ Ensure /health returns 200 and { "status": "ok" }.
2. Metrics
   ○ If using Prometheus, scrape /metrics and verify counters for
     jsonrpc_requests_total and jsonrpc_errors_total.
3. Log Inspection
   ○ Trigger an error (e.g., invalid JSON) and confirm the server logs include
     the request and error details.

By combining **manual smoke tests**, **automated pytest suites**, **schema
validation**, and **observability checks**, you'll have high confidence that your MCP
server handles both standard and edge-case scenarios correctly before moving on to
advanced configurations.

2.3 Advanced MCP Server Configurations

2.3.1 Setting Up Multiple Servers for Scalability

To handle high throughput and ensure high availability, run **multiple MCP server
instances** behind a load balancer. This section shows two common approaches: using
Docker Compose with NGINX and deploying on **Kubernetes**.

A. Stateless Server Design

1. Statelessness
   ○ Ensure each MCP server instance shares no in-memory state: store
     sessions, rate limits, and context in external stores (Redis, database).
2. Externalize Context
   ○ Use a **Context Store** (e.g., Redis) for session data and streaming state
     across servers.
3. Shared Adapters
   ○ Adapters must be idempotent and thread-safe so any instance can handle
     any request.

B. Docker Compose + NGINX Load Balancer

Project Structure
arduino

mcp-scaled/

├── docker-compose.yml

├── app/

│   ├── Dockerfile

│   ├── main.py

│   ├── config.py

│   └── adapters/···

└── nginx/

├── nginx.conf

└── Dockerfile

NGINX Configuration (nginx/nginx.conf)
nginx

events {}

http {

upstream mcp_servers {

server mcp1:8000;

server mcp2:8000;

}

```
server {

  listen 8000;


  location / {

    proxy_pass http://mcp_servers;

    proxy_http_version 1.1;

    proxy_set_header Connection "";

    proxy_set_header Host $host;

  }

 }

}
```

Docker Compose File (docker-compose.yml)
yaml

```yaml
version: '3.8'

services:

 mcp1:

  build: ./app

  environment:

    - MCP_SERVER_HOST=0.0.0.0

    - MCP_SERVER_PORT=8000
```

```yaml
    networks:
      - mcp-net

  mcp2:
    build: ./app
    environment:
      - MCP_SERVER_HOST=0.0.0.0
      - MCP_SERVER_PORT=8000
    networks:
      - mcp-net

  nginx:
    build: ./nginx
    ports:
      - "8000:8000"
    depends_on:
      - mcp1
      - mcp2
    networks:
      - mcp-net

networks:
```

```yaml
  mcp-net:

    driver: bridge
```

Build & Run
bash

```bash
docker-compose up --build
```

- ○ NGINX listens on **localhost:8000** and distributes requests in round-robin to mcp1 and mcp2.

C. Kubernetes Deployment

Deployment YAML (k8s/mcp-deployment.yaml)
yaml

```yaml
apiVersion: apps/v1

kind: Deployment

metadata:

  name: mcp-server

spec:

  replicas: 3

  selector:

    matchLabels:

      app: mcp

  template:

    metadata:
```

```yaml
  labels:
    app: mcp
 spec:
  containers:
   - name: mcp
     image: your-registry/mcp-server:latest
     env:
      - name: MCP_SERVER_HOST
        value: "0.0.0.0"
      - name: MCP_SERVER_PORT
        value: "8000"
     ports:
      - containerPort: 8000
```

Service YAML (k8s/mcp-service.yaml)
yaml

```yaml
apiVersion: v1
kind: Service
metadata:
 name: mcp-service
spec:
 selector:
```

```yaml
    app: mcp

  ports:

   - port: 80

     targetPort: 8000

     protocol: TCP

   type: LoadBalancer
```

Apply to Cluster
bash

```bash
kubectl apply -f k8s/mcp-deployment.yaml

kubectl apply -f k8s/mcp-service.yaml
```

- ○ Kubernetes creates a **LoadBalancer** (or NodePort) automatically distributing traffic to all replicas.

D. Best Practices

Aspect	Recommendation
Health Checks	Use /health endpoint for load-balancer probes to detect unhealthy pods.
Autoscaling	Configure **Horizontal Pod Autoscaler** (HPA) based on CPU/memory or QPS.
External State Stores	Offload session/rate-limit data to Redis or a shared database.

TLS Termination	Terminate TLS at the load balancer (NGINX, AWS ELB, or Ingress controller).
Logging & Metrics	Centralize logs (ELK, Fluentd) and metrics (Prometheus) for all instances.
Rolling Updates	Deploy new versions with zero downtime via rolling update strategies.

By running **multiple stateless MCP server instances** behind a load balancer and externalizing shared state, you achieve a horizontally scalable, highly available architecture. Whether you choose Docker Compose for small-scale setups or Kubernetes for production environments, the principles remain the same: keep servers stateless, centralize state, and let the orchestration layer handle traffic distribution.

2.3.2 Load Balancing and Fault Tolerance in MCP

To ensure your MCP infrastructure remains responsive under high traffic and resilient to failures, implement both **load balancing** and **fault-tolerance** mechanisms. Below are best-practice strategies and patterns.

A. Load Balancing Strategies

1. Layer-4 (TCP) vs. Layer-7 (HTTP) Balancing
   - **Layer-4** (e.g., AWS NLB, Kubernetes Service): fast, protocol-agnostic, but cannot inspect HTTP paths.
   - **Layer-7** (e.g., NGINX, AWS ALB, Ingress controller): routes based on URL, headers, or JSON-RPC path; supports advanced routing (canary, header-based).
2. Common Algorithms
   - **Round-Robin**: evenly distributes requests across all healthy instances.
   - **Least Connections**: sends each request to the instance with the fewest active connections—useful when call latency varies.

- **IP Hash / Sticky**: binds a client IP (or session) to a single instance; generally **not** recommended for MCP since servers should be stateless and interchangeable.
3. Health Checks
    - Configure readiness and liveness probes (HTTP GET /health) so the load balancer only sends traffic to healthy instances.
    - Set timeouts and failure thresholds to detect and remove unhealthy servers quickly.

B. Fault-Tolerance Patterns

1. Circuit Breaker
    - Prevents continuous calls to a failing adapter or downstream service. After a threshold of errors, new requests immediately fail or fallback without invoking the adapter.
    - Can be implemented at the adapter layer (e.g., using libraries like pybreaker) or via a service mesh (Istio, Linkerd).
2. Bulkhead Isolation
    - Separate resource pools for different adapters or request types, so failures in one integration (e.g., weather API) don't exhaust all server threads or connections.
3. Timeouts and Retries
    - Enforce per-call timeouts in both HTTP clients (httpx) and database drivers.
    - Implement exponential back-off with jitter for retryable errors (network timeouts, 5xx). Cap retries to prevent cascading delays.
4. Fallback Strategies
    - Return cached or default data when an adapter is unavailable.
    - For non-critical tools (e.g., logging), use **notifications** so failures don't block the main workflow.
5. Graceful Degradation
    - Detect high-error rates (via metrics) and switch to reduced-functionality mode (e.g., read-only context fetch) until issues resolve.

C. Observability and Auto-Remediation

1. Centralized Metrics
    - Track per-method QPS, error rates, latency, circuit-breaker state.

- Alert on anomalies (error rate > 5%, latency spikes) to trigger automated failovers or scale-ups.
2. Structured Logging
   - Include requestId, method, adapter, status, and durationMs in every log entry.
   - Correlate logs with load-balancer and service-mesh logs for end-to-end tracing.
3. Auto-Scaling and Healing
   - In Kubernetes, use a **Horizontal Pod Autoscaler** based on CPU, memory, or custom metrics (e.g., queue length).
   - Configure **Pod Disruption Budgets** to ensure a minimum number of instances remain during upgrades or failures.

D. Putting It All Together

Aspect	Implementation	Benefit
Load Balancing	NGINX/Ingress with round-robin or least-conn	Even traffic distribution, high throughput
Health Probes	/health readiness & liveness in each pod	Removes unhealthy instances automatically
Circuit Breaker	pybreaker or service mesh policy	Stops thrashing failing services
Timeouts & Retries	httpx timeouts + exponential back-off	Prevents hung requests and transient errors
Bulkheads	Thread- or connection-pool isolation per adapter	Limits blast radius of failures
Monitoring & Alerts	Prometheus + Alertmanager on error/latency	Rapid detection and response to service degradation

| Auto-Scaling | Kubernetes HPA on CPU or custom QPS metrics | Dynamically adjusts capacity to match load |

By combining **robust load-balancing**, **active health checks**, and **fault-tolerance patterns**, you'll create an MCP deployment that remains highly available, responsive, and maintainable—even under heavy traffic and partial failures.

2.3.3 Optimizing Server Performance for Large-Scale Applications

As your MCP server handles increasing traffic and heavier workloads, it's essential to tune both the server framework and your adapter implementations. The following strategies will help you achieve low latency, high throughput, and consistent performance at scale.

A. Asynchronous IO and Concurrency

1. Use Async-First Libraries
   - Ensure adapters rely on **async** HTTP and database clients (e.g., httpx.AsyncClient, asyncpg) to avoid blocking the event loop.
   - Avoid mixing synchronous code in adapters; if you must, isolate it in a threadpool with FastAPI's run_in_threadpool.
2. Configure Uvicorn/Gunicorn Workers

For pure async setups, run Uvicorn with multiple workers:
bash

```
uvicorn main:app --workers 4 --host 0.0.0.0 --port 8000
```

In CPU-bound scenarios, use **Gunicorn** with the Uvicorn worker class:
bash

```
gunicorn main:app -k uvicorn.workers.UvicornWorker -w 4 --bind 0.0.0.0:8000
```

3. Fine-Tune Concurrency Settings
   - Adjust --limit-concurrency and --timeout-keep-alive to prevent slow clients from consuming worker slots.
   - Use FIFO request queuing (--backlog) to smooth traffic spikes.

B. Connection Pooling and Resource Reuse

1. HTTP Connection Pooling
   o **Reuse** httpx.AsyncClient instances across requests rather than creating a new client per call.

Configure pool limits to match your expected concurrency:
python

```python
client = httpx.AsyncClient(limits=httpx.Limits(max_connections=100, max_keepalive_connections=20))
```

2. Database Pooling

Use an **asyncpg** connection pool:
python

```python
pool = await asyncpg.create_pool(dsn=DATABASE_URL, min_size=5, max_size=20)
```

   o Share the pool across adapter calls to avoid costly connect/disconnect overhead.
3. Redis and Cache Layers
   o Cache frequent or expensive tool calls (e.g., reference data, static lookups) in Redis with TTLs.
   o Use hashed keys combining method name and serialized args for collision-safe caching.

C. Batching, Caching, and Rate-Limiting

1. Batching Related Calls
   o For logical groups of requests (e.g., multi-record fetch), use JSON-RPC **batch** to reduce network round-trips.
   o Aggregate small queries into a single database or API call when possible.
2. Result Caching
   o At the adapter level, memoize idempotent calls to external services.

- Respect cache invalidation when underlying data changes (e.g., versioned keys, short TTLs).
3. Rate-Limiting to Protect Downstreams
    - Enforce per-method throttles in the MCP server to avoid overloading slow downstream APIs.
    - Return a standardized rate-limit error (-32029) with retryAfter hints, allowing clients to back off.

D. Profiling and Monitoring

1. Profiling Hot Paths
    - Integrate a lightweight Python profiler (e.g., pyinstrument) in development to identify slow adapter methods or JSON serialization bottlenecks.
    - Focus on reducing time in JSON-RPC dispatch and adapter IO operations.
2. Metrics Instrumentation
    - Use **Prometheus client** to track key metrics per method:
        - **Request latency** (histogram)
        - **Error rate** (counter)
        - **Concurrent in-flight calls** (gauge)
    - Expose /metrics endpoint and set up dashboards/alerts for anomalies.
3. Structured Logging
    - Log each request with method, id, duration_ms, and status (success/error).
    - Aggregate logs in ELK/Fluentd to analyze patterns and detect outliers.

E. JSON Serialization and Validation

1. Optimize JSON Encoding
    - Use orjson (if performance critical) as FastAPI's JSON backend for faster serialization.
    - Avoid deep or nested data structures; flatten responses where sensible.
2. Lazy Validation
    - Validate input schemas in the tool manifest only once per request, not repeatedly inside business logic.
    - Cache compiled JSON-Schema validators to avoid re-parsing schemas on every call.

F. Infrastructure-Level Optimizations

1. Horizontal Scaling
   - Automate instance scaling based on custom metrics (e.g., QPS, latency) via Kubernetes HPA or auto-scaling groups.
2. Edge Caching and CDN
   - For predominantly read-only tools (e.g., static metadata), consider fronting with a CDN or edge cache.
3. Service Mesh Features
   - Leverage mTLS, retries, and circuit breakers provided by Istio/Linkerd without changing application code.

By applying these optimizations—concurrent async patterns, pooled connections, intelligent caching and batching, rigorous profiling, and robust monitoring—you'll ensure your MCP server remains **highly performant**, **resilient**, and **cost-effective** as you scale to support large-scale, context-aware AI applications.

2.4 Interactive Q&A

2.4.1 Troubleshooting Common Server Setup Problems

Use these discussion points to diagnose and resolve frequent issues when getting your MCP server up and running:

- Server Won't Start
  - ✓☐ Have you activated your virtual environment and installed all dependencies (pip install -r requirements.txt)?
  - 🔍 Check the startup logs for import errors or syntax faults in main.py or imported modules.
- Environment Variables Not Loading
  - ✓☐ Does a .env file exist at the project root?
  - 🔍 Is load_dotenv() called before you reference settings in main.py?
- Incorrect RPC Path / 404 on /rpc
  - ✓☐ Is settings.rpc_path matching the route decorator (@app.post(settings.rpc_path)) and your curl/HTTP client URL?
  - 🔍 Print out settings.rpc_path at startup to confirm its value.
- Methods Not Registered ("Method not found")
  - ✓☐ Have you imported your adapter modules (e.g., import adapters.weather_api) so that @method-decorated functions are registered?
  - 🔍 Ensure each module lives in a Python package (an __init__.py file) and Python's working directory is correct.
- CORS or Browser Errors

- ○ ✓☐ Did you add the FastAPI CORSMiddleware if your client runs in a browser?
  - ○ 🔍 Review the browser's console for CORS-related messages and verify your allow_origins settings.
- Database Connection Failures
  - ○ ✓☐ Is the DATABASE_URL environment variable set correctly, and is the database server accessible?
  - ○ 🔍 Test the connection string manually (e.g., using psql or a Python REPL) to isolate network or credential issues.
- External API Adapter Errors
  - ○ ✓☐ Have you set and exported required API keys (e.g., WEATHER_API_KEY) in your .env?
  - ○ 🔍 Log the outgoing request URL and response status/body to verify authentication and endpoint correctness.
- JSON-RPC Schema Violations
  - ○ ✓☐ Are your requests including both context and args objects?
  - ○ 🔍 Use a JSON-RPC inspector (or dump the raw request/response) to check for missing fields or malformed JSON.
- Health Check Not Passing
  - ○ ✓☐ Is there a /health GET route defined, and does it return {"status":"ok"}?
  - ○ 🔍 Curl the health endpoint directly (curl http://localhost:8000/health) and inspect HTTP status.
- Logging Too Sparse to Debug
  - ○ ✓☐ Have you set an appropriate log level (LOG_LEVEL=debug) and added structured logging?
  - ○ 🔍 Temporarily increase verbosity to capture full request/response bodies and stack traces.

Reflect on each point—reproduce the failure, inspect logs or error messages, and apply the checks above. This systematic approach will help you quickly isolate configuration glitches, dependency mismatches, and integration faults before moving on to advanced features.

2.4.2 Discussion of Deployment Scenarios

ises vs. Cloud

- What trade-offs do you see between hosting MCP servers in your own data center (full control, compliance) versus a public cloud (elasticity, managed services)?
- How would network latency and data residency requirements influence your choice?

2. Containerized Deployments
   - In a Docker-Compose setup, what benefits and limitations arise compared to a full orchestration platform like Kubernetes?
   - How would you structure your Dockerfile and Compose services to cleanly separate MCP, Redis, and database layers?

3. Kubernetes & Service Mesh
   - If deploying on Kubernetes, which features (Pod autoscaling, rolling updates, health probes) are most valuable for MCP?
   - How might a service mesh (Istio, Linkerd) add observability, security (mTLS), and fault-tolerance to your deployment?

4. Serverless & FaaS
   - Could you run MCP handlers as serverless functions (AWS Lambda, Azure Functions)? What patterns would you adopt for cold-start mitigation and state storage?
   - Which use cases (sporadic workloads, very low traffic) might favor a serverless approach over always-on servers?

5. Multi-Region & Edge Deployments
   - For global applications, how would you replicate MCP servers across regions to minimize latency? What challenges arise with context or rate-limit synchronization?
   - When might you push lightweight MCP instances to the edge (e.g., on-prem gateways) versus centralizing them?

6. Hybrid & Air-Gapped Environments
   - In regulated industries, how could you support an air-gapped deployment where only adapters to internal systems run behind the firewall, and public adapters live in the cloud?
   - What strategies ensure secure proxying and minimal data leakage between environments?

7. CI/CD Pipeline Integration
   - How would you integrate MCP server builds, tests, and deployments into your existing CI/CD pipeline (e.g., GitHub Actions, GitLab CI)?
   - Which stages (linting, unit tests, integration tests, canary rollout) are essential to validate MCP adapters before they hit production?

8. High-Availability & Disaster Recovery

- Beyond load balancing, how would you design for disaster recovery—cross-zone failover, backup/restore of context stores, database replicas?
- What RPO/RTO targets make sense for your MCP-powered workflows, and how do they drive your infrastructure choices?

Reflect on these scenarios to identify the deployment pattern that best aligns with your architectural requirements, operational constraints, and organizational priorities.

Chapter 3: Building Context-Aware AI Systems with MCP

3.1 Understanding Context in AI

3.1.1 What Is Context in AI, and Why Does It Matter?

In AI applications, **context** refers to any information beyond the immediate input that shapes an AI model's reasoning and output. Rather than treating each request as an isolated, stateless event, context-aware systems draw on additional data—such as user history, environmental signals, or system state—to generate more relevant, accurate, and personalized responses.

What Forms Can Context Take?

Context Type	Description	Example
User History	Prior interactions, preferences, or profile data	A chatbot remembering that you prefer "dark mode."
Environmental	External conditions like time, location, or weather	A navigation assistant rerouting because of rain.
System State	Current application or workflow status	Resuming a multi-step form where you left off.
Real-Time Data	Live streams, sensor readings, or market feeds	A trading bot adjusting strategies based on stock ticks.
Session Metadata	Authentication tokens, session identifiers, user roles	Ensuring only admins can perform certain actions.

Why Context Matters

1. Relevance & Personalization
   - **Tailored Outputs**: By factoring in user preferences or past behavior, AI responses feel bespoke rather than generic.
   - **Improved Engagement**: Users are more likely to trust and continue using systems that "remember" their needs.
2. Continuity & Coherence
   - **Seamless Interactions**: Maintaining session state avoids repetitive prompts (e.g., re-asking for your name).
   - **Multi-Turn Dialogues**: Context lets chatbots carry information across turns, enabling meaningful conversations.
3. Accuracy & Informed Decisions
   - **Up-to-Date Information**: Incorporating live data (sensor feeds, market prices) helps models act on current facts, not stale training data.
   - **Reduced Ambiguity**: Context clarifies vague inputs (e.g., "book that" could refer to a flight, hotel, or restaurant based on prior steps).
4. Efficiency & Resource Optimization
   - **Selective Data Fetching**: Models request only the context they need—reducing redundant calls and network overhead.
   - **Proactive Preloading**: Anticipating likely data needs (e.g., caching next-step information) lowers latency.
5. Security & Governance
   - **Contextual Authorization**: Permission checks based on session tokens and user roles prevent unauthorized actions.
   - **Audit Trails**: Carrying metadata like timestamps and session IDs aids in compliance and debugging.

Illustrative Scenario

E-Commerce Chatbot

- **Without Context**: Every "What's my order status?" query requires you to re-enter your order number and identity.
- **With Context**: The bot remembers your authentication token and last 5 orders, immediately displaying relevant updates and suggesting related products.

By making context a **first-class concern**, context-aware AI systems—facilitated by MCP servers—deliver interactions that are not only more intelligent and user-friendly but also more robust and maintainable across complex, real-world workflows.

3.1.2 How MCP Enhances Context-Awareness in AI Applications

MCP provides the **infrastructure** and **patterns** that turn isolated AI model calls into truly context-aware interactions. Here's how MCP empowers richer, more dynamic AI behavior:

1. Uniform Context Propagation
   ○ Every JSON-RPC request includes a dedicated context object, so metadata (session IDs, user profiles, timestamps) is carried automatically to each tool call.
   ○ Adapters and downstream services receive all the information they need for authentication, auditing, or branching logic—without manual wiring in model code.
2. Stateful Multi-Turn Workflows
   ○ By externalizing session state into a **Context Store** (cache or database), MCP lets agents resume conversations or long-running tasks across multiple calls.
   ○ Models simply refer to context keys rather than re-fetching or re-verifying state, enabling seamless, coherent dialogs.
3. Dynamic Capability Discovery
   ○ AI clients can introspect available tools and their parameter schemas at runtime via listMethods, adapting behavior based on what context services are currently registered.
   ○ This flexibility allows workflows to evolve—new context sources (e.g., a new sensor feed) become immediately usable without client updates.
4. On-Demand, Granular Data Fetching
   ○ Instead of bulk pulling all possible context ahead of time, models issue fine-grained tool calls (e.g., getUserPreferences, fetchSensorData) only when that slice of context is required.
   ○ This minimizes latency, reduces unnecessary load, and ensures models work with the freshest data.
5. Streaming and Notifications for Real-Time Context
   ○ For real-time inputs (IoT sensor streams, live market feeds), MCP supports JSON-RPC notifications and chunked responses. Agents can subscribe to context streams and react instantly to changes.

- Streaming adapters push incremental updates, so AI systems maintain an up-to-the-moment view of their environment.
6. Consistent Error and Retry Semantics
    - When context-fetch calls fail (e.g., timeout fetching user data), MCP's standardized error codes and retry hints let agents implement uniform fallback strategies—caching, default values, or graceful degradation.
    - Agents need not reimplement bespoke error logic for each context source.
7. Caching and Batching Optimizations
    - MCP servers can batch multiple context requests into a single external call or cache frequent queries (e.g., static reference data), transparently improving performance without altering AI logic.
    - Caching adapters return context instantly when safe, further smoothing multi-turn workflows.
8. Separation of Concerns for Maintainability
    - AI models focus purely on **"what"** to ask for: their prompts and reasoning. All **"how"** to fetch, authenticate, parse, and secure context lives in adapters.
    - Teams can independently evolve context-gathering capabilities (e.g., swap a legacy database for a new microservice) without touching model code, keeping systems modular and resilient.

Example: Context-Aware Email Assistant

An email assistant might need:

- **User Preferences** (language, tone)
- **Calendar Availability** (free/busy slots)
- **Recent Sentiment** (tone analysis of last messages)

With MCP:

1. The assistant issues three tool calls—getPreferences, getCalendarFreeSlots, analyzeSentiment—each carrying the same context.sessionId.
2. MCP adapters handle auth (OAuth2 for calendar, API key for sentiment), parse responses, and return structured results.
3. The model merges these context slices into its prompt, producing an email draft that matches the user's style, fits their schedule, and responds appropriately to recent tone cues.

By providing this **standardized, flexible bridge** between AI and context sources, MCP transforms simple inference engines into **richly informed**, **responsive**, and **maintainable** context-aware applications.

3.1.3 Examples of Context-Aware AI in Practice

Below are several real-world systems that leverage context to deliver smarter, more personalized, and efficient AI experiences. In each case, MCP–style integrations could provide the bridge between models and the contextual data sources they rely on.

A. Customer Support Chatbots

- **Context Types**: User profile, order history, open support tickets
- **Behavior**:
    - Automatically fetches a customer's last five orders and active tickets.
    - Skips verification steps for returning users (based on sessionId and userId).
    - Suggests solutions pulled from past resolved cases for similar issues.
- **Benefit**: Faster resolution times, reduced agent hand-offs, and higher customer satisfaction.

B. Smart Home Automation

- **Context Types**: Time of day, occupancy sensor data, weather forecasts
- **Behavior**:
    - Arms or disarms security systems based on presence detected by motion sensors.
    - Adjusts lighting and thermostat schedules when residents arrive home.
    - Closes windows or adjusts shades ahead of imminent rain.
- **Benefit**: Improved energy efficiency, enhanced comfort, and proactive safety measures.

C. Healthcare Monitoring & Alerts

- **Context Types**: Patient vital signs (heart rate, blood pressure), medication schedules, activity levels
- **Behavior**:
    - Continuously streams sensor readings from wearable devices.

- - Triggers alerts when readings exceed patient-specific thresholds.
    - Sends medication reminders if a dose is overdue.
  - **Benefit**: Early detection of health anomalies and improved adherence to treatment plans.

D. Autonomous Vehicle Navigation

- **Context Types**: GPS location, traffic congestion data, weather and road conditions, LIDAR/camera sensor inputs
- **Behavior**:
    - Dynamically routes around traffic jams or road closures.
    - Modifies driving parameters (e.g., braking distance) in response to rain or fog.
    - Chooses optimal parking maneuvers based on curb-side availability.
- **Benefit**: Enhanced safety, optimized travel times, and more reliable autonomous operation.

E. Personalized E-Commerce Recommendations

- **Context Types**: Browsing history, real-time inventory status, user loyalty tier, geolocation
- **Behavior**:
    - Recommends products that are in stock at the nearest fulfillment center.
    - Shows region-specific promotions and coupons.
    - Adapts homepage banners based on local seasonal trends and past purchases.
- **Benefit**: Higher conversion rates, reduced cart abandonment, and more relevant marketing.

F. Industrial IoT & Predictive Maintenance

- **Context Types**: Machine vibration, temperature, operational hours, environmental conditions
- **Behavior**:
    - Streams real-time sensor data from factory equipment.

- Predicts equipment failures by comparing live readings against historical baselines.
- Automatically schedules maintenance during off-peak production windows.
- **Benefit**: Reduced unplanned downtime and lower maintenance costs.

In each scenario, an MCP server would manage the JSON-RPC–based calls that fetch or stream the needed context—abstracting away authentication, data parsing, and error handling—so that the AI models remain focused on delivering intelligent, context-aware responses.

3.2 Designing Context-Aware AI Workflows

3.2.1 Defining and Capturing Context Data

Building truly context-aware AI begins with a clear plan for **what** context you need and **how** you'll capture it. This section walks through the steps to define your context requirements, design schemas for context payloads, and implement adapters that gather context at runtime.

A. Identify Relevant Context Types

1. Business Goals & Use Cases
   - Map your AI workflow end-to-end. At each decision point, ask: "What additional information would improve this step?"
   - Example: In a support chatbot, you might need userTier, openTicketCount, and lastInteractionDate.
2. Context Categories
   - **User Context**: Identity, preferences, history
   - **Environmental Context**: Time, location, device
   - **System Context**: Workflow state, session variables
   - **Real-Time Context**: Live sensor or market data
3. Prioritize Context
   - Rank by **impact** (how much it changes AI output) and **cost** (latency and complexity to fetch).
   - Focus first on high-impact, low-cost items (e.g., user ID, session token) before adding heavy streaming data.

B. Define a Context Schema

Use a JSON Schema (or similar) to formalize the shape of your context block. This ensures adapters and clients agree on field names, types, and required values.

json

```json
{
  "type": "object",
  "properties": {
    "sessionId": { "type": "string" },
    "userId":   { "type": "string" },
    "timestamp": { "type": "string", "format": "date-time" },
    "userTier":  { "type": "string", "enum": ["free","silver","gold"] },
    "location": {
      "type": "object",
      "properties": {
        "lat": { "type": "number" },
        "lng": { "type": "number" }
      },
      "required": ["lat","lng"]
    }
  },
  "required": ["sessionId","userId","timestamp"]
```

}

- **Required vs. Optional**: Mark only truly essential fields (sessionId, userId, timestamp) as required to keep the payload minimal.

C. Capture Context at Ingress

1. Client-Side Injection
    - Middleware or wrapper libraries automatically populate context from request headers, cookies, or client state.

Example (Python pseudocode):
python

```python
def make_mcp_call(method, args):

    context = {

        "sessionId": request.headers.get("X-Session-ID"),

        "userId":   current_user.id,

        "timestamp": datetime.utcnow().isoformat()

    }

    return mcp_client.call(method, context, args)
```

2. API Gateway or Reverse Proxy
    - Terminate authentication at the edge (OAuth2, JWT), then inject userId and sessionId into downstream MCP requests.

D. Adapter-Level Enrichment

Some context requires fetching from external systems:

Profile Service Adapter
python

```python
@method

async def enrichUserContext(context: dict, args: dict):

    # context already has sessionId, userId

    profile = await profile_service.get(context["userId"])

    return { "userTier": profile.tier, "preferences": profile.prefs }
```

Location Lookup Adapter
python

```python
@method

def lookupGeo(context, args):

    ip = args.get("ip")

    geo = geoip.lookup(ip)

    return { "location": { "lat": geo.lat, "lng": geo.lng } }
```

E. Caching and State Management

- **Short-Lived Context** (session tokens, request time) can live only in memory.
- **Long-Lived Context** (user profile, preferences) should be cached (e.g., Redis) with TTLs to reduce repeated lookups.
- **Streaming Context** (sensor feeds) may require a dedicated context store that appends new events and serves windows of recent data.

F. Best Practices

Practice	Rationale
Minimal Required Fields	Reduces payload size and parsing overhead.
Version Your Schema	Use a contextVersion field to manage schema changes.
Validate Early	Reject malformed context at the server ingress.
Isolate Context Logic	Keep context formation in middleware/adapters, not in core AI code.
Monitor Context Latency	Track time to fetch/enrich context to avoid slowdowns.

By **systematically defining** your context needs, **formalizing schemas**, and **implementing adapters** that reliably capture and enrich context at runtime, you'll equip your AI workflows with the rich, relevant information they need—paving the way for truly context-aware intelligence.

3.2.2 Building Workflows That Adapt Based on Contextual Information

Adaptive workflows respond differently depending on the context supplied at runtime—enabling AI systems to make conditional decisions, branch logic, and invoke only the tools needed for a given scenario. With MCP, you express all interactions as JSON-RPC tool calls, and your orchestration layer uses context to select, sequence, and parameterize those calls.

A. Workflow Patterns for Context-Driven Logic

1. Rule-Based Branching
   - Define a set of conditional rules that inspect context and route execution accordingly.

Example:
python

```python
if context["userTier"] == "gold":

  result = await mcp.call("premiumRecommendation", context, args)

else:

  result = await mcp.call("standardRecommendation", context, args)
```

2. State Machine / Orchestration
   - Model the workflow as states; transitions depend on both prior results and context values.
   - Use a simple state-enum plus a dispatcher function to move between states.
3. Event-Driven Invocation
   - Use JSON-RPC **notifications** or streaming adapters to trigger certain tools when context events occur (e.g., a sensor reading crosses a threshold).
   - Example: an anomalyDetector adapter emits a notification that causes your orchestration logic to call sendAlert.
4. Parallel & Conditional Forks
   - Dispatch multiple context-dependent tool calls in **parallel** (via batch JSON-RPC) and wait for all results before proceeding.
   - Filter out non-applicable calls by examining context first to keep payloads lean.

B. Example: Context-Adaptive Support Workflow

Consider a support system that, upon receiving a new user message, adapts its steps based on customer status and issue severity:

python

```python
async def handleSupportRequest(mcp, context, args):

  # 1. Fetch user profile and open tickets in parallel
```

```python
calls = [

{"jsonrpc":"2.0","id":1,"method":"getUserProfile","params":{"context":context,"args":{}}},

{"jsonrpc":"2.0","id":2,"method":"getOpenTickets","params":{"context":context,"args":{}}}

]

responses = await mcp.batch_call(calls)

profile = responses[0]["result"]

tickets = responses[1]["result"]["tickets"]


# 2. Determine workflow path

if profile["tier"] == "gold" and args["issueLevel"] >= 3:

    # escalate immediately to human expert

    return await mcp.call("escalateToExpert", context, {"ticketId": tickets[0]["id"]})

elif tickets:

    # reply with existing ticket status

    return await mcp.call("replyWithTicketStatus", context, {"ticketId": tickets[0]["id"]})

else:

    # create a new ticket and provide troubleshooting

    new_ticket = await mcp.call("createTicket", context, {"issue": args["issue"]})
```

```python
    return await mcp.call("provideTroubleshooting", context, {"ticketId":
new_ticket["id"]})
```

- **Parallel calls** reduce overall latency.
- **Branching logic** uses both profile and issue severity to choose the next action.
- Each MCP call is a simple JSON-RPC invocation—core workflow code stays concise.

C. Dynamic Tool Discovery for Flexible Flows

Use the listMethods tool to discover available capabilities and adapt workflows accordingly:

python

```python
methods = await mcp.call("listMethods", context, {})

if "premiumRecommendation" in methods:

    rec_tool = "premiumRecommendation"

else:

    rec_tool = "standardRecommendation"


recommendation = await mcp.call(rec_tool, context, {"userId":
context["userId"]})
```

This lets you deploy new adapters/tools without changing client code.

D. Best Practices

Practice	Why It Matters
Minimize Context Checks	Group related conditions to avoid repeated branching
Centralize Orchestration Logic	Keep workflow code in one module for easier updates
Graceful Fallbacks	Always include a default branch to handle unexpected context values
Leverage Batch Calls	Combine related tool calls when possible to optimize throughput
Test All Paths	Write unit tests for each branch using mock contexts

By expressing all decision logic in terms of **context inspection**, **conditional branching**, and **JSON-RPC tool invocations**, you create workflows that are both **flexible** and **maintainable**—able to evolve as new context types or tools are added to your MCP ecosystem.

3.2.3 Integrating Context with Machine Learning Models

Bringing context into your ML models—whether a traditional classifier or a large language model—requires transforming raw context data into a form the model can consume. MCP shines here by making context readily available through simple tool calls, letting you focus on **how** to inject it into your model rather than **where** it comes from.

A. Context in Prompt-Based LLMs

Prompt Templates with Context Slots
Define prompts that include placeholders for each piece of context:
jinja

You are a support agent. Customer {{userName}} (tier: {{userTier}}) last ordered on {{lastOrderDate}}.

They say: "{{userMessage}}"

Provide a helpful, polite answer.

1. At runtime, fetch each context value via MCP calls (getUserProfile, getLastOrder) and render the template before sending to the LLM.
2. Dynamic Context Window Management
   - **Summarization**: If a user's history is long, call a summarization tool (summarizeHistory) to compress it into a concise paragraph.
   - **Chunking**: For knowledge-base documents, fetch only the top-K relevant chunks via RAG adapters and embed those into the prompt.

Chaining Tool Calls
Use a sequence of MCP calls to enrich context before the final inference:
python

```python
profile = await mcp.call("getUserProfile", context, {"userId": uid})

history = await mcp.call("summarizeHistory", context, {"userId": uid})

answer = await llm.generate(render_prompt(profile, history, message))
```

B. Context as Features in Classical ML

1. Feature Engineering via MCP

Call tools to fetch numerical context features (e.g., getAccountAge, getAvgSpend) and assemble them into a feature vector for your model:
python

```python
features = {

 **await mcp.call("getAccountMetrics", context, {"userId": uid}),

 "hourOfDay": datetime.utcnow().hour

}
```

```python
prediction = classifier.predict([features])
```

2. Real-Time Feature Updates
   ○ For streaming ML (e.g., fraud detection), subscribe to sensor or transaction streams via MCP notifications and update feature stores on the fly.

C. Context in Embedding & Retrieval Pipelines

1. Contextual Embeddings

When embedding user messages, prepend or append a learned "context token" vector:
python

```python
ctx_vec = await mcp.call("getUserEmbedding", context, {"userId": uid})

msg_vec = embedder.encode(message)

combined = concatenate([ctx_vec, msg_vec])
```

   ○ Use combined for similarity searches or classification.
2. Retrieval-Augmented Generation (RAG)

Query a vector store with both message and context embeddings to fetch highly relevant documents:
python

```python
docs = await mcp.call("vectorSearch", context, {"queryVec": combined, "topK": 5})
```

D. Best Practices

Practice	Rationale
Minimal Prompt Context	Include only the most relevant context to stay within token limits.

Preprocess & Sanitize	Normalize dates, remove PII, and format context consistently.
Cache Heavy Context	Summaries or embeddings that are costly to compute should be cached.
Validate Context Freshness	Track timestamp in context to avoid using stale data in critical decisions.
Monitor Model Drift	Log model outputs vs. context versions to detect when context fails to help.

By leveraging MCP to fetch and prepare context, you ensure that every model call—prompt-generation, feature construction, or embedding—starts from a **rich, accurate** data foundation. This integration turns static inference into a **dynamic, context-aware** decision pipeline.

3.3 Using MCP to Manage Context

3.3.1 Storing and Retrieving Context Data Efficiently

When building context-aware workflows, you need a fast, reliable store for session state, user metadata, or streaming context. Below are patterns and best practices for choosing a store, designing your key schema, and accessing context with minimal overhead.

A. Choosing the Right Context Store

Store Type	Use Case	Pros	Cons
In-Memory Cache (e.g., Python dict)	Single-instance development, ephemeral state	Zero latency, trivial API	Not shared across processes

Distributed Cache (e.g., Redis, Memcached)	Session data, short-lived context, pub/sub	Fast, multiplayer clients	Requires an external service
NoSQL Database (e.g., MongoDB, DynamoDB)	Complex or large state, flexible schemas	Durable, queryable	Higher latency than caches
Relational DB (e.g., PostgreSQL)	Strong consistency, transactional workflows	ACID guarantees, joins	Slower for high-QPS lookups

For most real-time context needs, a **Redis**-backed store strikes the best balance of speed, ease of use, and built-in TTL support.

B. Designing Your Key and Field Schema

1. Key Namespacing

Use clear prefixes to avoid collisions:
makefile

session:<sessionId>:state

user:<userId>:preferences

stream:<sessionId>:events

2. Field Structures

Hashes for grouped context:
redis

HSET session:abc123 state lastToolCalled "getProfile" userTier "gold"

o **JSON blobs** when fields are deeply nested (using RedisJSON module)

Sorted sets or lists for streaming sequences:
redis

RPUSH stream:abc123:events '{"evt":"temp","val":22.5,"ts":...}'

C. Managing TTL and Expiration

Set a sensible TTL on session keys to auto-expire idle contexts:
redis

EXPIRE session:abc123:state 3600 # 1 hour

- **Sliding expiration**: on each read/write, refresh the TTL if the session remains active.
- **Persistent vs. Ephemeral**: keep long-lived user preferences in a database without expiration; use short TTLs for transient session state.

D. Efficient Retrieval Patterns

1. Single-Hop Reads

Fetch only the fields you need:
python

state = await redis.hgetall(f"session:{sid}:state")

2. Batch Fetching

When you need multiple context types (state + preferences), pipeline your calls:
python

pipe = redis.pipeline()

pipe.hgetall(f"session:{sid}:state")

pipe.hgetall(f"user:{uid}:preferences")

state, prefs = await pipe.execute()

3. Pub/Sub for Streaming

Subscribe to a Redis channel for real-time context updates:
python

```python
pubsub = redis.pubsub()

await pubsub.subscribe(f"stream:{sid}:events")

async for msg in pubsub.listen():

  process(msg["data"])
```

E. Serialization and Versioning

- **JSON vs. Native Types**:
  - Use native hash fields for simple values; serialize complex objects to JSON only when necessary.
- **Schema Versioning**:
  - Store a contextVersion field so adapters know how to migrate old formats.
- **Compression**:
  - For very large blobs (e.g., long chat histories), compress before storing and decompress on retrieval.

F. Best Practices

Practice	Rationale
Minimal Footprint	Store only needed fields to keep lookups fast.
TTL Management	Prevent stale contexts consuming memory indefinitely.
Pipelining	Reduce network round-trips when fetching multiple keys.

Connection Pooling	Reuse your Redis or database connections.
Monitoring Evictions	Alert on high eviction rates—may indicate undersized cache.
Graceful Fallbacks	If the cache is unavailable, fall back to a database or default values.

By selecting an appropriate store, naming your keys methodically, and fetching only the context you need—ideally in batched or pipelined calls—you'll keep your context-aware workflows snappy and scalable, ready to serve high-QPS AI workloads.

3.3.2 Real-Time Context Updates and State Management

Keeping your AI agents continuously in sync with rapidly changing context—sensor readings, user actions, market feeds—requires a combination of **streaming updates**, **efficient state stores**, and **robust change management**. MCP's support for notifications and its separation of context logic into adapters make this tractable at scale.

A. Streaming Context via JSON-RPC Notifications

Fire-and-Forget Updates
JSON-RPC **notifications** (requests without an id) let adapters push context changes to the MCP server without waiting for a response:
json

```
{

  "jsonrpc": "2.0",

  "method": "streamSensorData",

  "params": {

    "context": { "sessionId": "abc123" },
```

"args": { "sensorId": "temp-42", "value": 22.7, "timestamp": "2025-04-18T14:05:00Z" }

    }

}

- The server simply hands each notification to the streamSensorData adapter, which writes it into the context store or triggers downstream logic.
- **Chunked/Incremental Responses**
  For long-running operations, adapters can respond with partial result chunks. The server relays each chunk to the client, enabling the AI agent to process data in real time without waiting for the full payload.

B. Underlying Transport for Live Updates

- **WebSockets / Server-Sent Events (SSE)**
  While HTTP POST + notifications suffice for many scenarios, you can layer WebSocket or SSE on top of your MCP server to maintain an open channel for high-frequency updates.
- **Message Brokers**
  Publishers (adapters) send context events to a broker (e.g., Kafka, Redis Pub/Sub). MCP server instances subscribe and translate incoming events into JSON-RPC notifications internally.

C. State Store Patterns

Pattern	Use Case	Trade-Offs
Append-Only Log	Event sourcing of all context changes	Full audit trail, higher storage
Snapshot-Plus-Deltas	Frequent state reads with occasional historical lookup	Fast reads, manageable size

| Time-Series DB | High-volume sensor data | Built-in retention & aggregation |
| In-Memory Cache | Ultra-low-latency, single-instance prototyping | Not durable, no cross-instance sync |

-
  Event Sourcing
  Record every context update as an immutable event. Build the current state by replaying or by loading periodic snapshots plus recent deltas.
- **Snapshots + Deltas**
  Persist a full state snapshot (e.g., user profile, machine state) periodically, and store only the most recent events in a short-lived queue for quick recoveries.
- **Time-Series Databases**
  When context is inherently temporal (IoT telemetry, market ticks), leverage a TSDB (InfluxDB, TimescaleDB) that optimizes writes and windowed queries.

D. Concurrency and Consistency

- **Atomic Updates**
  Use atomic data structures (Redis hashes, lists) or transactions (multi/EXEC) to prevent race conditions when multiple events arrive simultaneously.
- **Optimistic Locking**
  Store a version counter with your context object. Adapters read–modify–write only if the version matches, retrying on conflicts.
- **Ordering Guarantees**
  Ensure events are applied in timestamp or sequence order. Message brokers often include offsets or partitions to help preserve ordering per key (e.g., per session).

E. Example: Streaming Sensor Feed into Context Store

python

```python
# adapters/stream_adapter.py
import asyncio, json
from jsonrpcserver import method
from redis.asyncio import Redis


redis = Redis()


@method
async def streamSensorData(context, args):
    key = f"stream:{context['sessionId']}:latest"
    # Store only the most recent value for quick lookups
    await redis.hset(key, mapping={
        "sensorId": args["sensorId"],
        "value": args["value"],
        "ts": args["timestamp"]
    })
    # Optionally, push to a list for history
    await redis.rpush(f"stream:{context['sessionId']}:history",
json.dumps(args))
    # Trim history to last N entries
    await redis.ltrim(f"stream:{context['sessionId']}:history", -1000, -1)
    return None  # notifications need no response
```

- **Latest State** lives in a hash for O(1) retrieval of current values.
- **Historical Window** kept in a capped list for occasional backtesting or anomaly detection.

F. Best Practices

Practice	Why It Matters
Separate Hot & Cold Paths	Keep high-frequency updates in a fast cache; archive older events elsewhere.
TTL for Temporal Data	Auto-expire outdated context (e.g., short-lived session info).
Backpressure Handling	Drop or queue events if the server is overloaded; signal clients to slow down.
Resilience to Failures	On adapter or store outage, buffer events locally and retry—avoid data loss.
Monitoring Lag & Throughput	Track time between event generation and application; alert on slowdowns.

By combining **JSON-RPC notifications, efficient state stores**, and **solid concurrency controls**, MCP lets you maintain an up-to-the-millisecond view of context—empowering your AI agents to react instantly to the world around them.

3.3.3 Synchronizing Context Across Different AI Systems and Agents

When you run multiple AI agents or services that share parts of the same workflow, it's crucial that they see a **consistent view** of context. Synchronization ensures that one agent's update to session state or user data is immediately available to others, preventing stale or conflicting behavior.

A. Centralized Context Repository

1. Single Source of Truth
   - Store all shared context in a **centralized data store** (Redis cache, NoSQL database, or relational DB).
   - Every agent reads from and writes to this common repository, avoiding in-memory divergence.
2. Namespaces and Keys
   - Use clear, hierarchical key patterns (session:<id>, user:<id>, workflow:<id>) to isolate context domains.
   - Include a version or lastUpdated timestamp on each context object.

B. Event-Driven Context Propagation

1. Publish–Subscribe Model
   - When an agent updates context (e.g., advances a workflow step), it **publishes** a context-changed event to a message broker (Kafka, Redis Pub/Sub).
   - Other agents **subscribe** to relevant channels and update their local caches or take immediate action.

Event Payloads
json

```json
{

  "type": "ContextUpdated",

  "domain": "session",

  "id": "abc123",

  "changes": { "lastTool": "verifyIdentity", "state": "verified" },

  "timestamp": "2025-04-18T14:30:00Z"
```

}

- o Payload includes domain, id, the changes map, and a timestamp for ordering.

C. Versioning and Conflict Resolution

1. Optimistic Concurrency
    - o Agents read the current version of a context object before applying updates.
    - o On write, they include the expected version; the store accepts the update only if versions match, incrementing the version atomically.
2. Merge Strategies
    - o **Last-Write-Wins**: Simplest, but may overwrite concurrent changes.
    - o **Field-Level Merging**: Only overwrite the fields you're responsible for, leaving other fields intact.
    - o **Custom Resolution**: For complex objects (e.g., lists of events), apply application-specific merge logic in adapters.

D. Hybrid Push–Pull Approach

1. Pull Model for Initial Load
    - o On startup or session join, an agent **pulls** the full context snapshot from the centralized store.
2. Push Model for Deltas
    - o Subsequent updates are pushed via **Pub/Sub** so agents can apply **only the diffs**, reducing bandwidth and speeding up reaction times.

E. Example: Orchestrating a Multi-Agent Workflow

python

Agent A: Verifies user and updates context

```
await mcp.call("updateSessionState", context, {"sessionId": sid, "state":
"verified"})

# Publish event

await mcp.call("publishEvent", context, {

  "channel": f"session:{sid}:events",

  "event": {"type": "stateChange", "state": "verified", "version":
new_version}

})


# Agent B: Listens to context changes

async for evt in subscribe(f"session:{sid}:events"):

  if evt["type"] == "stateChange" and evt["state"] == "verified":

    # Proceed with next step

    await mcp.call("startNextTask", context, {"sessionId": sid})
```

- **Agent A** updates the shared context and emits a notification.
- **Agent B** receives the notification and continues the workflow without polling.

F. Best Practices

Practice	Benefit
Atomic Versioned Updates	Prevents race conditions and lost writes
Event Ordering Guarantees	Use broker features (partitions, offsets) to maintain order

Field-Level Context Design	Limits merge conflicts by scoping each agent to its fields
TTL and Cleanup	Expire or archive stale sessions to free resources
Monitoring Consistency Lag	Track time between write and subscriber receipt, alert on delays

By combining a **centralized store**, **event-driven propagation**, and **versioned updates**, you'll ensure all your AI agents and services operate on a **synchronized, up-to-date** context—enabling coherent, multi-agent workflows that scale reliably.

3.4 Industry Case Study: Healthcare AI Systems

3.4.1 Implementing MCP in Healthcare for Patient Data Integration

In healthcare, AI systems often need to integrate multiple patient data sources— electronic health records (EHR), medical imaging archives, wearable device feeds, and real-time monitoring systems—while meeting strict privacy and compliance requirements. MCP provides a standardized, secure way to fetch, update, and synchronize this data.

A. Common Patient Data Sources

Data Source	Protocol / API	Typical Context Fields
EHR (FHIR)	RESTful FHIR APIs	patientId, encounterId, authToken

Lab Systems (HL7 v2)	MLLP or HTTP Interface	orderId, labTestCode, timestamp
PACS (DICOM)	DICOMweb or DICOM C-STORE	studyInstanceUID, modality
Wearables & IoT	MQTT, WebSockets, REST	deviceId, sensorType, value, ts

B. Building FHIR Adapters

Adapter: fetchPatientRecord

python

```python
# adapters/fhir_adapter.py
import os, httpx
from jsonrpcserver import method


FHIR_BASE = os.getenv("FHIR_BASE_URL")    # e.g.,
"https://ehr.example.com/fhir"

FHIR_TOKEN = os.getenv("FHIR_API_TOKEN")


@method
async def fetchPatientRecord(context: dict, args: dict):
    """"""
```

```python
    Retrieves a patient's FHIR record by patientId.
    Params:
      args["patientId"]: string
    """

    pid = args.get("patientId")
    if not pid:
        raise ValueError("Missing patientId")


    headers = {
        "Authorization": f"Bearer {FHIR_TOKEN}",
        "Accept": "application/fhir+json"
    }
    async with httpx.AsyncClient(timeout=10) as client:
        resp = await client.get(f"{FHIR_BASE}/Patient/{pid}", headers=headers)
        resp.raise_for_status()
        data = resp.json()


    # Extract relevant fields for AI context
    return {
        "id": data["id"],
        "name": " ".join([n["given"][0] for n in data["name"]] + [data["name"][0]["family"]]),
        "gender": data.get("gender"),
```

```
    "birthDate": data.get("birthDate")

}
```

Security: TLS, OAuth2 Bearer tokens

Compliance: Scopes limited to Patient.read

C. Enriching Clinical Context

Fetch Active Encounters
python

```python
@method

async def fetchActiveEncounters(context, args):

    pid = args["patientId"]

    # GET /Encounter?patient={pid}&status=active

    ...

    return {"encounters": [...]}
```

Retrieve Lab Results
python

```python
@method

async def fetchLabResults(context, args):

    order = args["orderId"]

    # HL7 v2 or REST endpoint call

    ...

    return {"results": [{ "test": "CBC", "value": 5.4, "unit": "10^3/µL" }]}
```

1. **Streaming Vital Signs**
   - Use JSON-RPC notifications to push heart rate or SpO_2 readings in real time into a time-series store.

D. Orchestrating a Patient Summary Workflow

python

```python
async def buildPatientSummary(mcp, context, args):

    pid = args["patientId"]

    # 1. Batch fetch record and active encounters

    calls = [

{"jsonrpc":"2.0","id":1,"method":"fetchPatientRecord","params":{"context":context,"args":{"patientId":pid}}},

{"jsonrpc":"2.0","id":2,"method":"fetchActiveEncounters","params":{"context":context,"args":{"patientId":pid}}}

    ]

    rec, enc = await mcp.batch_call(calls)

    # 2. If no active encounter, create one

    if not enc["result"]["encounters"]:

        new_enc = await mcp.call("createEncounter", context, {"patientId": pid, "type": "inpatient"})

        enc_data = new_enc["result"]

    else:
```

```
enc_data = enc["result"]["encounters"][0]

# 3. Summarize labs if any

labs = await mcp.call("fetchLabResults", context, {"orderId":
enc_data["orderId"]})

return {

 "patient": rec["result"],

 "encounter": enc_data,

 "labs": labs["result"]["results"]

}
```

E. Best Practices in Healthcare Context Integration

Practice	Rationale
Least Privilege	Grant adapters only the minimal IAM/FHIR scopes needed.
Audit Logging	Record every MCP call with context.userId, sessionId, and timestamp for compliance.
Data Minimization	Only fetch and expose fields required for AI reasoning.
Encryption & TLS	Protect PHI in transit; enforce strong cipher suites.

Cache with Caution	Cache non-PII reference data; avoid caching sensitive details longer than necessary.
Schema Validation	Use JSON Schema to validate FHIR payloads before use.
Fail-Safe Defaults	On adapter failure, return anonymized or null context to avoid PHI leaks.

By encapsulating each clinical data source behind MCP adapters and orchestrating calls with context-aware branching, you can build robust healthcare AI systems that respect privacy, ensure data consistency, and deliver timely, personalized insights to clinicians and patients alike.

3.4.2 Context-Aware AI for Diagnosis and Treatment Planning

In clinical settings, AI can support diagnosis and personalized treatment by weaving together diverse patient data—medical history, vitals, lab results, imaging—and external knowledge sources (clinical guidelines, drug databases). MCP provides the scaffolding for fetching, updating, and synchronizing this contextual information through simple, composable tool calls.

A. Defining Clinical Context

- **Patient Demographics & History**
  patientId, age, sex, known comorbidities, allergy list
- **Current Presentation**
  Chief complaint, reported symptoms, triage vitals (heart rate, blood pressure, temperature)
- **Investigations**
  Recent lab panels (CBC, BMP), imaging summaries (CT/MRI reports), genetic markers

- **Treatment Constraints**
  Medication history, current prescriptions, renal/hepatic function, insurance/formulary restrictions

Each of these context elements is exposed via a dedicated MCP adapter (e.g., fetchPatientHistory, fetchLatestVitals, fetchImagingReport).

B. Clinical Decision Support Adapters

1. **Guidelines Engine** (fetchGuidelineRecommendations)
   - Calls a clinical decision-support API (e.g., CDS Hooks) with context to receive evidence-based recommendations.
2. **Drug Interaction Checker** (checkDrugInteractions)
   - Receives current medication list and proposed drugs; returns alerts for contraindications.
3. **Risk Scoring Service** (calculateSepsisRisk, calculateStrokeRisk)
   - Ingests vitals, labs, and history; returns a numeric risk score and severity category.

C. Diagnostic Workflow Orchestration

python

```python
async def diagnosticWorkflow(mcp, context, args):

    # 1. Gather core context in parallel

    results = await mcp.batch_call([

        {"jsonrpc":"2.0","id":1,"method":"fetchPatientHistory","params":{"context":context,"args":{"patientId":args["patientId"]}}},

        {"jsonrpc":"2.0","id":2,"method":"fetchLatestVitals","params":{"context":context,"args":{"patientId":args["patientId"]}}},
```

```
{"jsonrpc":"2.0","id":3,"method":"fetchLabResults","params":{"context":context,"args":{"patientId":args["patientId"]}}}
```

```
])

history = results[0]["result"]

vitals  = results[1]["result"]

labs    = results[2]["result"]



# 2. Compute risk scores

sepsis = await mcp.call("calculateSepsisRisk", context, {"vitals": vitals, "labs": labs})

stroke = await mcp.call("calculateStrokeRisk", context, {"history": history, "vitals": vitals})



# 3. Branch based on high-risk threshold

if sepsis["risk"] >= 8:

    await mcp.call("alertCareTeam", context, {"patientId": args["patientId"], "reason": "High sepsis risk"})

```

D. Treatment Planning & Personalization

1. **Evidence-Based Recommendations**

   - Invoke `fetchGuidelineRecommendations` with the patient's diagnosis code and comorbidities to retrieve first-line therapy options.

2. **Medication Safety Checks**

   - Before prescribing, call `checkDrugInteractions` and present any flags to the clinician.

3. **Patient Preference Integration**

   - Use a `fetchAdvanceDirectives` tool to respect do-not-resuscitate orders or treatment refusals.

E. Continuous Monitoring & Plan Adjustment

- **Streaming Vitals**: Use JSON-RPC notifications (`streamVitalSign`) from bedside monitors.

- **Adaptive Alerts**: If vitals cross critical thresholds, dynamically escalate via `alertCareTeam`.

- **Recompute Treatment**: Periodically re-invoke `calculateSepsisRisk` or `fetchGuidelineRecommendations` as new data arrives.

F. Best Practices

Practice	Rationale
Audit Trails	Log every MCP call with `context.userId`, `timestamp`, and tool name to meet compliance.
Explainability	Surface scoring inputs and guideline rationale to clinicians for trust.
Data Minimization	Fetch only required context fields; avoid over-exposing PHI.
Fail-Safe Defaults	If an adapter fails, degrade to an offline clinical protocol rather than blocking care.
Versioned Guidelines	Tag guideline fetches with `version` to ensure consistency over time.

By organizing diagnosis and treatment steps as a sequence of context-driven MCP tool calls, you build an AI system that is **modular**, **auditable**, and **responsive**—empowering clinicians with up-to-date, personalized decision support while maintaining strict governance over patient data.

3.5 Interactive Q&A

3.5.1 How Would You Apply Context in an AI-Driven Healthcare System?

1. **Identify Critical Context Elements**
   - Which pieces of patient data (e.g., allergies, comorbidities, recent lab values) would most influence your AI's recommendations?
   - How would you rank them by impact and timeliness?
2. **Designing Adapters for Clinical Systems**
   - What adapters would you build to fetch FHIR resources (Patient, Encounter, Observation) from an EHR?

- How would you handle HL7 v2 messages or DICOMweb calls in a consistent MCP interface?

3. **Session vs. Long-Lived Context**
   - What belongs in the per-request session context (e.g., current encounter ID, request timestamp) versus patient-level context (e.g., demographics, history)?
   - How would you manage TTLs and cache invalidation for each?

4. **Real-Time Monitoring**
   - For streaming vital signs from bedside monitors, would you use JSON-RPC notifications or a separate pub/sub channel?
   - How would your MCP workflow react to a critical threshold breach in real time?

5. **Privacy and Compliance**
   - Which context fields contain PHI, and how would you ensure they're encrypted in transit and at rest?
   - How would you audit every MCP call for HIPAA or GDPR compliance?

6. **Error Handling & Fallbacks**
   - If a context-fetch adapter (e.g., lab results) fails, what default or fallback would you provide to avoid blocking critical decision support?
   - How would you surface that failure to the clinician?

7. **Adaptive Treatment Paths**
   - How could you branch your treatment-planning workflow based on context (e.g., renal function from labs alters medication choice)?
   - What rules or risk-scoring adapters would you invoke conditionally?

8. **Context Synchronization Across Teams**
   - If multiple AI agents (triage bot, diagnostic assistant, discharge planner) share patient context, how would you keep them in sync?
   - What event-driven pattern or versioning scheme would you adopt?

9. **Performance and Scalability**
   - Which context calls are high-frequency (e.g., streaming vitals) versus low-frequency (e.g., demographics lookup), and how would you optimize each?
   - Would you batch or cache certain context fetches to reduce EHR API load?

10. **Measuring Impact**
    - What metrics (time-to-alert, guideline adherence, clinician satisfaction) would you track to evaluate the effectiveness of your context-aware AI workflows?
    - How would you design A/B experiments to validate that adding context improves patient outcomes?

Reflect on these points—or discuss them with your team—to craft a robust, secure, and high-impact context-aware AI solution in the healthcare domain.

3.5.2 Discussion on Real-Time Context Updates in AI Workflows

1. Use Cases for Streaming Context
   - Which AI scenarios in your domain benefit most from real-time data (e.g., predictive maintenance, live trading signals, telehealth monitoring)?
   - How would latency requirements differ between, say, anomaly detection in factory sensors vs. personalized recommendations in an e-commerce chat?
2. Choosing an Update Mechanism
   - When is a JSON-RPC **notification** sufficient versus a persistent channel like WebSocket or message queue?
   - How do you balance the simplicity of HTTP-based notifications with the efficiency of a brokered pub/sub system?
3. State Consistency and Ordering
   - What guarantees do you need around event ordering? If two sensors fire concurrently, how do you ensure your AI sees them in the correct sequence?
   - Would you include sequence numbers or timestamps in each event to reconcile out-of-order arrivals?
4. Backpressure and Throttling
   - How would you handle bursts of high-frequency updates that could overwhelm your context store or AI agents?
   - Would you drop, buffer, or sample events, and what criteria would guide that decision?
5. Concurrency Control
   - If multiple adapters publish updates for the same context key (e.g., two different IoT feeds for "room temperature"), how do you prevent races?
   - Would you use atomic operations, optimistic locking, or a dedicated sequencer to serialize writes?
6. Efficient Retrieval and Caching
   - For AI steps that need both the latest and recent history, how do you fetch these without multiple round-trips?
   - Would you maintain both a "current state" hash and a capped event list, and how would you pipeline those calls?
7. Error Handling in Streams
   - If a streaming adapter temporarily fails (e.g., network glitch), how does your workflow detect gaps in the context feed?

- Would you implement sequence-based checks, or compare expected vs. actual event rates to trigger recovery?

8. Integration with Inference Logic
   - At what points in your AI pipeline do you poll for new context vs. react immediately on receipt?
   - How do you design your inference loop to interleave context-processing and model calls without blocking?

9. Monitoring & Alerting for Context Health
   - Which metrics (event throughput, processing lag, error rate) will you track to ensure your real-time context layer is healthy?
   - How would you surface context starvation (no updates when expected) or overload (too many events) to your operations team?

10. Security and Compliance for Live Data
   - How do you authenticate and authorize each real-time context update, especially when the data contains sensitive information?
   - What encryption and audit mechanisms are necessary to comply with domain regulations (HIPAA, GDPR, PCI)?

Reflecting on these points will help you architect robust, low-latency AI workflows that stay in sync with rapidly changing contexts—ensuring your models make decisions on the freshest, most accurate data available.

Chapter 4: Data Integration and External System Connectivity

4.1 Connecting to Databases and File Systems

4.1.1 How to Configure MCP Servers to Access Databases (SQL, NoSQL)

Connecting your MCP server to both relational and document stores follows the same general pattern: externalize your connection settings, create a shared connection pool at startup, and write adapters that borrow from the pool to execute queries or commands. Below is a step-by-step guide for both SQL (PostgreSQL via **asyncpg**) and NoSQL (MongoDB via **motor**).

A. Extract Configuration into Settings

Use a Pydantic settings class to centralize your database URLs and pool parameters:

python

```python
# config.py

from pydantic import BaseSettings, Field, AnyUrl


class MCPSettings(BaseSettings):
    # PostgreSQL (asyncpg)
    sql_dsn: AnyUrl = Field(..., env="SQL_DSN")
    sql_min_size: int = Field(5, env="SQL_POOL_MIN")
    sql_max_size: int = Field(20, env="SQL_POOL_MAX")


    # MongoDB (motor)
```

```python
    mongo_uri: AnyUrl = Field(..., env="MONGO_URI")

    mongo_max_pool: int = Field(10, env="MONGO_POOL_MAX")


    class Config:

        env_file = ".env"

        env_file_encoding = "utf-8"


settings = MCPSettings()
```

env

```
# .env
SQL_DSN=postgresql://user:pass@db-host:5432/mydb

SQL_POOL_MIN=5

SQL_POOL_MAX=20


MONGO_URI=mongodb://user:pass@mongo-host:27017/mydb

MONGO_POOL_MAX=10
```

B. Initialize Connection Pools on Startup

In your main application module, establish shared pools that adapters can import:

python

```python
# db.py

import asyncio

import asyncpg

from motor.motor_asyncio import AsyncIOMotorClient

from config import settings


# SQL pool (PostgreSQL)

_sql_pool: asyncpg.Pool = None


async def init_sql_pool():
    global _sql_pool
    _sql_pool = await asyncpg.create_pool(
        dsn=str(settings.sql_dsn),
        min_size=settings.sql_min_size,
        max_size=settings.sql_max_size
    )


def get_sql_pool() -> asyncpg.Pool:
    return _sql_pool


# NoSQL client (MongoDB)
```

```python
_mongo_client: AsyncIOMotorClient = None


def init_mongo_client():
    global _mongo_client
    _mongo_client = AsyncIOMotorClient(
        settings.mongo_uri,
        maxPoolSize=settings.mongo_max_pool
    )


def get_mongo_db():
    return _mongo_client.get_default_database()
```

Hook these into your FastAPI startup events:

python

```python
# main.py (excerpt)
from fastapi import FastAPI
from db import init_sql_pool, init_mongo_client

app = FastAPI()


@app.on_event("startup")
```

```python
async def startup_event():

    await init_sql_pool()

    init_mongo_client()
```

C. Write Adapters That Use the Pools

SQL Adapter Example
python

```python
# adapters/user_sql.py

from jsonrpcserver import method

from db import get_sql_pool


@method
async def getUserById(context: dict, args: dict):
    user_id = args.get("userId")
    if not user_id:
        raise ValueError("userId is required")

    pool = get_sql_pool()
    async with pool.acquire() as conn:
        row = await conn.fetchrow(
            "SELECT id, name, email FROM users WHERE id = $1", user_id
        )
```

```python
    if not row:

        return None

    return dict(row)
```

NoSQL Adapter Example
python

```python
# adapters/order_mongo.py

from jsonrpcserver import method

from db import get_mongo_db


@method
async def fetchRecentOrders(context: dict, args: dict):

    user_id = args.get("userId")

    limit = args.get("limit", 5)


    db = get_mongo_db()

    cursor = db.orders.find({"userId": user_id}).sort("createdAt", -1).limit(limit)

    docs = await cursor.to_list(length=limit)

    # Convert ObjectId to string if needed

    for doc in docs:

        doc["_id"] = str(doc["_id"])

    return {"orders": docs}
```

D. Best Practices for Database Access

Practice	Benefit
Single Shared Pool	Avoids overhead of repeatedly opening/closing connections.
Acquire with async with	Ensures connections are returned to the pool even on errors.
Parameterize Queries	Prevents SQL injection and leverages query caching.
Indexing & Projection	In NoSQL, limit fields returned (.find({}, {"_id":1, "status":1})) to reduce payload.
Timeouts & Retries	Wrap adapter calls with retry/back-off logic for transient failures.
Credentials Management	Store sensitive DSNs in environment, not source code.
Monitoring Pool Metrics	Track pool usage, waiting clients, and connection errors via application metrics.
Schema Validation	Validate args against JSON Schema to catch bad input early (e.g., missing userId).

By externalizing your database configuration, bootstrapping robust connection pools at startup, and writing idempotent adapters that borrow and release connections cleanly, you'll equip your MCP server to handle both SQL and NoSQL loads with high efficiency, safety, and maintainability.

4.1.2 Reading and Writing to File Systems Using MCP

MCP lets you treat file I/O—whether configuration files, document stores, or user uploads—as "tools" just like databases or APIs. The pattern is to isolate all filesystem logic in adapters, validate paths, and stream large files when needed.

A. Configure a Safe Base Directory

Define in your settings the root directory your adapters may access:

python

```python
# config.py (excerpt)

from pydantic import BaseSettings, Field


class MCPSettings(BaseSettings):

    file_root: str = Field("/var/mcp/files", env="FILE_ROOT")


    class Config:

        env_file = ".env"


settings = MCPSettings()
```

env

```
# .env
```

FILE_ROOT=/srv/mcp_data

—this prevents accidental traversal outside an approved folder.

B. Adapter: Reading Files

python

```python
# adapters/file_reader.py
from pathlib import Path
from jsonrpcserver import method
from config import settings


@method
async def readFile(context: dict, args: dict):
    """

    Reads the entire contents of a text file under FILE_ROOT.
    Args:
      args["path"]: relative path under settings.file_root
    """
    rel = args.get("path")
    if not rel:
        raise ValueError("Missing required argument: path")
```

```python
    base = Path(settings.file_root).resolve()

    target = (base / rel).resolve()

    if not str(target).startswith(str(base)):

        # prevent directory traversal

        raise PermissionError(f"Access to {rel} is forbidden")


    content = target.read_text(encoding="utf-8")

    return {"content": content}
```

C. Adapter: Writing Files

python

```python
# adapters/file_writer.py

from pathlib import Path

from jsonrpcserver import method

from config import settings


@method

async def writeFile(context: dict, args: dict):

    """""
```

Writes content to a file under FILE_ROOT, creating directories as needed.

Args:

args["path"]: relative path under settings.file_root

args["content"]: string data to write

"""

```python
rel = args.get("path")

data = args.get("content", "")

if not rel:

    raise ValueError("Missing required argument: path")


base = Path(settings.file_root).resolve()

target = (base / rel).resolve()

if not str(target).startswith(str(base)):

    raise PermissionError(f"Access to {rel} is forbidden")


target.parent.mkdir(parents=True, exist_ok=True)

target.write_text(data, encoding="utf-8")

return {"status": "ok", "path": rel}
```

D. Streaming Large Files

For very large files, stream in chunks via JSON-RPC **notifications** or by returning an async generator:

python

```python
# adapters/file_streamer.py

from pathlib import Path

from jsonrpcserver import method, stream

from config import settings


@method
async def streamFile(context: dict, args: dict):
    """

    Streams a file's bytes in base64-encoded chunks.
    Args:
      args["path"]: relative file path
      args["chunkSize"]: integer chunk size in bytes (default: 65536)
    """

    rel = args.get("path")

    size = args.get("chunkSize", 64 * 1024)

    base = Path(settings.file_root).resolve()

    target = (base / rel).resolve()

    if not str(target).startswith(str(base)):

        raise PermissionError(f"Access to {rel} is forbidden")
```

```python
async def generator():

    with target.open("rb") as f:

        while True:

            chunk = f.read(size)

            if not chunk:

                break

            yield {"chunk": chunk.hex()}  # or use base64


    return stream(generator())
```

Clients can consume each streamed partial result as it arrives.

E. Error Handling

- **Missing Files**: Catch FileNotFoundError and return a JSON-RPC error code -32004 with a message "File not found".
- **Permission Denied**: Translate PermissionError to -32003 with "Access denied".
- **I/O Errors**: Map general OSError to -32000 and include e.strerror in the data field.

Implement a decorator or centralized exception handler in your MCP server to map Python exceptions to standardized JSON-RPC errors.

F. Best Practices

Practice	Rationale

Sanitize Paths	Prevent directory traversal by resolving and checking prefixes
Limit File Types & Sizes	Reject unknown extensions or enforce max-size to avoid abuse
Use Async I/O for Large Files	Keeps the event loop responsive when streaming data
Centralize Error Mapping	Ensure consistent JSON-RPC codes and messages across adapters
Log File Access	Audit which files are read or written for security and debugging
Monitor Disk Usage	Alert on low disk space in your file_root directory
Versioning Output Files	Include timestamps or UUIDs in filenames to avoid overwrites

By encapsulating filesystem operations in well-defined MCP adapters and following these patterns, you provide your AI clients with robust, secure, and efficient file-based context and data storage.

4.1.3 Best Practices for Secure Data Handling

When your MCP adapters bridge to sensitive data—whether in databases, file systems, or external APIs—it's vital to enforce strong security measures at every layer. Below are key practices to protect data confidentiality, integrity, and auditability.

A. Principle of Least Privilege

- **Database Credentials**: Grant adapters only the minimum SQL privileges they need (e.g., SELECT on specific tables; avoid DROP/ALTER).

- **File System Access**: Restrict file-system adapters to a dedicated directory (FILE_ROOT) and disallow write access if only reads are required.
- **API Scopes**: Use scoped API tokens (e.g., OAuth2 scopes limited to Patient.read for EHR calls).

B. Secure Credential Management

- **Environment Variables & Secrets Vaults**: Store DB URIs, API keys, and certificates in environment variables or a secrets manager (Vault, AWS Secrets Manager), not in source code or config files.
- **Automated Rotation**: Implement credential rotation policies and integrate adapters to fetch fresh secrets dynamically where possible.
- **Encryption at Rest**: Ensure any on-disk credential store (e.g., .env files on servers) is encrypted or accessible only by privileged processes.

C. Transport Security

- **TLS Everywhere**: Enforce HTTPS/TLS for all external calls (databases with SSL, REST APIs, file transfers).
- **Strong Ciphers & Cert Validation**: Configure clients to reject weak ciphers and validate server certificates (hostname, CA chain).
- **Mutual TLS**: Where supported (e.g., internal microservices), use mTLS to authenticate both client and server.

D. Input Validation & Sanitization

- **SQL Parameterization**: Never build queries by concatenating strings. Always use parameterized queries or ORM bindings to avoid injection attacks.
- **Path Sanitization**: Resolve file paths against FILE_ROOT and reject any attempt at directory traversal (..).
- **JSON Schema Enforcement**: Validate incoming args and context against your tool manifest's JSON Schema before processing.

E. Encryption of Sensitive Data

- **At Rest**: Encrypt sensitive database tables (TDE) or file-system directories (e.g., using LUKS, EFS).
- **In Transit**: For especially sensitive context (PHI, PII), consider double-encrypting payloads or using application-level encryption before passing through MCP.

F. Audit Logging & Monitoring

- **Structured Logs**: Log every MCP call with timestamp, method, context.userId (or anonymized hash), and adapter outcome (success/error).
- **Immutable Audit Trails**: Ship logs to a write-only, centralized system (ELK, Splunk) to prevent tampering.
- **Access Audits**: Record who accessed or modified critical data, and regularly review logs for unusual patterns.

G. Rate Limiting & Quotas

- **Protect Downstream**: Enforce per-client and per-method rate limits in the MCP server to prevent abusive or accidental overloads.
- **Global Throttles**: Apply overall caps to protect sensitive systems (e.g., EHR services) from unexpected spikes.

H. Secure Defaults & Error Handling

- **Fail-Closed**: On security-related errors (invalid token, missing auth), deny access rather than falling back to permissive behavior.
- **Non-Verbose Errors**: Avoid leaking sensitive details in error messages; log the full stack trace server-side but return only generic messages client-side.

I. Regular Security Reviews

- **Dependency Audits**: Scan dependencies (e.g., pip-audit, Snyk) for vulnerabilities and apply patches promptly.

- **Penetration Testing**: Periodically perform pen tests on your MCP server endpoints and adapter logic.
- **Configuration Drift Detection**: Monitor your infrastructure for unapproved changes to security settings (firewalls, TLS configs, IAM policies).

By weaving these security practices into your MCP server and adapter development, you'll build a robust, defensible layer for data integration—ensuring that sensitive databases, file systems, and APIs remain protected while delivering context-aware AI services.

4.2 Integrating Web APIs and Services

4.2.1 Using MCP to Connect AI Systems to Third-Party APIs

Third-party APIs—from mapping services and payment gateways to social-media feeds and specialized ML endpoints—are vital context sources and action targets for AI applications. MCP lets you encapsulate every external API interaction behind a uniform "tool" interface, isolating authentication, request formatting, rate-limiting, and error handling in standalone adapters.

A. Adapter Anatomy for an External REST API

1. Configuration

Store the API base URL and credentials in your environment (or secrets manager) and load them via your settings class:
env

WEATHER_API_KEY=...

WEATHER_BASE_URL=https://api.openweathermap.org/data/2.5

2. HTTP Client Setup

Use an async HTTP client (e.g., httpx.AsyncClient) to support high concurrency:
python

client = httpx.AsyncClient(

```python
    base_url=settings.weather_base_url,

    timeout=5.0,

    headers={"Authorization": f"Bearer {settings.weather_api_key}"}

)
```

3. Method Definition

Decorate a function with @method that unpacks args, calls the API, handles status codes, parses JSON, and returns a normalized result:

python

```python
# adapters/weather.py

from jsonrpcserver import method

from config import settings

import httpx


@method
async def fetchWeather(context: dict, args: dict):
    city = args.get("city")
    if not city:
        raise ValueError("Missing city parameter")
    resp = await httpx.AsyncClient().get(
        f"{settings.weather_base_url}/weather",
        params={"q": city, "appid": settings.weather_api_key, "units": "metric"}
```

```
)

resp.raise_for_status()

data = resp.json()

return {

   "city": data["name"],

   "temp": data["main"]["temp"],

   "desc": data["weather"][0]["description"]

}
```

4. Registration

Import the adapter module in your main.py so MCP registers the new tool:
python

```
import adapters.weather  # registers fetchWeather
```

B. Handling Authentication & Security

- OAuth2 Flows
  - For APIs requiring OAuth2, implement token-refresh logic inside your adapter or a helper class.
  - Cache tokens with expiration to avoid unnecessary refresh calls.
- API Keys
  - Rotate keys periodically. Store them in a vault or as Kubernetes secrets.
  - Avoid logging raw keys or including them in error messages.
- mTLS or Client Certificates

When APIs require mutual TLS, configure your HTTP client with cert paths:
python

```
client = httpx.AsyncClient(
```

```
    cert=(settings.client_cert, settings.client_key),

    verify=settings.ca_bundle

)
```

C. Rate Limiting and Back-Off

- Server-Side Throttles

Configure MCP's rate-limiter to enforce per-API quotas (e.g., 60 calls/minute):
python

```
from mcp_server.rate_limit import RateLimiter

limiter = RateLimiter(method="fetchWeather", max_calls=60, period=60)
```

- Client-Side Retry

On 429 or 5xx responses, catch the exception and implement exponential back-off with jitter:
python

```
for attempt in range(3):
    try:
        return await client.get(...)
    except httpx.HTTPStatusError as e:
        if e.response.status_code in (429, 502, 503):
            await asyncio.sleep(2 ** attempt + random.random())
        else:
            raise
```

```
raise RuntimeError("API unavailable after retries")
```

D. Input Validation and Schema Enforcement

- JSON Schema for args
  - Define a JSON Schema for each tool in your manifest so MCP can validate incoming parameters before calling the API.
- Sanitize Inputs
  - Strip unexpected fields, enforce length limits, and normalize strings to guard against injection.

E. Caching and Response Normalization

- Result Caching
  - For idempotent API calls (e.g., currency rates, weather), cache responses in Redis with a TTL to reduce external traffic.
- Data Mapping
  - Convert third-party field names into your canonical schema to decouple client code from API changes.

F. Example Invocation from an AI Workflow

python

```python
# In your orchestration code

context = {"sessionId": sid, "userId": uid, "timestamp": now_iso()}

weather = await mcp.call("fetchWeather", context, {"city": "Paris,FR"})

prompt = f"The current weather in {weather['city']} is {weather['temp']}°C with {weather['desc']}."

response = await llm.generate(prompt)
```

G. Best Practices Summary

Practice	Why It Matters
Isolate API Logic in Adapters	Keeps AI workflow code clean and focused on inference
Secure Credential Storage	Prevents accidental leaks of sensitive API keys
Rate Limiting & Retries	Protects both your system and the third-party service
Parameter & Response Validation	Catches issues early and normalizes data for downstream use
Caching for Idempotent Calls	Improves performance and reduces external dependencies
Version Your API Clients	Facilitates rollbacks and safe upgrades as APIs evolve

By wrapping every external HTTP call in an MCP adapter, you create a **uniform, testable**, and **secure** mechanism for AI models to interact with the rich ecosystem of third-party services—while ensuring all integration concerns stay neatly encapsulated.

4.2.2 Examples: Integrating with RESTful APIs, GraphQL APIs, and WebSockets

Below are three MCP adapter patterns illustrating how to wrap common third-party connectivity scenarios as uniform JSON-RPC tools.

A. RESTful API Integration

Use Case: Fetch stock quotes from a public REST endpoint.

python

```python
# adapters/stock_rest.py

import os, httpx

from jsonrpcserver import method

from config import settings


API_KEY = os.getenv("STOCKS_API_KEY")

BASE_URL = "https://api.example.com/v1"


@method
async def fetchStockQuote(context: dict, args: dict):
    """

    Retrieves the latest price for a given ticker.

    args["symbol"]: string, e.g. "AAPL"

    """

    symbol = args.get("symbol")

    if not symbol:

        raise ValueError("Missing required argument: symbol")


    url = f"{BASE_URL}/quotes/{symbol}"

    headers = {"Authorization": f"Bearer {API_KEY}"}
```

```python
    async with httpx.AsyncClient(timeout=5.0) as client:

        resp = await client.get(url, headers=headers)

        resp.raise_for_status()

        data = resp.json()


    return {

        "symbol": symbol,

        "price": data["price"],

        "timestamp": data["timestamp"]

    }
```

- **Error Handling:** resp.raise_for_status() maps HTTP errors to exceptions.
- **Security:** API key in header, loaded from env.

B. GraphQL API Integration

Use Case: Query user profile via a GraphQL endpoint.

python

```python
# adapters/user_graphql.py

import os, httpx

from jsonrpcserver import method

from config import settings
```

```python
GQL_URL = os.getenv("GQL_ENDPOINT")

GQL_TOKEN = os.getenv("GQL_API_TOKEN")


PROFILE_QUERY = """
query GetUserProfile($id: ID!) {
  user(id: $id) {
    id
    name
    email
    preferences { theme, notifications }
  }
}
"""


@method
async def fetchUserProfileGQL(context: dict, args: dict):
    """
    Fetches a user profile using GraphQL.
    args["userId"]: string ID
    """
    uid = args.get("userId")
```

```python
if not uid:
    raise ValueError("Missing required argument: userId")


payload = {"query": PROFILE_QUERY, "variables": {"id": uid}}
headers = {
    "Authorization": f"Bearer {GQL_TOKEN}",
    "Content-Type": "application/json"
}


async with httpx.AsyncClient(timeout=5.0) as client:
    resp = await client.post(GQL_URL, json=payload, headers=headers)
    resp.raise_for_status()
    result = resp.json()


if errors := result.get("errors"):
    raise RuntimeError(f"GraphQL error: {errors}")


user = result["data"]["user"]
return {
    "id": user["id"],
    "name": user["name"],
    "email": user["email"],
```

```
            "preferences": user["preferences"]

    }
```

- **Batching:** GraphQL can fetch nested data in one round-trip.
- **Error Mapping:** Inspect errors field for business logic failures.

C. WebSocket Integration

Use Case: Subscribe to real-time cryptocurrency price updates.

python

```python
# adapters/crypto_ws.py

import asyncio, os, json, websockets

from jsonrpcserver import method, stream

from config import settings


WS_URL = os.getenv("CRYPTO_WS_URL")  # e.g.
"wss://stream.example.com/prices"


@method
async def streamCryptoPrices(context: dict, args: dict):
    """

    Streams live price updates for a given symbol.

    args["symbol"]: e.g. "BTC-USD"
```

Returns a JSON-RPC stream of partial results.

"""

```python
symbol = args.get("symbol")
if not symbol:
    raise ValueError("Missing required argument: symbol")


async def generator():
    async with websockets.connect(WS_URL) as ws:
        # Subscribe message
        await ws.send(json.dumps({"type": "subscribe", "symbol": symbol}))
        async for message in ws:
            data = json.loads(message)
            # Emit each update as a partial result
            yield {"symbol": symbol,
                "price": data["price"],
                "ts": data["timestamp"]}
return stream(generator())
```

- **Streaming:** Uses JSON-RPC partial results to push updates.
- **Backpressure:** Client can cancel the stream to unsubscribe.

D. General Best Practices

Practice	Rationale
Validate args Early	Reject missing or invalid parameters before making external calls.
Centralize Credentials	Keep API URLs and tokens in environment/config, not in code.
Handle Timeouts & Retries	Wrap HTTP/WebSocket calls with sensible timeouts and back-off.
Normalize Responses	Map provider-specific fields into your canonical schema.
Rate-Limit at Server	Throttle MCP calls to third-party APIs to respect provider quotas.
Monitor External Health	Track success/error rates and latency for each adapter.
Secure Transport	Enforce TLS/mTLS and validate certificates.

By encapsulating REST, GraphQL, and WebSocket interactions in dedicated MCP adapters, your AI workflows can uniformly **call**, **stream**, and **compose** these services—keeping core model logic clean and focused on inference.

4.2.3 API Authentication and Security Considerations

When your MCP adapters call third-party APIs, you must guard credentials, enforce strong authentication, and protect data both in transit and at rest. Below are key considerations and best practices:

A. Credential Management

Practice	Rationale
Secrets in Vaults	Store API keys, tokens, and certificates in a managed secrets store (e.g., HashiCorp Vault, AWS Secrets Manager) rather than in code or plaintext files.
Environment Variables	Load secrets at runtime from env vars injected by your orchestration layer; avoid committing .env files to source control.
Automated Rotation	Rotate API keys and tokens on a schedule; ensure adapters can fetch new credentials dynamically without redeploy.

B. Authentication Schemes

1. API Keys
   - Suitable for simple services.
   - Always send over HTTPS, and scope keys to minimal permissions if supported.
2. OAuth2 / OpenID Connect
   - For user-delegated access (e.g., on behalf of a clinician).
   - Implement token-refresh logic inside adapters; cache access tokens until expiration.
3. Bearer Tokens / JWTs
   - Validate token signatures and expiration before calling downstream services.
   - Use short-lived tokens to limit exposure.
4. Mutual TLS (mTLS)
   - Require client certificates for strong two-way authentication.
   - Store certs and keys securely, and pin certificates to prevent MITM.
5. HMAC Signatures
   - Sign request payloads (e.g., AWS Signature v4) to verify integrity and authenticity.
   - Keep signing secrets in a secure vault; rotate periodically.

C. Transport Layer Security

- **TLS 1.2+**: Enforce modern TLS versions, disable legacy ciphers (SSL, TLS 1.0/1.1).
- **Certificate Validation**: Verify server certificates against a trusted CA bundle; optionally pin critical certificates.
- **HTTP Security Headers**: For any MCP-exposed endpoints, use Strict-Transport-Security, X-Frame-Options, X-Content-Type-Options, etc.

D. Least Privilege and Scoping

- **Narrow Scopes**: Request only the scopes you need (e.g., read:orders rather than full access).
- **Role-Based Tokens**: Use separate service accounts for different adapters, each with minimal ACLs.
- **Network ACLs**: Restrict outbound access via network policies or firewall rules— only allow requests to known API endpoints.

E. Secure Defaults and Error Handling

- **Fail-Closed Behavior**: On authentication failure, deny the operation rather than returning stale or default data.
- **Non-Verbose Errors**: Return generic error messages (e.g., "Unauthorized") to clients; log full details internally for debugging.
- **Circuit Breakers**: Prevent repeated credential errors from overwhelming downstream services by opening the circuit on repeated 401/403 responses.

F. Auditing and Monitoring

- **Request Logging**: Log each API call with metadata (method, endpoint, context.userId, timestamp) but never log raw credentials or tokens.
- **Access Audits**: Retain audit logs for compliance (HIPAA, PCI-DSS, GDPR) and periodically review for suspicious patterns.

- **Metrics and Alerts**: Track authentication failure rates and latency; alert on anomalies (e.g., sudden spike in 401 errors).

G. Refresh and Revoke Strategies

- **Token Caching**: Cache access tokens until their TTL; handle refresh proactively before expiration.
- **Revocation Handling**: Detect and react to token revocation (e.g., 401 errors) by clearing caches and obtaining fresh credentials.
- **Graceful Degradation**: If an adapter can't authenticate, fallback to read-only data or a safe default rather than blocking the entire workflow.

By embedding these authentication and security practices into your MCP adapters and server configuration, you'll ensure that every third-party API call is made with **strong protection**, **minimal privileges**, and **full auditability**, keeping both your system and your users' data safe.

4.3 Extending MCP with Custom Data Sources
4.3.1 How to Build Custom Tools for Data Integration

When your AI workflows need to reach beyond standard SQL, REST, or file systems—whether it's reading from a legacy CSV archive, connecting to an internal SOAP service, or ingesting messages from a proprietary queue—MCP lets you package each integration as a **custom tool**. Follow these steps to design, implement, and register your data-integration adapters:

A. Define Your Tool Contract

1. Name & Purpose
   o Choose a clear, imperative method name (e.g. importLegacyCsv, querySoapService, consumeQueueMessage).
2. Parameters (args)
   o List inputs needed: file path, record ID, query parameters, or queue name.
   o Decide which go into args versus which come from context (e.g. userId, sessionId).
3. Return Schema

- ○ Design a JSON schema for the result—e.g., an array of objects for CSV rows, a nested object for SOAP responses, or a single message payload.

B. Scaffold the Adapter Module

Create a new module under adapters/, and import @method from your JSON-RPC library:

python

```python
# adapters/legacy_csv.py

from pathlib import Path

import csv

from jsonrpcserver import method

from config import settings


@method
async def importLegacyCsv(context: dict, args: dict):
    """

    Reads a legacy CSV file and returns its rows as JSON objects.

    args:

      - path: relative path under settings.file_root

      - delimiter: optional, default ','

    result:

      - rows: list of dicts
```

```python
    """
    rel_path = args.get("path")
    delimiter = args.get("delimiter", ",")
    if not rel_path:
        raise ValueError("Missing required argument: path")

    base = Path(settings.file_root).resolve()
    file_path = (base / rel_path).resolve()
    if not str(file_path).startswith(str(base)):
        raise PermissionError(f"Access to {rel_path} is forbidden")

    rows = []
    with file_path.open(newline="", encoding="utf-8") as f:
        reader = csv.DictReader(f, delimiter=delimiter)
        for row in reader:
            rows.append(row)
    return {"rows": rows}
```

C. Handle Complex Protocols (e.g. SOAP)

python

```python
# adapters/soap_adapter.py
```

```python
import os

from zeep import AsyncClient, helpers

from jsonrpcserver import method

from config import settings


WSDL_URL = os.getenv("SOAP_WSDL_URL")


@method
async def querySoapService(context: dict, args: dict):
    """
    Calls a SOAP operation and normalizes the response.
    args:
      - operation: name of the SOAP method
      - params: dict of parameters for that operation
    """
    op_name = args.get("operation")
    params = args.get("params", {})
    if not op_name:
        raise ValueError("Missing required argument: operation")

    client = AsyncClient(wsdl=WSDL_URL)
    service = client.service
```

```python
    operation = getattr(service, op_name, None)

    if operation is None:

        raise ValueError(f"Operation {op_name} not found")


    raw = await operation(**params)

    # Convert to Python primitives

    result = helpers.serialize_object(raw)

    return {"data": result}
```

D. Consuming Message Queues

python

```python
# adapters/queue_adapter.py

import asyncio, json

from jsonrpcserver import method, stream

from aiokafka import AIOKafkaConsumer

from config import settings


@method

async def streamQueueMessages(context: dict, args: dict):

    """

    Streams messages from a Kafka topic.
```

```python
    args:
      - topic: string
      - group_id: string
    """

    topic = args.get("topic")
    group = args.get("group_id", "mcp-group")
    if not topic:
        raise ValueError("Missing required argument: topic")


    consumer = AIOKafkaConsumer(
        topic, bootstrap_servers=settings.kafka_bootstrap, group_id=group
    )
    await consumer.start()
    async def generator():
        try:
            async for msg in consumer:
                yield {"topic": topic, "value": json.loads(msg.value)}
        finally:
            await consumer.stop()
    return stream(generator())
```

E. Register and Document

Import in main.py
python

```python
import adapters.legacy_csv     # registers importLegacyCsv

import adapters.soap_adapter    # registers querySoapService

import adapters.queue_adapter    # registers streamQueueMessages
```

1. Manifest Entry
   ○ Update your tool manifest to include the new methods, their parameter schemas, return types, and descriptions, enabling clients to discover and validate them at runtime.

F. Testing Your Custom Tools

- **Unit Tests**: Mock file contents, SOAP endpoints, or Kafka brokers to validate success and error paths.
- **Integration Tests**: Run against a test environment or sample data folder.
- **Schema Validation**: Use jsonschema to validate args before processing in each adapter.

G. Best Practices

Practice	Reason
Path & Input Sanitization	Prevent directory traversal, injection, or malformed parameters
Timeouts & Retries	Wrap external calls with back-off logic for resilience
Error Mapping	Catch native exceptions and raise JSON-RPC errors with codes/messages

Logging & Metrics	Record adapter invocation counts, latencies, and failures
Version Control	Tag adapters with versions if the external protocol or schema evolves
Secure Credentials	Load secrets from a vault; never embed in code

By packaging each data source behind a **self-contained MCP tool**, you create a modular, testable integration layer—making it trivial for AI clients to "call" any custom data endpoint through a consistent JSON-RPC interface.

4.3.1 How to Build Custom Tools for Data Integration

When your AI workflows need to reach beyond standard SQL, REST, or file systems—whether it's reading from a legacy CSV archive, connecting to an internal SOAP service, or ingesting messages from a proprietary queue—MCP lets you package each integration as a **custom tool**. Follow these steps to design, implement, and register your data-integration adapters:

A. Define Your Tool Contract

1. Name & Purpose
   - Choose a clear, imperative method name (e.g. importLegacyCsv, querySoapService, consumeQueueMessage).
2. Parameters (args)
   - List inputs needed: file path, record ID, query parameters, or queue name.
   - Decide which go into args versus which come from context (e.g. userId, sessionId).
3. Return Schema
   - Design a JSON schema for the result—e.g., an array of objects for CSV rows, a nested object for SOAP responses, or a single message payload.

B. Scaffold the Adapter Module

Create a new module under adapters/, and import @method from your JSON-RPC library:

python

```python
# adapters/legacy_csv.py

from pathlib import Path

import csv

from jsonrpcserver import method

from config import settings


@method
async def importLegacyCsv(context: dict, args: dict):
    """
    Reads a legacy CSV file and returns its rows as JSON objects.
    args:
      - path: relative path under settings.file_root
      - delimiter: optional, default ','
    result:
      - rows: list of dicts
    """
    rel_path = args.get("path")
    delimiter = args.get("delimiter", ",")
```

```python
    if not rel_path:

        raise ValueError("Missing required argument: path")


    base = Path(settings.file_root).resolve()

    file_path = (base / rel_path).resolve()

    if not str(file_path).startswith(str(base)):

        raise PermissionError(f"Access to {rel_path} is forbidden")


    rows = []

    with file_path.open(newline="", encoding="utf-8") as f:

        reader = csv.DictReader(f, delimiter=delimiter)

        for row in reader:

            rows.append(row)

    return {"rows": rows}
```

C. Handle Complex Protocols (e.g. SOAP)

python

```python
# adapters/soap_adapter.py

import os

from zeep import AsyncClient, helpers

from jsonrpcserver import method
```

```python
from config import settings


WSDL_URL = os.getenv("SOAP_WSDL_URL")


@method
async def querySoapService(context: dict, args: dict):
    """
    Calls a SOAP operation and normalizes the response.
    args:
      - operation: name of the SOAP method
      - params: dict of parameters for that operation
    """
    op_name = args.get("operation")
    params = args.get("params", {})
    if not op_name:
        raise ValueError("Missing required argument: operation")


    client = AsyncClient(wsdl=WSDL_URL)
    service = client.service
    operation = getattr(service, op_name, None)
    if operation is None:
        raise ValueError(f"Operation {op_name} not found")
```

```python
    raw = await operation(**params)

    # Convert to Python primitives

    result = helpers.serialize_object(raw)

    return {"data": result}
```

D. Consuming Message Queues

python

```python
# adapters/queue_adapter.py

import asyncio, json

from jsonrpcserver import method, stream

from aiokafka import AIOKafkaConsumer

from config import settings


@method
async def streamQueueMessages(context: dict, args: dict):
    """

    Streams messages from a Kafka topic.

    args:

      - topic: string

      - group_id: string
```

```python
    """

    topic = args.get("topic")

    group = args.get("group_id", "mcp-group")

    if not topic:

        raise ValueError("Missing required argument: topic")


    consumer = AIOKafkaConsumer(

        topic, bootstrap_servers=settings.kafka_bootstrap, group_id=group

    )

    await consumer.start()

    async def generator():

        try:

            async for msg in consumer:

                yield {"topic": topic, "value": json.loads(msg.value)}

        finally:

            await consumer.stop()

    return stream(generator())
```

E. Register and Document

Import in main.py
python

```python
import adapters.legacy_csv      # registers importLegacyCsv
```

```
import adapters.soap_adapter    # registers querySoapService

import adapters.queue_adapter    # registers streamQueueMessages
```

1. Manifest Entry
   ○ Update your tool manifest to include the new methods, their parameter schemas, return types, and descriptions, enabling clients to discover and validate them at runtime.

F. Testing Your Custom Tools

- **Unit Tests**: Mock file contents, SOAP endpoints, or Kafka brokers to validate success and error paths.
- **Integration Tests**: Run against a test environment or sample data folder.
- **Schema Validation**: Use jsonschema to validate args before processing in each adapter.

G. Best Practices

Practice	Reason
Path & Input Sanitization	Prevent directory traversal, injection, or malformed parameters
Timeouts & Retries	Wrap external calls with back-off logic for resilience
Error Mapping	Catch native exceptions and raise JSON-RPC errors with codes/messages
Logging & Metrics	Record adapter invocation counts, latencies, and failures

Version Control	Tag adapters with versions if the external protocol or schema evolves
Secure Credentials	Load secrets from a vault; never embed in code

By packaging each data source behind a **self-contained MCP tool**, you create a modular, testable integration layer—making it trivial for AI clients to "call" any custom data endpoint through a consistent JSON-RPC interface.

4.3.2 Connecting to IoT Devices, Sensors, and Other External Data Sources

IoT devices and sensors often use protocols and transports (MQTT, CoAP, HTTP, WebSockets, BLE) that differ from traditional REST or database interfaces. With MCP, you wrap each integration in an adapter—exposing sensor reads, command topics, and streaming updates as uniform JSON-RPC tools.

A. MQTT-Based Sensor Streaming

1. **Use Case**: Subscribe to temperature readings published on an MQTT broker.

Adapter Example (adapters/iot_mqtt.py):
python

```python
import os, json, asyncio

from jsonrpcserver import method, stream

from asyncio_mqtt import Client, MqttError

from config import settings


@method

async def streamMqttSensor(context: dict, args: dict):

    """"""
```

Streams live MQTT messages from a given topic.

args:

  - broker: str, e.g., "mqtt.example.com"

  - topic: str, e.g., "sensors/room1/temperature"

  - qos: int (0, 1, 2), default 0

"""

```python
broker = args["broker"]

topic  = args["topic"]

qos    = args.get("qos", 0)


async def generator():
    try:
        async with Client(broker) as client:
            async with client.unfiltered_messages() as messages:
                await client.subscribe(topic, qos)
                async for msg in messages:
                    yield {"topic": msg.topic,
                        "payload": json.loads(msg.payload.decode()),
                        "timestamp": msg.timestamp}
    except MqttError as e:
        # map to JSON-RPC error
        raise RuntimeError(f"MQTT error: {e}")
```

```
return stream(generator())
```

2. **Notes**:
   - Use **streaming partial results** for low latency.
   - Handle reconnects and back-pressure with client QoS and error handling.

B. CoAP for Constrained Devices

1. **Use Case**: Poll a temperature sensor over CoAP (Constrained Application Protocol).

Adapter Example (adapters/iot_coap.py):
python

```python
from jsonrpcserver import method

import asyncio

from aiocoap import Context, Message, GET

from config import settings


@method
async def fetchCoapResource(context: dict, args: dict):

    """

    Retrieves a CoAP resource.

    args:

      - uri: str, e.g., "coap://[fe80::1]/sensors/temp"

    """

    uri = args.get("uri")
```

```python
    if not uri:

        raise ValueError("Missing required argument: uri")


    protocol = await Context.create_client_context()

    request = Message(code=GET, uri=uri)

    try:

        response = await protocol.request(request).response

    except Exception as e:

        raise RuntimeError(f"CoAP request failed: {e}")


    payload = response.payload.decode()

    # assume JSON payload

    return {"uri": uri, "data": json.loads(payload)}
```

2. **Notes**:
   - CoAP over DTLS when security is required.
   - Use block-wise transfers for large payloads.

C. HTTP-Polling and RESTful Sensor APIs

1. **Use Case**: Poll a REST endpoint on a gateway that aggregates sensor data.

Adapter Example (adapters/iot_http.py):
python

```python
import httpx
```

```python
from jsonrpcserver import method

from config import settings


@method
async def fetchHttpSensor(context: dict, args: dict):
    """
    Polls an HTTP sensor gateway.
    args:
     - url: str, full endpoint, e.g., "https://api.gateway.local/sensor/42"
    """

    url = args.get("url")
    if not url:
        raise ValueError("Missing required argument: url")
    try:
        async with httpx.AsyncClient(timeout=3.0) as client:
            resp = await client.get(url)
            resp.raise_for_status()
            data = resp.json()
    except httpx.HTTPError as e:
        raise RuntimeError(f"HTTP sensor call failed: {e}")
    return {"url": url, "data": data, "fetchedAt": resp.headers.get("Date")}
```

2. **Notes**:
    - ○ Implement adaptive polling intervals based on freshness requirements.
    - ○ Cache recent readings if downstream workflows require look-back.

D. WebSocket-Driven Updates

1. **Use Case**: Receive a live feed of device events over WebSocket.

Adapter Example (adapters/iot_ws.py):
python

```python
import json, websockets

from jsonrpcserver import method, stream


@method
async def streamWsEvents(context: dict, args: dict):
    """

    Streams JSON messages from a WebSocket endpoint.

    args:

     - uri: str, e.g., "wss://devices.example.com/events"

    """

    uri = args.get("uri")

    if not uri:

        raise ValueError("Missing required argument: uri")


    async def generator():
```

```
    async with websockets.connect(uri) as ws:

        async for msg in ws:

            yield json.loads(msg)

    return stream(generator())
```

2. **Notes**:
   - Support back-pressure by allowing the client to cancel the stream.
   - Secure WebSockets with TLS and JWT subprotocols.

E. Best Practices for IoT Integrations

Practice	Why It Matters
Protocol-Specific Libraries	Use battle-tested clients (paho-mqtt, aiocoap, websockets).
TLS/DTLS Encryption	Always encrypt sensor traffic to protect integrity and privacy.
Authentication & ACLs	Employ broker/server ACLs; use per-device credentials or JWTs.
Reconnect & Retry Logic	Handle intermittent connectivity common in IoT networks.
Data Validation	Validate sensor schema (units, ranges) to avoid garbage inputs.
Rate Limiting & Throttling	Prevent floods of noisy sensors from overwhelming your server.

Topic & URI Sanitization	Reject unexpected topics/paths to avoid injection attacks.
Back-Pressure Handling	Use streaming cancellation and QoS settings to manage flow.
Edge vs. Cloud Processing	Offload pre-aggregation or filtering to gateways to reduce volume.
Monitoring & Metrics	Track per-device message rates, error counts, and latency.

By encapsulating each IoT protocol in its own MCP adapter—exposing both pull-style reads and push-style streams—you provide your AI agents with a **consistent**, **secure**, and **high-performance** way to consume real-world sensor data and external device feeds.

4.3.3 Case Study: Building a Real-Time Data Pipeline Using MCP

In this case study, we'll build a real-time IoT pipeline for monitoring factory temperature sensors. As readings arrive, MCP adapters ingest them, store the latest state, and trigger alerts when thresholds are exceeded—demonstrating end-to-end context flow in a streaming AI workflow.

A. Scenario Overview

- **Devices**: Networked temperature sensors publish JSON messages to an MQTT broker.
- **Goal**: Continuously monitor sensor values, maintain the latest reading in a shared context store, and invoke an AI-powered anomaly detector when readings spike.
- **Outcomes**:
    1. Real-time ingestion of sensor data via MCP notifications.
    2. Centralized storage of "current temperature" per sensor.
    3. Conditional alerts routed through an AI model when values exceed safe limits.

B. Architecture

plaintext

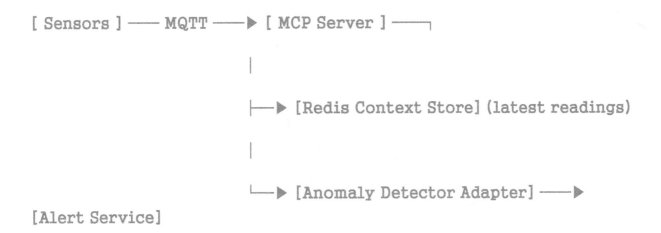

```
[ Sensors ] —— MQTT ——▶ [ MCP Server ] ——┐
                              |
                              ├——▶ [Redis Context Store] (latest readings)
                              |
                              └——▶ [Anomaly Detector Adapter] ——▶
[Alert Service]
```

1. **MCP Server** receives JSON-RPC **notifications** (streamSensorData).
2. **Stream Adapter** writes each reading to Redis under sensor:<id>:current.
3. When a reading exceeds a threshold, the adapter issues a downstream call to detectAnomaly—another MCP tool wrapping an AI model.
4. If an anomaly is detected, sendAlert is invoked to notify engineers.

C. Step 1: Ingesting Data with a Streaming Adapter

python

```python
# adapters/stream_adapter.py

import json

from jsonrpcserver import method

from redis.asyncio import Redis
```

```python
from config import settings

redis = Redis.from_url(settings.redis_url)

@method
async def streamSensorData(context: dict, args: dict):
    """
    JSON-RPC notification for live MQTT readings.
    args: {"sensorId": str, "value": float, "timestamp": ISO8601}
    """
    sensor = args["sensorId"]
    val    = args["value"]
    ts     = args["timestamp"]

    # Store latest reading
    key = f"sensor:{sensor}:current"
    await redis.hset(key, mapping={"value": val, "ts": ts})

    # Trigger anomaly detection if above a threshold
    if val > settings.temperature_threshold:
        await context["mcp_client"].call(
```

```
    "detectAnomaly", context, {"sensorId": sensor, "value": val,
"timestamp": ts}
    )

    # No response for notifications

    return None
```

- **Mechanics**: The MCP client library injects itself into context["mcp_client"].
- **Threshold**: Configured in settings.temperature_threshold.

D. Step 2: Storing and Managing Context

python

```python
# db.py (excerpt)

from redis.asyncio import Redis

from config import settings


redis = Redis.from_url(settings.redis_url)


async def get_current_reading(sensor_id: str) -> dict:

    data = await redis.hgetall(f"sensor:{sensor_id}:current")

    # Convert bytes to appropriate types

    return {"sensorId": sensor_id, "value": float(data[b"value"]), "ts":
data[b"ts"].decode()}
```

- **Key Schema**: sensor:<id>:current holds a hash of latest value and ts.
- **TTL (Optional)**: You may set an expiry (redis.expire(key, 3600)) to clear stale contexts.

E. Step 3: Processing and Alerting via AI

python

```python
# adapters/anomaly_detector.py

from jsonrpcserver import method

from transformers import pipeline  # example AI model


# Preload an out-of-the-box anomaly detection model

detector = pipeline("anomaly-detection", model="your-org/temp-anomaly-model")


@method
async def detectAnomaly(context: dict, args: dict):
    """
    Runs an AI model to determine if a temperature reading is anomalous.
    args: {"sensorId": str, "value": float, "timestamp": ISO8601}
    """
    reading = args["value"]
```

```python
    result  = detector(reading)  # returns e.g.
{"label":"anomaly","score":0.95}


    if result["label"] == "anomaly" and result["score"] >
settings.anomaly_score_threshold:

        # Invoke alert tool

        await context["mcp_client"].call(

            "sendAlert", context,

                {"sensorId": args["sensorId"], "score": result["score"], "timestamp":
args["timestamp"]}

        )

    return {"anomaly": result}
```

- **Model**: A pretrained anomaly detection pipeline.
- **Alert**: Calls sendAlert only when confidence is high.

python

```python
# adapters/alert_adapter.py

from jsonrpcserver import method

import httpx


ALERT_WEBHOOK = settings.alert_webhook_url


@method
```

```python
async def sendAlert(context: dict, args: dict):
    """

    Sends an HTTP POST to an alerting service.

    args: {"sensorId","score","timestamp"}

    """

    payload = {"sensor": args["sensorId"], "score": args["score"], "time": args["timestamp"]}

    async with httpx.AsyncClient(timeout=3) as client:

        resp = await client.post(ALERT_WEBHOOK, json=payload)

        resp.raise_for_status()

    return {"status": "alert_sent"}
```

F. Putting It All Together: Orchestration

python

```python
# main.py (excerpt)

import adapters.stream_adapter

import adapters.anomaly_detector

import adapters.alert_adapter
```

MQTT→MCP Bridge: Use an external bridge (e.g., MQTT→HTTP webhook) to forward sensor JSON into MCP's /rpc endpoint as notifications:
bash

```
mosquitto_sub -h mqtt.example.com -t sensors/+/temperature | \

 xargs -I{} curl -d
'{"jsonrpc":"2.0","method":"streamSensorData","params":'"{}"'}' \

 -H 'Content-Type:application/json' http://localhost:8000/rpc
```

G. Best Practices

Practice	Benefit
Notification Pattern	Low-latency, non-blocking ingestion of high-rate data
Context Store TTLs	Automatically expire stale sensor states
Back-pressure Handling	Use MQTT QoS and client-side buffering to smooth bursts
Model Warm-Up	Load anomaly model at startup to avoid first-call latency
Circuit Breakers	Prevent alert storms by limiting sendAlert calls
Monitoring & Metrics	Track ingestion rate, detection latency, and alert volume

This pipeline showcases how MCP's **streaming notifications**, **context storage**, and **composable tool calls** enable a robust, real-time data flow—turning simple sensor readings into intelligent, responsive alerts with minimal glue code.

4.4 Interactive Q&A

4.4.1 How Do You Handle Authentication in API Integrations?

1. Secure Credential Storage
   - Store API keys, tokens, and client certificates in a dedicated secrets manager (Vault, AWS Secrets Manager, Kubernetes Secrets) rather than in source code or plaintext files.
   - Inject them into your MCP server via environment variables or mounted files at runtime.
2. Choose the Right Scheme
   - **API Keys** for simple services—pass in headers or query params, rotate regularly.
   - **OAuth 2.0 / OpenID Connect** for user-delegated access—implement token fetch and automatic refresh inside the adapter.
   - **mTLS (Mutual TLS)** when both client and server need strong identity assurance—store certs securely and configure your HTTP client accordingly.
   - **HMAC Signatures** (e.g., AWS Signature v4) for payload integrity and source authentication.
3. Token Management & Rotation
   - Cache access tokens until just before expiration, then proactively refresh them to avoid mid-request failures.
   - Automate periodic rotation of API keys and client certificates, and ensure your adapters can seamlessly load new credentials without downtime.
4. Scope & Least Privilege
   - Request only the minimal scopes or permissions needed (e.g., read:orders rather than full admin access).
   - Use separate service accounts or credentials for different adapters to limit blast radius if a secret is compromised.
5. Secure Transport
   - Enforce TLS 1.2+ for all outbound API calls; disable legacy ciphers.
   - Validate server certificates (hostname checks, CA pinning) to prevent man-in-the-middle attacks.
6. Error Handling & Fail-Safe Defaults
   - On authentication failures (401/403), return a standardized JSON-RPC error and avoid leaking credential details in messages.
   - Fail closed—deny the request rather than returning stale or default data when credentials are invalid.
7. Audit & Monitoring

- Log each authenticated API call with metadata (method, endpoint, context.userId, timestamp), but never log raw secrets.
- Monitor authentication error rates and alert if they spike—indicative of expired tokens, revoked credentials, or misconfiguration.

8. Testing & Validation
    - Include automated tests that simulate token expiration, 401 responses, and secret rotation.
    - Validate in staging with real-world authentication flows (e.g., OAuth 2.0 "refresh token" exchanges) before production rollout.

By embedding these practices in your MCP adapters and server configuration, you'll ensure your AI systems connect to third-party APIs in a way that's both **secure** and **resilient**.

4.4.2 Discussion Points on Data Integration Challenges

1. Heterogeneous Schemas and Formats
    - How do you reconcile differing field names, types, and nested structures when merging data from SQL, NoSQL, CSV, and custom APIs?
    - What tooling or schema-mapping strategies help reduce friction?
2. Data Quality and Validation
    - What checks (schema validation, range checks, null handling) do you enforce at ingestion to catch bad data early?
    - How do you handle incomplete or inconsistent records without blocking downstream workflows?
3. Latency vs. Freshness Trade-Offs
    - Which integrations must be real-time (sensor streams, trading feeds) versus those that tolerate batch updates (overnight reports)?
    - How do you architect to meet conflicting SLAs for freshness and response time?
4. Error Handling Across Diverse Systems
    - How do you standardize retry logic, fallback values, and circuit breakers when some sources are flaky or overloaded?
    - What user-visible behavior (e.g., default messages) ensures graceful degradation?
5. Authentication and Authorization Complexities
    - When different sources use different auth schemes (API keys, OAuth2, mTLS), how do you manage and rotate multiple credentials safely?
    - How do you enforce consistent permission checks across adapters?
6. Scalability and Throttling

- Which upstream services impose rate limits, and how do you aggregate or queue requests to stay within quotas?
- How do you throttle bursty traffic (e.g., IoT spikes) without losing critical data?

7. Data Consistency and Synchronization
   - In a multi-agent setup, how do you ensure all components see the same view of "current" context when two sources update the same key?
   - What versioning or event-sourcing patterns help reconcile concurrent writes?

8. Security, Privacy, and Compliance
   - How do you mask or encrypt PII/PHI and maintain audit trails when integrating with sensitive systems?
   - What governance processes validate an adapter before it goes live?

9. Observability and Monitoring
   - Which metrics (ingestion throughput, error rates, data lag) are critical to track for each integration?
   - How do you alert on silent failures—when data simply stops arriving?

10. Evolution and Backward Compatibility
    - When an external API changes (new version, deprecated fields), how do you update adapters without breaking clients?
    - What deprecation and version-negotiation strategies keep your MCP ecosystem stable?

Reflect on these challenges in the context of your own environment to identify where your integration layer needs reinforcement, process improvements, or new tooling.

Chapter 5: Advanced MCP Server Implementations

5.1 Dynamic Capabilities and Custom Tool Development

5.1.1 Extending MCP Functionality with Custom Tools

While MCP includes built-in adapters for common systems (databases, REST APIs, file I/O), real-world applications often demand bespoke integrations. Custom tools let you expose any functionality—legacy systems, domain-specific services, or in-process utilities—via MCP's JSON-RPC interface.

A. Plugin Architecture for Custom Tools

1. Modular Organization
   - Place each custom tool in its own module under adapters/ (or a dedicated plugins/ folder).
   - Use clear naming conventions (e.g., adapters/my_custom_tool.py) to reflect purpose.
2. Dynamic Discovery
   - MCP servers can import all modules in adapters/ at startup, registering any function decorated with @method.
   - For large deployments, support a PLUGINS environment variable listing modules to load, reducing startup overhead.
3. Entry-Point Based Loading (Optional)
   - Use Python packaging entry-points (setup.py / pyproject.toml) so third-party packages can register MCP tools without modifying the server code.
   - At startup, MCP scans installed distributions for the mcp.adapters entry-point group and imports each.

B. Writing a Custom Tool

Define the Method Signature
python

```
from jsonrpcserver import method


@method

async def myCustomTool(context: dict, args: dict):

    """

    Brief description: What the tool does.

    args:

      - param1: type, description

      - param2: type, description

    result:

      - key1: type, description

      - key2: type, description

    """

    # Your integration logic here...

    return { "key1": value1, "key2": value2 }
```

1. Argument Validation
   ○ Perform explicit checks on args at the top of the function, raising
     ValueError or a JSON-RPC error code for missing/invalid inputs.
   ○ For complex schemas, use jsonschema to validate the entire params block
     against a shared schema.
2. Leverage Context Metadata
   ○ Extract context["userId"], context["sessionId"], or custom metadata (e.g.,
     context["roles"]) to apply authorization or per-user logic.
   ○ Avoid reading state directly from external stores; instead, encapsulate that
     in separate adapters or helper functions.

3. Error Handling and Mapping
   ○ Catch domain-specific exceptions (e.g., DatabaseError, PermissionError) and raise a JsonRpcError(code, message, data) to return structured errors.
   ○ Keep error codes in the -32000 to -32099 range for server errors, reserving >=1000 for application-specific codes.

C. Registering and Documenting Tools

1. Automatic Registration
   ○ Ensure your module is imported in main.py (e.g., import adapters.my_custom_tool).
   ○ The @method decorator registers the function name as the JSON-RPC method.
2. Tool Manifest Updates

Append an entry to your MCP server's tool_manifest.json:
json

```json
{

  "name": "myCustomTool",

  "description": "Fetches domain-specific data",

  "params": {

   "type": "object",

   "properties": {

    "param1": { "type": "string", "description": "..." },

    "param2": { "type": "integer", "description": "..." }

   },

   "required": ["param1"]

  },
```

```
  "result": {

    "type": "object",

    "properties": {

      "key1": { "type": "string" },

      "key2": { "type": "number" }

    }

  },

  "version": "1.0.0"

}
```

- ○ This allows clients to discover and validate myCustomTool at runtime.
3. Versioning and Deprecation
    - ○ Include a version field for each tool entry.
    - ○ When deprecating a tool, introduce a new version and retire the old after a transition period; signal clients via manifest metadata.

D. Hot-Reloading and Runtime Updates

1. Development Mode
    - ○ In dev, run MCP with --reload so new or changed adapter modules are picked up automatically.
2. Production Considerations
    - ○ For safety, disable hot-reload and deploy new adapters via rolling-restart pipelines.
    - ○ Use health checks to ensure new plugins load without errors before promoting instances.
3. Conditional Capability Exposure
    - ○ Dynamically add or remove tools based on configuration flags or feature toggles (e.g., for A/B testing).
    - ○ Expose only approved tools to clients by filtering the manifest based on client roles or environments.

E. Advanced Patterns

Pattern	Description
Composite Tools	Tools that orchestrate multiple sub-tools in a single call, hiding complexity from the client.
Streaming Tools	Implement stream(generator()) for custom data streams (e.g., live logs).
Plugin Isolation	Run untrusted or resource-heavy tools in sandboxed subprocesses or containers for safety.
Dependency Injection	Use a DI framework to supply shared resources (DB pools, clients) to adapters.
Pre- and Post-Hooks	Wrap tools with middleware for logging, metrics, authorization—applied uniformly.

By following these guidelines, you'll turn your MCP server into a flexible platform where new capabilities can be added rapidly and safely—enabling your AI clients to leverage an ever-growing ecosystem of domain-specific tools without altering core inference code.

5.1.2 Writing and Registering New Tools for Integration

Once you've designed your custom tool contract (name, inputs, outputs), follow these steps to implement and make it available to MCP clients.

A. Implementing the Tool Adapter

1. Create the Module
   - Under your adapters/ directory, add a new file, e.g. adapters/my_tool.py.

Define and Decorate the Method
python

```python
# adapters/my_tool.py

from jsonrpcserver import method

from config import settings


@method

async def myTool(context: dict, args: dict):

    """

    Brief description of what myTool does.

    args:

      - foo: string, description

      - bar: integer, description

    result:

      - baz: boolean, description

    """

    foo = args.get("foo")

    bar = args.get("bar")

    if foo is None or not isinstance(bar, int):

        raise ValueError("foo (str) and bar (int) are required")

    # --- Your integration logic here ---
```

```python
baz = (len(foo) > bar)

return {"baz": baz}
```

2. Handle Errors Cleanly
    ○ Raise ValueError for client mistakes (mapped to -32602 Invalid params).
    ○ For downstream failures, catch exceptions and re-raise a JsonRpcError with code in -32000–-32099.

B. Registering the Tool with Your MCP Server

Import the Adapter
In your main.py, add:
python

```python
import adapters.my_tool  # noqa: F401
```

1. This ensures the @method decorator registers myTool at startup.
2. Verify Discovery

Call the built-in listMethods tool:
bash

```bash
curl -X POST http://localhost:8000/rpc \

 -H "Content-Type: application/json" \

 -d
'{"jsonrpc":"2.0","id":1,"method":"listMethods","params":{"context":{},"args":{}}}'
```

    ○ Confirm myTool appears in the returned manifest.

C. Updating the Tool Manifest

If you maintain an external manifest (e.g., tool_manifest.json), append an entry for myTool:

jsonc

```jsonc
{
  "name": "myTool",
  "description": "Returns whether foo's length exceeds bar",
  "params": {
    "type": "object",
    "properties": {
      "foo": { "type": "string", "description": "Input string" },
      "bar": { "type": "integer", "description": "Threshold length" }
    },
    "required": ["foo","bar"]
  },
  "result": {
    "type": "object",
    "properties": {
      "baz": { "type": "boolean", "description": "True if foo length > bar" }
    }
  },
  "version": "1.0.0"
```

}

Clients can fetch this manifest at runtime to auto-generate validation and invocation code.

D. Testing Your New Tool

1. Unit Tests

Write a pytest function to call myTool directly:
python

```python
from adapters.my_tool import myTool

import pytest


@pytest.mark.asyncio
async def test_my_tool_success():
    res = await myTool({}, {"foo":"hello","bar":3})

    assert res["baz"] is True


@pytest.mark.asyncio
async def test_my_tool_invalid():
    with pytest.raises(ValueError):

        await myTool({}, {"foo":None,"bar":"x"})
```

Integration Test via RPC
bash

```
curl -X POST http://localhost:8000/rpc \

 -H "Content-Type: application/json" \

 -d '{

  "jsonrpc":"2.0","id":2,"method":"myTool",

  "params":{"context":{},"args":{"foo":"hi","bar":5}}

 }'
```

- Expect "result":{"baz":false}.
2. Manifest Validation
    - Ensure your params and result align with your JSON Schema; use automated schema checks if available.

By following this pattern—implement, import, document, and test—you'll seamlessly introduce new capabilities into your MCP server, keeping your AI clients' integration logic both uniform and discoverable.

5.1.3 Managing Dynamic Capabilities for Flexible AI Systems

As your application evolves, you'll want to add, remove, or update tools—sometimes without restarting the entire MCP server. Dynamic capability management allows AI clients to discover and use new functionality at runtime, enabling feature roll-outs, A/B experiments, and pluggable architectures.

A. Runtime Tool Discovery

1. listMethods Endpoint
    - Clients call listMethods to obtain the current set of available tools and their schemas.

- By polling or subscribing to manifest changes, clients can adapt to new capabilities on the fly.
2. Manifest Versioning
   - Embed a manifestVersion or timestamp in the response so clients know when to refresh.

Example schema:
json

```json
{

  "manifestVersion": "2025-04-18T15:00:00Z",

  "tools": [ /* array of tool definitions */ ]

}
```

B. Hot-Reloadable Plugins

1. Filesystem Watcher
   - Monitor the adapters/ directory for file changes (using watchdog or similar).
   - On new or updated modules, import them dynamically and register new @method functions.
2. Safe Reload Pattern

Load each plugin in an isolated namespace:
python

```python
import importlib, sys

def load_plugin(path):

  spec = importlib.util.spec_from_file_location(path.stem, path)

  mod = importlib.util.module_from_spec(spec)

  spec.loader.exec_module(mod)

  sys.modules[path.stem] = mod
```

  ○ Unregister old methods before loading updated code to avoid duplicates.

C. Feature Flags & Capability Toggles

 1. Configuration-Driven Exposure

Use environment variables or a feature-toggle service to enable or disable tools per environment or user cohort:
yaml

```yaml
FEATURE_FLAGS:

  enableAdvancedAnalytics: true

  enableLegacyCsvImport: false
```

Conditional Registration
python

```python
if settings.feature_flags.enableAdvancedAnalytics:

  import adapters.advanced_analytics
```

 2. Runtime Toggle Updates
  ○ Fetch flags from a remote service at startup and periodically; reconfigure the server to add/remove adapters without downtime.

D. Deprecation and Backward Compatibility

 1. Deprecation Notices
  ○ Mark old tools as deprecated in the manifest with a deprecated: true flag and include a removalDate.
 2. Client Grace Period
  ○ Allow clients to continue using deprecated methods until the removal date; log warnings to drive migration.

3. Version Negotiation
   ○ Support a clientSupportedVersions field in context; the server can route calls to the appropriate tool version.

E. Composite and Meta-Tools

1. Capability Aggregators
   ○ Expose tools like getAllContextTools that return only tools matching certain tags or categories (e.g., "analytics", "ingestion").
2. Dynamic Workflows
   ○ AI orchestrators can assemble pipelines by querying the manifest for tools with specific capabilities (e.g., "streaming", "batch", "auth-required").

F. Best Practices

Practice	Benefit
Centralize Plugin Loading Logic	Avoid scattering dynamic import code across the server.
Graceful Failure on Missing Tools	Clients should handle "Method not found" and fallback safely.
Audit Plugin Changes	Log plugin add/remove events with timestamps and user IDs.
Automated Compatibility Tests	Run integration tests whenever plugins change to detect breaks early.
Limit Hot-Reload Scope	Only reload adapters; keep core server code immutable.

By managing dynamic capabilities—through runtime discovery, hot-reloadable plugins, feature flags, and clear deprecation policies—you'll keep your MCP server both **stable** and **extensible**, enabling AI systems to seamlessly leverage new tools as they emerge.

5.2 Managing Streaming Data with MCP

5.2.1 Real-Time Data Processing and Stream Handling

Modern AI systems often need to consume and react to high-velocity data streams—whether financial ticks, IoT sensor feeds, or user interaction events. MCP's support for JSON-RPC **notifications**, **partial responses**, and **streaming tools**enables real-time pipelines that remain both scalable and maintainable.

A. Streaming via JSON-RPC Notifications

Fire-and-Forget Ingestion
Clients or external bridges send **notifications** (no id) whenever new data arrives. MCP delivers each notification to a @method-decorated handler without blocking:
json

```
{

  "jsonrpc":"2.0",

  "method":"streamSensorData",

  "params":{

    "context":{"sessionId":"s1"},

    "args":{"sensorId":"temp-1","value":22.5,"timestamp":"2025-04-18T15:00:00Z"}

  }

}
```

Adapter Logic
The handler writes into a context store or triggers downstream logic:
python

```
@method
```

```python
async def streamSensorData(context, args):
    await redis.hset(f"sensor:{args['sensorId']}:current", mapping={
        "value": args["value"], "ts": args["timestamp"]
    })
    return None  # notifications need no response
```

B. Partial Responses and Chunked Streams

Long-Running Operations
For adapters that push large or continuous outputs (e.g., log tails, video frames), return a **stream** of partial results:
python

```python
from jsonrpcserver import method, stream


@method
async def streamLogLines(context, args):
    async def generator():
        with open("/var/log/app.log") as f:
            for line in f:
                yield {"line": line.rstrip("\n")}
                await asyncio.sleep(0.1)
    return stream(generator())
```

- **Client Consumption**
  The client library yields each chunk as soon as it arrives, allowing real-time processing without waiting for the entire payload.

C. Integrating with Message Brokers

Kafka / PubSub
Use an async consumer to fetch messages and yield via a JSON-RPC stream:
python

```python
@method

async def streamKafka(context, args):

  async def generator():

    await consumer.start()

    try:

      async for msg in consumer:

        yield {"topic": msg.topic, "value": msg.value.decode()}

    finally:

      await consumer.stop()

  return stream(generator())
```

- **MQTT**
  Similarly subscribe to topics and push each packet as a stream element.

D. Back-Pressure and Flow Control

Cancellation Support
Clients may cancel a streaming call—ensure your generator checks for cancellation and closes resources:
python

```python
try:

  async for chunk in generator():
```

```python
    yield chunk

except asyncio.CancelledError:

  await cleanup()

  raise
```

- **Rate Limiting**
  Apply per-stream quotas to avoid overwhelming downstream systems (e.g., drop or sample messages when beyond a threshold).

E. Windowing, Aggregation, and State

Sliding Windows
Maintain in-memory or Redis-backed queues of the last N events for real-time aggregates (e.g., moving average):
python

```python
buffer = deque(maxlen=100)

@method

async def aggregateStream(context, args):

  for reading in await subscribe_stream(args["streamId"]):

    buffer.append(reading["value"])

    avg = sum(buffer)/len(buffer)

    yield {"average": avg}
```

- **Stateful Stream Processing**
  Use external state stores to maintain counters, histograms, or event-time watermarks across adapter invocations.

F. Error Handling and Resilience

- **Transient Errors**
  Wrap broker connections with retry/back-off—reconnect on network failures.
- **Poison-Message Handling**
  Detect malformed messages, log them, and optionally forward to a dead-letter queue to prevent stream interruption.
- **Health Checks**
  Expose metrics on active stream count, lag, and error rate; alert if consumers fall behind real time.

G. Best Practices

Practice	Benefit
Use Async I/O End-to-End	Keep the event loop free; avoid blocking calls in adapters.
Support Stream Cancellation	Allow clients to stop stale or unneeded streams and free resources.
Implement Back-Pressure	Throttle or sample high-volume feeds to prevent overload.
Maintain Minimal Working State	Keep per-stream state lightweight (fixed-size buffers, TTL caches).
Graceful Reconnection	Handle broker outages with exponential back-off and jitter.

Metrics & Monitoring	Track stream throughput, processing latency, and error rates.
Security & Authentication	Secure broker connections (TLS, ACLs) and validate incoming messages.

By leveraging MCP's streaming capabilities—notifications for ingestion, partial responses for long-running or continuous outputs, and robust back-pressure handling—you can build real-time AI workflows that ingest, process, and react to data with minimal latency and maximum resilience.

5.2.2 MCP's Role in Handling Event-Driven Architectures

Event-driven systems emit and react to discrete happenings—user clicks, sensor thresholds, external webhooks—rather than polling for state. MCP fits naturally into this paradigm by treating each event as a JSON-RPC **notification** or **stream**, decoupling producers from consumers and providing a uniform programming model.

A. Ingestion via JSON-RPC Notifications

- **Loose Coupling**: Producers (IoT gateways, webhooks, message brokers) send one-way MCP notifications (id omitted) to the server's RPC endpoint.
- **Stateless Handlers**: Each @method-decorated adapter processes the event, updating context stores or triggering further tool calls without blocking the caller.

Example:
json

```json
{

"jsonrpc":"2.0",

"method":"userSignedUp",

"params":{
```

```json
    "context":{"sessionId":"abc"},

    "args":{"userId":"u123","timestamp":"2025-04-18T16:00:00Z"}

  }

}
```

B. Declarative Subscriptions & Manifest Extensions

- **Event-Tool Mapping**: Include an events section in your tool manifest to declare which adapters handle which event types. Clients and orchestrators can query this to wire up event flows dynamically.

Example Manifest Snippet:
json

```json
{

  "methods": [ /* ... */ ],

  "events": [

    { "name":"userSignedUp", "handler":"handleNewUser", "schema":{/*...*/} },

    { "name":"orderPlaced", "handler":"processOrder", "schema":{/*...*/} }

  ]

}
```

C. Broker Integration & At-Least-Once Delivery

- **Message Brokers**: Use Kafka, RabbitMQ, or MQTT as the durable transport. An external bridge or lightweight adapter pulls from the broker and forwards events into MCP notifications.
- **Retry Semantics**: If a notification handler fails, the bridge can requeue the event—leveraging broker delivery guarantees—while MCP's uniform error codes make it easy to detect transient vs. permanent failures.

D. Composable Event Pipelines

- **Chaining Tools**: An event adapter can invoke downstream MCP calls to other tools, building a pipeline:
  userSignedUp notification → fetchWelcomeTemplate → sendWelcomeEmail
- **Conditional Routing**: Within the adapter, inspect args or enriched context metadata to route events to different handlers (e.g., premium vs. free users).

E. Stateful vs. Stateless Event Handlers

- **Stateless Handlers**: Pure functions that transform events into actions, ideal for idempotent or purely computational tasks.
- **Stateful Handlers**: Those that update a context store (Redis, database) to track session progress, aggregates, or sliding-window metrics. MCP keeps state concerns separate from core logic via adapters.

F. Back-Pressure and Flow Control

- **Consumer Throttling**: Adapters can signal the bridge to slow consumption (e.g., pause Kafka partition) when downstream MCP calls lag.
- **Batch Notifications**: For bursts, group events into JSON-RPC batch calls, reducing overhead and smoothing processing.

G. Best Practices for Event-Driven MCP

Practice	Benefit
Define Clear Event Schemas	Validates incoming notifications and surfaces errors early.
Use Durable Brokers	Guarantees delivery and decouples producers from MCP availability.

Idempotent Handlers	Allow safe retries without duplicating side-effects.
Centralize Error Policies	Apply uniform retry/back-off and poison-message handling.
Monitor End-to-End Latency	Track time from event arrival to adapter completion.
Document Event Catalog	Provide clients and integrators with a clear list of supported events and handlers.

By leveraging JSON-RPC notifications, declarative manifests, and a clear separation between event ingestion and processing, MCP provides a **flexible**, **scalable**, and **observable** foundation for building robust event-driven AI architectures.

5.2.3 Best Practices for Managing Streaming Data in AI Workflows

1. End-to-End Asynchronous I/O
   - Use fully **async** libraries (e.g., httpx.AsyncClient, asyncio_mqtt, AIOKafkaConsumer) from ingestion through processing to avoid blocking the event loop.
   - Offload any blocking work (e.g., heavy CPU tasks) to thread or process pools.
2. Idempotent, Stateless Handlers
   - Design streaming adapters so that replaying the same event produces the same outcome without duplication.
   - Keep per-event logic pure; store state (aggregates, counters) in an external store rather than in memory.
3. Back-Pressure and Flow Control
   - Honor broker QoS or pause/resume consumption when downstream processing lags (e.g., consumer.pause()).
   - Buffer and batch bursts of events where possible, or sample/drop low-priority messages under overload.
4. Schema Versioning & Validation

- Define JSON Schema for each stream's message format; reject or route malformed events to a dead-letter queue.
- Include a schemaVersion field in each message to support incremental upgrades.
5. Sliding Window & Aggregation Patterns
   - For rolling metrics (e.g., moving average), maintain fixed-size buffers (in memory or Redis) and update incrementally.
   - Emit pre-aggregated summaries at intervals to reduce downstream load.
6. Resource-Aware Concurrency Tuning
   - Tune consumer partition counts, parallel handler tasks, and connection pool sizes to match your hardware and workload.
   - Monitor task queue lengths and automatically scale out via container orchestration when thresholds are breached.
7. Graceful Shutdown & Cancellation
   - Support clean shutdown by catching asyncio.CancelledError in generators, closing broker connections, and draining in-flight messages.
   - Expose a health/ready endpoint so orchestrators can wait before killing a pod.
8. Observability: Metrics & Tracing
   - Instrument throughput (events/sec), processing latency (end-to-end), lag (consumer offset lag), and error rates.
   - Correlate events with tracing IDs carried in context to debug multi-stage pipelines.
9. Durability & Delivery Guarantees
   - Choose at-least-once vs. exactly-once semantics based on use case; use idempotent writes and de-duplication keys for critical data.
   - Persist streaming state (offsets, watermarks) externally so you can resume after restarts.
10. Security & Compliance
    - Encrypt streams in transit (TLS/DTLS, mTLS for MQTT, SSL for Kafka).
    - Authenticate producers and consumers with per-device or per-service credentials, limiting topic or partition access via ACLs.
11. Edge Pre-Processing
    - Where possible, perform filtering, aggregation, or anomaly detection at the edge (gateway devices) to reduce central processing load and bandwidth.
12. Testing and Simulation
    - Build test harnesses that replay recorded or synthetic streams at controlled rates to validate behavior under varying load and failure modes.

- Include fault-injection tests (broker outages, malformed messages) to verify resilience.

By adhering to these best practices, you'll ensure your MCP-powered streaming pipelines remain **low-latency**, **fault-tolerant**, and **scalable**, empowering AI models to react reliably to real-time data.

5.3 Security and Rate-Limiting in MCP Servers

5.3.1 Implementing Rate-Limiting to Prevent Abuse

Uncontrolled usage of your MCP server—whether by buggy clients, malicious actors, or unexpected traffic spikes—can overwhelm downstream services and degrade performance. A robust rate-limiting layer protects your system by enforcing quotas at multiple levels. Below are patterns, code examples, and best practices for adding rate-limits to your FastAPI-based MCP server.

A. Rate-Limiting Strategies

Scope	Description	Use Case
Global	Caps total requests across all clients	Prevent overall overload during spikes
Per-Client	Limits by context.userId or IP address	Protect fair use by each user/service
Per-Method	Quotas for individual JSON-RPC methods (e.g., fetchWeather)	Throttle expensive or rate-limited tools
Burst vs. Steady	Allow short bursts above steady-state rate (token bucket)	Smooth out traffic bursts

| Leaky Bucket | Enforce a fixed processing rate, dropping or delaying excess calls | Strict throughput control |

B. Implementation Example Using Redis and Token Buckets

Install Dependencies
bash

```bash
pip install aioredis
```

Middleware Setup
Create a FastAPI middleware that intercepts each /rpc request, extracts a client key (e.g., userId or IP), and applies token-bucket logic in Redis:
python

```python
# rate_limit.py

import time

from fastapi import Request, HTTPException

from starlette.middleware.base import BaseHTTPMiddleware

from aioredis import from_url

from config import settings


redis = from_url(settings.redis_url, encoding="utf-8",
decode_responses=True)


class RateLimiterMiddleware(BaseHTTPMiddleware):

    async def dispatch(self, request: Request, call_next):
```

```python
# Only apply to /rpc endpoint
if request.url.path != settings.rpc_path:
    return await call_next(request)


# Identify client (fallback to IP)
context = await request.json()
user_id = context.get("params", {}).get("context", {}).get("userId")
client_key = user_id or request.client.host


# Method-specific key
method = context.get("method", "unknown")
key = f"rate:{client_key}:{method}"


# Token bucket parameters
rate = settings.rate_limits.get(method, settings.default_rate)
bucket_size = settings.bucket_sizes.get(method,
settings.default_bucket)
now = int(time.time())


# Lua script: refill tokens, attempt to consume 1
script = """
local tokens_key = KEYS[1]
```

```
local timestamp_key = KEYS[2]

local rate = tonumber(ARGV[1])

local capacity = tonumber(ARGV[2])

local now = tonumber(ARGV[3])


local last_ts = tonumber(redis.call("get", timestamp_key) or 0)

local tokens = tonumber(redis.call("get", tokens_key) or capacity)

local delta = math.max(0, now - last_ts)

local refill = delta * rate

tokens = math.min(capacity, tokens + refill)

if tokens < 1 then

    return tokens

else

    tokens = tokens - 1

    redis.call("set", tokens_key, tokens)

    redis.call("set", timestamp_key, now)

    return tokens

end
"""

remaining = await redis.eval(

    script,

    keys=[key, key + ":ts"],
```

```python
        args=[rate, bucket_size, now]
    )


    if float(remaining) < 0:
        # Rate limit exceeded
        raise HTTPException(
            status_code=429,
            detail="Rate limit exceeded. Try again later."
        )


    # Proceed to dispatch
    response = await call_next(request)
    return response
```

Configuring Limits
In config.py, define default and per-method rates:
python

```python
from pydantic import BaseSettings, Field

from typing import Dict


class Settings(BaseSettings):
    rate_limits: Dict[str, float] = Field(
        default_factory=lambda: {"fetchWeather": 1.0},  # tokens per second
```

```python
        env="RATE_LIMITS_JSON"  # JSON string in env
    )

    bucket_sizes: Dict[str, int] = Field(

        default_factory=lambda: {"fetchWeather": 5},    # burst capacity

        env="BUCKET_SIZES_JSON"

    )

    default_rate: float = 0.2   # 0.2 tokens/sec = 1 call per 5s

    default_bucket: int = 1     # no bursting by default

    redis_url: str = Field(..., env="REDIS_URL")

    rpc_path: str = Field("/rpc", env="MCP_RPC_PATH")

    class Config:

        env_file = ".env"
```

Register Middleware
In main.py, add before route definitions:
python

```python
from fastapi import FastAPI

from rate_limit import RateLimiterMiddleware


app = FastAPI()

app.add_middleware(RateLimiterMiddleware)
```

Error Mapping for JSON-RPC

Convert HTTP 429 into a JSON-RPC error within the /rpc endpoint:

python

```python
from jsonrpcserver import async_dispatch, InvalidParams

from fastapi.responses import JSONResponse


@app.post(settings.rpc_path)

async def rpc_endpoint(request: Request):

    try:

        body = await request.body()

        response = await async_dispatch(body.decode())

        return response

    except HTTPException as e:

        # Map to JSON-RPC rate-limit error code

        return JSONResponse({

            "jsonrpc": "2.0",

            "id": None,

            "error": {

                "code": -32029,

                "message": "Rate limit exceeded",

                "data": {"retryAfter": 1/rate_limits.get(method,1)}

            }

        }, status_code=429)
```

C. Alternative: FastAPI Limiter Library

For faster setup, you can use the slowapi extension:

bash

```bash
pip install slowapi
```

python

```python
from slowapi import Limiter
from slowapi.util import get_remote_address

limiter = Limiter(key_func=get_remote_address)
app.state.limiter = limiter
app.add_exception_handler(429, lambda req, exc: JSONResponse(...))

@app.post("/rpc")
@limiter.limit("5/minute")
async def rpc(request: Request):
    # your RPC logic
```

D. Best Practices

1. Granular Quotas
    - Tighten limits on costly or third-party methods; relax on lightweight ones.
2. Adaptive Limits
    - Increase quotas for trusted clients (context.userId in a whitelist).
3. Retry-After Hints
    - Return data.retryAfter in the JSON-RPC error to guide clients.
4. Monitoring & Alerts
    - Track 429 errors per method to identify misbehaving clients or capacity issues.
5. Documentation
    - Publish your rate-limit policies in your API docs so integrators code defensively.
6. Global vs. Local
    - Combine in-process middleware with upstream/load-balancer rate-limits for defense in depth.

By applying these patterns, you'll prevent abusive or runaway MCP usage, safeguard downstream services, and provide predictable, fair access for all clients.

5.3.2 Authentication and Authorization Strategies for MCP

Secure MCP deployments rely on both **authentication** (verifying who you are) and **authorization** (verifying what you're allowed to do). Below are patterns and best practices you can layer into your FastAPI-based MCP server.

A. Authentication Mechanisms

1. API Keys
    - **How**: Clients present a static key in an Authorization: ApiKey <key> header.
    - **Where**: Validate against a database or in-memory map.
    - **Use Case**: Machine-to-machine integrations with moderate security needs.
2. OAuth 2.0 / OpenID Connect (OIDC)
    - **How**: Clients send a bearer token (Authorization: Bearer <JWT>).
    - **Validate**: Verify signature, issuer, audience, and expiry via your OIDC provider's JWKS.
    - **Use Case**: User-delegated flows, single sign-on, scopes per method.
3. JWTs with Custom Claims
    - **How**: JWTs carry user identity, roles, or permissions in claims.
    - **Validate**: Use a shared secret or public key to verify.

- Use Case: Stateless, scalable auth with embedded authorization data.
4. mTLS (Mutual TLS)
   - How: Clients and server exchange certificates during the TLS handshake.
   - Validate: Map client certificate CN/subject to an application identity.
   - Use Case: Highest assurance for service-to-service communication.

B. Authorization Models

1. Role-Based Access Control (RBAC)
   - Define: Roles (e.g., reader, writer, admin) and map them to allowed MCP methods.
   - Enforce: In a middleware or dependency, check context["claims"]["role"] against a per-method ACL.
2. Attribute-Based Access Control (ABAC)
   - Define: Policies based on user attributes (department, clearance level) and resource attributes (method sensitivity).
   - Enforce: Evaluate a policy engine (e.g., OPA) at request time.
3. Scope-Based Permissions
   - Define: OAuth2 scopes like mcp:readOrders or mcp:manageUsers.
   - Enforce: Inspect the token's scopes claim and verify coverage before dispatching the method.
4. Per-Method API Keys
   - Define: Issue separate API keys scoped to individual methods or namespaces.
   - Enforce: Associate each key with an allow-list of methods in your key store.

C. FastAPI Integration Patterns

Dependency Injection
python

```python
from fastapi import Depends, HTTPException, Security

from fastapi.security import HTTPBearer, HTTPAuthorizationCredentials



auth_scheme = HTTPBearer()
```

```python
async def authenticate(creds: HTTPAuthorizationCredentials =
Depends(auth_scheme)):

    token = creds.credentials

    payload = verify_jwt(token)

    if not payload:

        raise HTTPException(401, "Invalid token")

    return payload  # e.g., {"userId": "...", "roles": [...], "scopes": [...]}



app = FastAPI()

@app.post("/rpc")

async def rpc(req: Request, user=Depends(authenticate)):

    context = extract_context(req)

    context["claims"] = user

    return await async_dispatch(...)
```

1. Middleware
   - Insert a middleware to authenticate early and attach a request.state.user for downstream access.
   - Reject unauthenticated requests with 401 before invoking JSON-RPC dispatch.

Per-Method Guards
python

```python
from jsonrpcserver import method, JsonRpcError



@method
```

```
async def deleteUser(context, args):

    if "admin" not in context["claims"]["roles"]:

    raise JsonRpcError(-32604, "Insufficient permissions")

    # ... perform deletion ...
```

D. Auditing and Token Management

- Audit Logs
  - Log every invocation with userId, sessionId, method, and outcome.
  - Ship logs to a WORM (write-once) store for compliance.
- Token Revocation
  - Maintain a short revocation list for JWTs or API keys.
  - Check tokens against that list on each request (or rely on short TTLs).
- Key Rotation
  - Roll API keys periodically.
  - Support multiple active key versions to allow smooth rollover.

E. Best Practices

Practice	Benefit
Least-Privilege Keys & Tokens	Limit each credential to only the methods it needs.
Short-Lived Tokens	Reduce risk of leaked credentials; enforce frequent refresh.
Centralized Auth Service	Delegate token issuance and validation to a single component.
Consistent Error Codes	Map auth failures to standard JSON-RPC codes (e.g., -32604).

Rate-Limit Sensitive Methods	Apply tighter quotas to high-risk operations.
Encrypted In-Transit	Always use TLS/mTLS for API and broker communications.
Periodic Pen-Testing	Validate that your auth and authorization logic cannot be bypassed.

By combining strong authentication, fine-grained authorization, centralized token management, and clear enforcement in your MCP server, you'll protect both your AI workflows and the sensitive data they access—ensuring only the right clients can invoke the right tools.

5.3.3 Encrypting Data Transmission and Securing Sensitive Data

Protecting sensitive information—whether in transit between AI clients and MCP servers, or within adapters calling external systems—is crucial for compliance, trust, and security. Below are practices and patterns to ensure end-to-end encryption and data protection.

A. Transport Layer Encryption

1. TLS for HTTP/JSON-RPC
   - **Server-Side**: Configure Uvicorn or your reverse proxy (NGINX, Traefik) with strong TLS (>= 1.2, prefer 1.3) and disable weak ciphers.
   - **Clients**: Reject self-signed or expired certificates; validate the full certificate chain.
   - **HSTS**: Enforce HTTP Strict Transport Security on any HTTP endpoints used by clients.
2. mTLS for Service-to-Service
   - Require client certificates in addition to server certificates to authenticate both ends.
   - Use a private CA or a certificate management service (e.g., Vault PKI) to issue short-lived certs.
   - Map certificate subjects to service identities and attach them to context for auditing.

3. Secure WebSockets / MQTT
    - Use WSS (WebSocket over TLS) or MQTTS (MQTT over TLS).
    - Validate server certs and optionally require client certs.
    - Enforce TLS renegotiation limits to prevent DoS.

B. Encryption at Rest

1. Context Store & Caches
    - Enable encryption on disk for Redis or database instances (e.g., AWS ElastiCache encryption at rest).
    - Use file-system encryption (LUKS, EFS) for any on-disk context snapshots or logs.
2. Sensitive Configuration
    - Store secrets (DB passwords, API keys) in a secrets manager—never in plaintext .env.
    - For local development, use encrypted vault files (e.g., Ansible Vault, git-crypt) with per-developer keys.
3. Database & Message Broker
    - Turn on Transparent Data Encryption (TDE) for relational DBs.
    - Enable disk-level encryption and topic-level encryption for Kafka, RabbitMQ.

C. Field-Level and Application-Level Encryption

1. Encrypting PII/PHI in Payloads

For highly sensitive fields (SSNs, medical records), apply application-level encryption before sending through MCP:

python

```python
from cryptography.fernet import Fernet

cipher = Fernet(settings.field_encryption_key)

encrypted = cipher.encrypt(pii_data.encode())
```

- Decrypt only within the adapter that needs the cleartext.
2. Tokenization
  - Replace sensitive values with tokens or surrogate keys; store the mapping in a secure vault or HSM.
3. Selective Disclosure
  - Only decrypt or reveal fields when absolutely necessary; propagate masked or hashed values elsewhere.

D. Key Management and Rotation

1. Centralized Key Vaults
   - Use an HSM or managed key service (AWS KMS, Azure Key Vault) to generate, store, and rotate encryption keys.
   - Grant each adapter only the minimal IAM permissions to access needed keys.
2. Automatic Rotation
   - Rotate data-encryption keys on a schedule; support key-versioning so old data can still be decrypted as needed.
   - For TLS/mTLS, issue short-lived certificates and rotate automatically via ACME or your PKI.
3. Audit and Access Control
   - Log every key-access event (which adapter, timestamp, operation).
   - Enforce MFA and strict approval workflows for key-vault administration.

E. Secure Logging and Auditing

1. Redact Sensitive Fields
   - Before writing structured logs, mask or omit PII/PHI fields.
   - Use a logging filter that automatically scrubs known sensitive keys (e.g., "ssn", "patientId").
2. Encrypted Log Storage
   - Ship logs to a centralized system that encrypts data at rest (e.g., ELK on encrypted EBS).
   - Restrict access to logs to authorized security and compliance teams.
3. Immutable Audit Trails

- For compliance, store audit events in a write-once medium (WORM storage) or append-only ledger (e.g., blockchain, dedicated append service).

F. End-to-End Security Verification

1. Penetration Testing
   - Periodically test your TLS configurations (e.g., using SSL Labs), simulate MITM attempts, and probe for weak ciphers.
   - Conduct app-layer pentests on your MCP server and adapters to uncover injection or misconfiguration issues.
2. Configuration Drift Detection
   - Monitor TLS and encryption settings in CI/CD; reject changes that downgrade security.
   - Use infrastructure-as-code scanning (e.g., Terraform Sentinel) to enforce encryption policies.
3. Certificate and Key Expiry Monitoring
   - Automate alerts for upcoming certificate or key expirations to prevent outages.
   - Integrate with your observability stack to surface any decryption failures in adapters.

By combining **strong transport encryption**, **at-rest safeguards**, **application-level data protection**, and **robust key management**, you ensure that sensitive data in your MCP-powered AI workflows remains confidential, integral, and auditable from end to end.

5.4 Industry Case Study: Robotics

5.4.1 Using MCP to Integrate Real-Time Data from Robots

Robotic systems require tight feedback loops—streaming telemetry, issuing control commands, and coordinating multiple agents in real time. MCP's JSON-RPC notifications and streaming support let you treat each robot as an MCP "tool," abstracting away the low-level protocol while maintaining end-to-end context awareness.

A. Scenario Overview

- **Robots:** Autonomous mobile robots (AMRs) in a warehouse, each publishing state (position, battery level, obstacle detections) at 10 Hz over MQTT.
- **Goal:** Ingest telemetry, update a central context store, detect anomalies (e.g., low battery or stalled motion), and dispatch control adjustments or human alerts.
- **Key Requirements:**
  1. **Low Latency:** Telemetry ingestion → decision in < 100 ms
  2. **Scalability:** Support hundreds of robots concurrently
  3. **Reliability:** Guarantee at-least-once delivery; idempotent processing

B. Architectural Components

1. **Robot MQTT Broker**: Robots publish JSON messages to topics like robot/{id}/telemetry.
2. **MQTT→MCP Bridge**: Small service that subscribes to all telemetry topics and forwards each message as a JSON-RPC **notification** to MCP.
3. **MCP Server**: Hosts adapters for ingestion, context store updates, anomaly detection, and command issuing.
4. **Context Store**: Fast cache (Redis) holding each robot's "latest state" hash.
5. **Anomaly Detector Adapter**: Runs lightweight rules or ML models to detect problems.
6. **Command Adapter**: Sends JSON-RPC calls back through the bridge to publish commands onto robot command topics.

C. Streaming Telemetry via Notifications

python

```python
# adapters/robot_stream.py

import json

from jsonrpcserver import method
```

```python
from redis.asyncio import Redis
from config import settings


redis = Redis.from_url(settings.redis_url)


@method
async def streamRobotTelemetry(context: dict, args: dict):
    """
    Notification handler for robot telemetry.
    args: {
      "robotId": str,
      "position": {"x": float, "y": float},
      "battery": float,
      "obstacles": [ { "angle": float, "distance": float }, ... ],
      "timestamp": ISO8601
    }
    """
    rid = args["robotId"]
    key = f"robot:{rid}:state"
    # Update latest state
    await redis.hset(key, mapping={
        "x": args["position"]["x"],
        "y": args["position"]["y"],
```

```python
    "battery": args["battery"],

    "ts": args["timestamp"]

  })
  # Store obstacles as a JSON string for further analysis
  await redis.set(f"{key}:obs", json.dumps(args["obstacles"]))


  # Trigger anomaly detection
  await context["mcp_client"].call(

    "detectRobotAnomaly", context,

    {"robotId": rid, "battery": args["battery"], "position": args["position"]}

  )

  return None  # notifications don't require responses
```

D. Anomaly Detection and Alerting

python

```python
# adapters/robot_anomaly.py

from jsonrpcserver import method

from math import hypot


@method

async def detectRobotAnomaly(context: dict, args: dict):

  """""
```

```python
Simple rule-based anomaly detection.
args: {"robotId","battery","position"}
"""

alerts = []
if args["battery"] < settings.low_battery_threshold:
    alerts.append("low_battery")
# If position change since last above a threshold is zero => stalled
prev = await context["mcp_client"].call(
    "getRobotState", context, {"robotId": args["robotId"]}
)
dx = args["position"]["x"] - prev["result"]["x"]
dy = args["position"]["y"] - prev["result"]["y"]
if hypot(dx, dy) < settings.stall_distance_threshold:
    alerts.append("stalled")

for alert in alerts:
    await context["mcp_client"].call(
        "sendRobotAlert", context,
        {"robotId": args["robotId"], "type": alert, "timestamp": args["timestamp"]}
    )
return {"alerts": alerts}
```

E. Commanding Robots

python

```python
# adapters/robot_commands.py
import json
from jsonrpcserver import method


@method
async def sendRobotCommand(context: dict, args: dict):
    """
    Issues a control command to a robot.
    args: {"robotId": str, "command": str, "params": dict}
    """
    # Use the same MQTT→MCP bridge in reverse: publish to `robot/{id}/commands`
    await context["mcp_client"].call(
        "mqttPublish", context,
        {
            "topic": f"robot/{args['robotId']}/commands",
            "message": json.dumps({
                "command": args["command"],
                "params": args.get("params", {}),
                "timestamp": context["timestamp"]
            })
        }
```

```
)
return {"status": "command_sent"}
```

F. Best Practices

Practice	Benefit
High-Frequency Notifications	Use lightweight JSON-RPC notifications to minimize latency.
Idempotent Handlers	Replaying the same telemetry shouldn't corrupt state.
Buffered State Windows	Maintain short sliding windows (Redis lists) for trend analysis.
Separate Ingestion & Control	Decouple telemetry adapters from command adapters for clarity.
Context-Driven Branching	Use context (e.g., robot role, zone) to adjust detection thresholds.
Throttled Commands	Prevent flooding the robot with too many commands per second.
Monitoring & Metrics	Track per-robot message rates, processing latency, and alert counts.

| Secure MQTT | Use MQTT over TLS with client certificates for robot authentication. |

By modeling each robot's telemetry and commands as MCP tools—leveraging JSON-RPC notifications for ingestion, context stores for state, and composable tool calls for anomaly detection and control—you achieve a **clean**, **scalable**, and **robust** integration layer that supports real-time robotic workflows with minimal boilerplate.

5.4.2 Context-Aware Systems in Autonomous Robots

Autonomous robots must perceive and react to a constantly changing environment, mission directives, and internal state. By treating every sensory input, map update, and command as a first-class "context" object via MCP, you can build robots that adapt their behavior in real time, maintain coherent world models, and execute complex tasks with minimal bespoke glue code.

A. Key Context Domains

Context Type	Description	Examples
Perceptual	Raw or processed sensor data	LIDAR point clouds, camera frames, IMU ticks
Environmental	World model, maps, dynamic obstacles	Occupancy grids, moving obstacle lists
Mission	High-level goals, waypoints, task queues	"Inspect zone A", delivery destination points
Robot State	Internal diagnostics, battery level, actuator status	Battery %, wheel encoder counts, error flags

| Collaborative | Peer robot positions, shared tasks, human directives | Fleet status, shared map of free docking bays |

B. Context Propagation via MCP

1. Sensor Adapters
   - Wrap each sensor feed as a streaming MCP tool (e.g., streamLidar, streamCameraFrame).
   - Downstream adapters normalize and fuse these into a common format (e.g., obstacle list).
2. Map Updates

Use JSON-RPC notifications for incremental map patches:
json

```json
{ "jsonrpc":"2.0", "method":"updateMapPatch",

  "params":{"context":{...},"args":{"patch":{...},"frameId":123}} }
```

   - A map manager adapter applies patches to a central occupancy grid in Redis.
3. State Synchronization
   - Each control cycle, the motion planner calls getRobotState and getLatestObstacles to build a context snapshot before planning the next motion primitive.

C. Adaptive Behavior Patterns

1. Context-Driven Mode Switching

E.g., switch between **exploration mode** and **obstacle-avoidance mode** based on proximity sensors:
python

```
dist = await mcp.call("getMinObstacleDistance", context, {})

if dist < settings.avoidance_threshold:

    behavior = "avoidObstacle"

else:

    behavior = "followPath"

await mcp.call(behavior, context, {"goal": next_waypoint})
```

2. Reactive Triggers
   - Define event handlers for critical thresholds (low battery, sensor fault) that immediately invoke emergency adapters like returnToBase or selfDiagnose.
3. Multi-Modal Fusion
   - Combine visual and LIDAR context within an "objectDetection" adapter to improve robustness under challenging lighting or dust.
4. Collaborative Context
   - Fleet robots publish their planned paths via streamPlannedPath and subscribe to getPeerPaths to deconflict and optimize traffic.

D. Best Practices

Practice	Benefit
Minimal Context Snapshots	Fetch only the fields needed for each decision to reduce latency.
Synchronized Timestamps	Use a common time base (e.g., NTP) so all context events align.
Graceful Degradation	On sensor failure, fall back to secondary modality (e.g., IMU-only navigation).

Schema-Validated Context	Define JSON Schemas for each context type to catch anomalies early.
Predictive Pre-Fetching	Preload map sections or sensor data when approaching new areas.
Real-Time Monitoring	Expose /metrics for control-loop durations and context freshness.

By structuring each sensor feed, map update, and mission directive as MCP tools—then composing them in your control logic—you create robots capable of **real-time adaptation**, **safe collaboration**, and **clean separation** of perception, planning, and actuation concerns.

5.5 Interactive Q&A

5.5.1 What Security Measures Would You Implement for a Robotics Application?

1. **Mutual TLS for All Robot-Server Traffic**
   • Enforce mTLS on MQTT/WebSocket/HTTP channels so both robots and your MCP server authenticate each other and prevent man-in-the-middle attacks.
   • Use short-lived certificates issued by your private PKI, rotated automatically.

2. **Strong Authentication & Authorization**
   • Assign each robot its own identity (client certificate or API key) and restrict its permissions to only the topics/methods it needs (principle of least privilege).
   • Use RBAC or fine-grained scopes so, for example, only "fleet manager" services can issue movement commands, while "telemetry collector" roles can only publish sensor data.

3. **Encrypted Payloads & Field-Level Protection**
   • Encrypt highly sensitive fields (e.g., cryptographic keys, location coordinates) in the JSON-RPC payload itself—only the intended adapter can decrypt.
   • Prevent accidental data leaks if logs or message queues are exposed.

4. **Network Segmentation & Firewalls**
   • Place robots, the MCP server, and external services (databases, dashboards) in separate network zones with strict ingress/egress rules.
   • Only allow specific ports (e.g., 8883 for MQTT over TLS) and IP whitelisting for control traffic.

5. **Secure Boot and Firmware Integrity**
   • Ensure each robot's OS and firmware verify signatures on boot to block unauthorized code and mitigate supply-chain attacks.
   • Automate secure, signed OTA updates over an encrypted channel.

6. **Input Validation & Schema Enforcement**
   • Validate every incoming JSON-RPC notification or request against a strict JSON Schema to guard against malformed or malicious data (e.g., extremely large payloads, unexpected fields).
   • Reject any messages that fail schema checks before they reach business logic.

7. **Rate Limiting & Anomaly Detection**
   • Apply per-robot and per-method rate limits to avoid flooding (e.g., a malfunctioning robot spamming telemetry).
   • Monitor for unusual patterns—sudden high-frequency logs, repeated failed commands—and trigger alerts or circuit breakers.

8. **Immutable Audit Logging**
   • Log every command and telemetry event with robot ID, timestamp, and user/agent identity to a write-once store (WORM) for forensic analysis and compliance (e.g., ISO 27001, NIST).
   • Include log integrity checks (hash chaining) so tampering is detectable.

9. **Runtime Integrity Checks**
   • Embed a lightweight watchdog or TPM on each robot to detect code tampering or memory corruption at runtime.
   • Periodically attest the robot's software stack back to a centralized verification service via a secure channel.

10. **Physical Security & Tamper Detection**
    • Equip robots with tamper-evident seals, intrusion sensors, or chassis-mounted accelerometers that report unauthorized access attempts.
    • Force a safe-mode shutdown or alert if physical tampering is detected.

11. **Secure Development Lifecycle (SDL)**
    • Conduct threat modeling for each component (robot firmware, network bridge, MCP adapters).
    • Integrate static code analysis, dependency vulnerability scanning (e.g., SBOM auditing), and regular penetration testing into your CI/CD pipeline.

12. **Emergency "Kill Switch"**
    • Implement a secure, out-of-band mechanism to immediately halt all robot motion (e.g., an HTTPS endpoint with MFA) in the event of a detected compromise or safety incident.

By layering these measures—from cryptographic protections and network controls to code integrity and physical safeguards—you'll build a comprehensive security posture that keeps both your robotic fleet and the people around it safe.

5.5.2 Discussion on Real-Time Data Processing in Autonomous Systems

1. Latency Budgets & End-to-End Deadlines
   - What is your maximum allowable processing delay from sensor capture to control action?
   - How do you allocate that total budget across acquisition, network transport, decoding, inference, and actuation?
2. Sensor Fusion & Time Alignment
   - How do you synchronize heterogeneous streams (LIDAR, IMU, cameras) to a common timebase?
   - What interpolation or buffering techniques ensure data coherence without undue lag?
3. Edge vs. Cloud Processing
   - Which computations must run locally on the robot (for safety and low latency) versus offloading to an edge or cloud service?
   - How do you handle intermittent connectivity or bandwidth constraints?
4. Back-Pressure and Flow Control
   - When upstream sensors produce bursts faster than your pipeline can consume, do you buffer, sample, or drop frames?
   - How do you signal producers (e.g., adjust lidar scan rate) to throttle output dynamically?
5. Fault Tolerance & Graceful Degradation
   - If a processing stage (e.g., object detection) becomes overloaded or fails, what fallback mode (e.g., reduced autonomy or safe stop) do you enter?
   - How do you detect and recover from stuck pipelines or memory leaks in streaming adapters?
6. Stateful vs. Stateless Pipelines
   - Which components maintain sliding-window state (e.g., motion history for odometry) and which operate purely on the current frame?
   - How do you checkpoint or snapshot state to resume after a restart without losing continuity?
7. Scalability Across Fleets
   - When multiple robots share a common context store or broker, how do you prevent one robot's high throughput from starving others?
   - Would you partition streams by robot-ID or dedicate separate channels for critical data types?
8. Quality of Service (QoS) Levels

- What QoS guarantees (e.g., exactly-once, at-least-once) do you need for different message types—telemetry versus commands?
- How does chosen QoS impact latency, bandwidth, and resource usage?

9. Monitoring, Metrics, and Alerting
   - Which real-time metrics (processing latency percentiles, frame drop rate, end-to-end jitter) will you track?
   - How quickly must you detect and alert on anomalies in the data pipeline before it affects robot safety?

10. Security and Data Integrity
   - How do you authenticate streams and ensure data hasn't been tampered with in transit?
   - Do you need encryption at the message level to protect sensitive context (e.g., map or mission data)?

11. Testing with Synthetic & Recorded Streams
   - How will you simulate edge conditions—network lag, message reordering, or corrupted packets—to validate resilience?
   - What replay mechanisms allow you to reproduce and debug intermittent real-world issues?

12. Continuous Optimization & Adaptive Sampling
   - Can your system learn which data channels are most critical in a given scenario and dynamically adjust sampling rates or processing fidelity?
   - How do you balance the trade-off between richer data (e.g., high-resolution images) and real-time constraints?

Reflecting on these points will help you architect a robust, low-latency data processing pipeline—one that keeps autonomous systems both performant and safe under the demands of real-world operation.

Chapter 6: Troubleshooting and Debugging MCP Servers

6.1 Common MCP Server Issues and Their Solutions

6.1.1 Connectivity Problems and How to Fix Them

Connectivity issues are among the most frequent obstacles when standing up or operating an MCP server. Below are common scenarios you'll encounter—each with symptoms, root causes, and targeted fixes.

A. RPC Endpoint Unreachable

- Symptoms
  1. curl or client requests to /rpc time out or return connection refused.
  2. No log entries for incoming requests.
- Causes & Fixes
  1. Server Not Listening on Expected Host/Port
     - **Check**: Are MCP_SERVER_HOST and MCP_SERVER_PORT correctly set in .env and loaded by config.py?
     - **Fix**: Print settings.host/settings.port at startup; ensure Uvicorn is bound to that address.
  2. Firewall / Security Group Blocking
     - **Check**: Can you telnet or nc to the host:port from the client machine?
     - **Fix**: Open the port in your OS firewall or cloud security group.
  3. Wrong RPC Path
     - **Check**: Is the client POSTing to the same path configured by settings.rpc_path?
     - **Fix**: Align the client URL (/rpc vs. /jsonrpc) with your FastAPI route decorator.

B. Database Connection Failures

- Symptoms
  1. Adapter calls to SQL methods hang, time out, or return "connection refused" or "authentication failed."
- Causes & Fixes
  1. Invalid DSN / Credentials
     - **Check**: Test psql $SQL_DSN (or equivalent) outside the app.

- **Fix**: Correct username/password, database name, or host in SQL_DSN.

2. Pool Exhaustion
   - **Check**: Examine Redis or Postgres logs for "too many connections."
   - **Fix**: Lower your max_size or scale the database; use a connection pool timeout.

3. Network Partition
   - **Check**: Can you ping or nc to the DB port from the MCP host?
   - **Fix**: Adjust network ACLs or VPN settings to restore connectivity.

C. Cache & Message Broker Unreachable

- Symptoms
  1. Streaming adapters fail with connection errors to Redis, Kafka, or MQTT.
  2. Errors like Connection refused or Timeout during connect.
- Causes & Fixes
  1. Wrong Broker URL
     - **Check**: Is REDIS_URL, KAFKA_BOOTSTRAP_SERVERS, or MQTT_BROKER correct?
     - **Fix**: Update the environment variable to the proper host:port (and protocol prefix, e.g., redis://).
  2. TLS / Authentication Mismatch
     - **Check**: Are you connecting with or without TLS when the broker expects the opposite?
     - **Fix**: Configure your client with the correct ssl settings or certificates.
  3. Broker Offline
     - **Check**: Is the broker process up and healthy?
     - **Fix**: Restart or scale the broker cluster; ensure it's registered in your service discovery.

D. External API Connectivity Issues

- Symptoms
  1. HTTP adapters return DNS errors, 5xx, or timeouts.
- Causes & Fixes
  1. DNS Resolution Failures

- **Check**: dig api.example.com from the server host.
- **Fix**: Update /etc/resolv.conf, your DNS service, or add an entry in /etc/hosts for testing.
2. Missing Proxy / Firewall Rules
   - **Check**: Are outbound HTTP(S) calls allowed?
   - **Fix**: Configure corporate proxy settings in httpx.AsyncClient(proxies=...) or open egress ports.
3. TLS Certificate Errors
   - **Check**: Does the client raise SSL: CERTIFICATE_VERIFY_FAILED?
   - **Fix**: Provide the correct CA bundle (verify= parameter) or pin certificates as needed.

E. CORS and Browser-Based Clients

- Symptoms
  1. Browser console shows "CORS policy: No 'Access-Control-Allow-Origin' header."
- Causes & Fixes
  1. Missing CORS Middleware
     - **Fix**: Add FastAPI's CORSMiddleware with appropriate allow_origins, allow_methods, and allow_headers.
  2. Wrong Origins Configured
     - **Check**: Are you allowing the exact front-end URL (including port)?
     - **Fix**: Use "*" for wide testing or list all allowed origins precisely.

Troubleshooting Checklist

1. **Confirm Service Status**: ps aux | grep uvicorn, systemctl status redis, kubectl get pods.
2. **Network Diagnostics**: ping, telnet, nc, curl -v.
3. **Log Inspection**: Tail server, adapter, and broker logs for error messages.
4. **Environment Verification**: printenv | grep -E 'MCP_SERVER|SQL|REDIS'.
5. **Health Endpoints**: Hit /health and /metrics to confirm liveness and discover any downstream errors.

By systematically walking through these connectivity checks—verifying configuration, network reachability, and correct protocols—you can quickly isolate and resolve the majority of MCP server connectivity problems.

6.1.2 Debugging Server Crashes and Timeouts

Crashes and timeouts can be particularly disruptive in MCP servers, interrupting AI workflows and degrading responsiveness. Below are common failure modes, diagnostic steps, and targeted fixes.

A. Identifying the Failure Mode

1. Crash vs. Timeout
   - **Crash**: Process exits unexpectedly (segfault, unhandled exception, OOM kill).
   - **Timeout**: Request hangs until client or server times out (HTTP 504, JSON-RPC no reply).
2. Gather Evidence
   - **Server Logs**: Look for stack traces, exception dumps, "Out of memory" messages, or signals (SIGSEGV, SIGKILL).
   - **System Logs**: Check dmesg or container runtime logs for OOM-killer events.
   - **Metrics**: Spike in CPU, memory, or event-loop latency preceding the failure.

B. Common Crash Causes & Remedies

Cause	Symptoms	Remedies
Unhandled Exceptions	Tracebacks in logs; server restarts	Wrap adapter code in try/except, map to JsonRpcError, add global exception handler.
Memory Leaks	Gradual memory growth; OOM-killer termination	Profile with tracemalloc/py-spy; fix unbounded caches or lingering references.

Threadpool Exhaustion	Server hangs then crashes under load	Avoid blocking I/O in adapters; use asyncio or offload to limited thread pool.
Segfaults in Native Extensions	SIGSEGV with no Python traceback	Update or replace faulty C extension (e.g., asyncpg, uvloop); pin to known good versions.
Improper Resource Cleanup	FD/socket leaks; "too many open files" errors	Ensure generators and clients close connections; use context managers (async with).

C. Timeout Scenarios & Solutions

1. HTTP Request Timeouts
   - **Symptom**: Clients get 504 Gateway Timeout or no JSON-RPC response.
   - **Fixes**:
     - Configure Uvicorn/Gunicorn --timeout-keep-alive and --timeout-graceful-shutdown.
     - On adapters, set sensible httpx.AsyncClient(timeout=...) or DB driver timeouts.
2. JSON-RPC Dispatch Timeouts
   - **Symptom**: jsonrpcserver hangs on a long-running method.

Fixes:
python

```python
response = await asyncio.wait_for(

    async_dispatch(request_text),

    timeout=settings.rpc_method_timeout

)
```

- Catch asyncio.TimeoutError and return a JSON-RPC error (-32001).

3. Database & External Service Timeouts
   - **Symptom**: Adapters block while waiting on slow queries or API calls.
   - **Fixes**:
     - Use connection pools with per-operation timeouts (e.g., asyncpg.create_pool(timeout=5)).
     - Implement retry with exponential back-off and a maximum total wait time.

D. Diagnostic Techniques

1. Request Tracing & Logging
   - Inject a unique requestId into context, log entry/exit times of each adapter.
   - Correlate logs with latency spikes or errors.
2. Profiling Under Load
   - Use tools like **py-spy**, **pyinstrument**, or **async-profiler** in production-like scenarios to find hot spots.
   - Profile memory with tracemalloc to identify growing allocations.
3. Health Probes & Canary Releases
   - Deploy a small subset of traffic to a canary instance with verbose logging and diagnostics enabled.
   - Use readiness/liveness endpoints to automatically eject unhealthy pods.

E. Automated Recovery Strategies

- Graceful Restart
  - On detecting high error rates or timeouts, restart worker processes one at a time to reclaim resources.
- Circuit Breakers
  - Temporarily disable problematic adapters after repeated failures to prevent cascading crashes.
- Bulkhead Isolation
  - Run heavy or unstable adapters in separate processes or containers so their failures don't bring down the main server.

By combining thorough log analysis, proactive profiling, sensible timeouts, and automated containment mechanisms, you'll minimize downtime and ensure your MCP server remains both robust and responsive under diverse failure conditions.

6.1.3 Handling Inconsistent Data and Failed Requests

In distributed MCP deployments, you'll inevitably encounter data that's missing, stale, or malformed—and requests that fail partway through. Robust handling of these scenarios prevents cascading errors and keeps your workflows resilient.

A. Symptoms of Inconsistent Data

- **Empty or Partial Results**
  – A `method returns` {} or missing fields.
- **Stale Context**
  – getUserState returns out-of-date values relative to downstream data sources.
- **Schema Mismatches**
  – `Upstream changes lead to JSON parse errors or unexpected types in adapters.`
- **Silent Failures**
  – `Adapters swallow exceptions and return default values without logging.`

B. Common Causes

Cause	Explanation
Late-Arriving Events	Streaming updates arrive out-of-order or after a related batch call.
Partial Network Outages	Some adapters succeed while others time out, leading to mixed state.

Schema Evolution	Downstream API or database schema changed without adapter update.
Improper Error Handling	Exceptions caught too broadly or not surfaced to the client.
Race Conditions	Concurrent writes to the same context key overwrite each other.

C. Strategies and Fixes

1. Input & Output Validation
   - **JSON Schema**: Validate both incoming params and outgoing result against a schema. Reject or fail early on mismatches.
   - **Type Checks**: Assert required fields exist and types are correct; raise JsonRpcError(-32602, "Invalid params") when validation fails.
2. Idempotency and Retries
   - **Idempotent Methods**: Design adapters so that retrying a failed call has no side effects or duplicate actions.
   - **Retry Policies**: Implement retry with exponential back-off for transient errors, capping the number of attempts.
3. Versioned Context and Schemas
   - Include a contextVersion or schemaVersion field in each context payload to detect stale clients or adapters.
   - Maintain backward-compatible transforms for older versions or migrate data on read.
4. Atomic Transactions
   - For multi-step operations (e.g., DB updates + cache writes), wrap in a transaction or two-phase commit so partial failures roll back cleanly.
5. Stale Data Detection
   - **Timestamps**: Tag each context update with a timestamp; ignore or reconcile out-of-order events based on time.
   - **Vector Clocks or Version Counters**: Reject older updates if a newer version is already applied.

6. Graceful Fallbacks
   - **Default Values**: Return safe defaults (empty lists, zeros) when non-critical data is missing.
   - **Error Indicators**: In the JSON-RPC result, include an errors array describing which sub-calls failed.
7. Centralized Error Reporting
   - Log every failed sub-call with context (method, args, error code, stack trace) to your observability backend.
   - Expose a /errors metrics endpoint or send alerts when error rates exceed a threshold.

D. Example: Composite Workflow with Partial Failures

python

```python
async def buildDashboard(mcp, context, args):

    calls = [

{"jsonrpc":"2.0","id":1,"method":"getUserProfile","params":{"context":context,"args":{}}},

{"jsonrpc":"2.0","id":2,"method":"getRecentTransactions","params":{"context":context,"args":{}}},

{"jsonrpc":"2.0","id":3,"method":"getRewardPoints","params":{"context":context,"args":{}}}
    ]

    responses = await mcp.batch_call(calls)

    profile = responses[0].get("result")

    transactions = responses[1].get("result", {}).get("transactions", [])

    points = responses[2].get("result", {}).get("points", 0)
```

```
errors = [r["error"] for r in responses if "error" in r]

return {

  "profile": profile,

  "transactions": transactions,

  "points": points,

  "partialFailures": errors

}
```

- Here, missing transactions or points won't block the entire dashboard; failures are surfaced in partialFailures.

E. Best Practices Checklist

- **Define and enforce JSON Schemas** for all methods.
- **Implement idempotent logic** to safely retry failed calls.
- **Tag context updates** with versions/timestamps to detect and reconcile stale data.
- **Use transactions** for multi-step operations affecting multiple stores.
- **Log and alert** on every adapter failure, including context and args.
- **Design workflows** to tolerate partial failures, surfacing errors without total abort.

By proactively validating data, handling partial failures, and surfacing errors in a structured way, you ensure your MCP server continues to operate reliably—even when individual data sources or requests fail.

6.2 Debugging JSON-RPC Requests and Responses

6.2.1 Step-by-Step Guide to Debugging JSON-RPC Calls

1. Capture the Raw HTTP Exchange

- Use curl -v, Postman, or your browser's dev tools to record the full request and response, including headers and body.
- In FastAPI, enable request/response logging middleware to dump payloads to your console or a file.

bash

```
curl -v -X POST http://localhost:8000/rpc \

 -H "Content-Type: application/json" \

 -d @request.json
```

2. Validate JSON Syntax and Structure
   - Paste the request body into a JSON linter (e.g., https://jsonlint.com) to catch stray commas or unescaped characters.
   - Ensure the top-level has "jsonrpc":"2.0", an "id", a valid "method" string, and a "params" object containing both "context" and "args".
3. Verify Method Availability

Invoke the built-in listMethods to confirm the server knows your target method:
bash

```
curl -s -X POST http://localhost:8000/rpc \

 -H "Content-Type: application/json" \

 -d
'{"jsonrpc":"2.0","id":0,"method":"listMethods","params":{"context":{},"args":{}}}'
```

- If your method isn't listed, check that you imported its adapter module and that the @method decorator executed.
4. Check Parameter Names and Types
   - Compare your request's args against the tool manifest or JSON Schema.
   - A mismatched type (e.g., string instead of integer) will produce a -32602 Invalid params error—adjust your payload accordingly.
5. Reproduce with a Minimal "Ping" Call

Test the simplest endpoint to isolate server vs. adapter issues:
bash

```
{"jsonrpc":"2.0","id":1,"method":"ping","params":{"context":{},"args":{}}}
```

- o A successful "result":{"message":"pong"} rules out core server problems.
6. Inspect JSON-RPC Error Codes
    - o -32700: Parse error (malformed JSON)
    - o -32600: Invalid Request (bad envelope)
    - o -32601: Method not found
    - o -32602: Invalid params
    - o -32000 **to** -32099: Server errors (adapter or infrastructure)
7. Enable Detailed Logging in Adapters
    - o Wrap your adapter logic with try/catch and log method name, args, and full exception stack trace.
    - o Return structured JsonRpcError with helpful data fields for context.
8. Use an Interactive JSON-RPC Client

In Python REPL or a small script, use jsonrpcclient to invoke methods and inspect exceptions programmatically:
python

```
from jsonrpcclient import request, parse

from httpx import AsyncClient


async with AsyncClient() as client:

    response = await client.post("http://localhost:8000/rpc",
json=request("myMethod"))

    print(parse(response.json()))
```

9. Automate Test Cases
    - o Write pytest tests that cover valid calls, missing params, and adapter exceptions; fail tests if unexpected error codes are returned.
10. Monitor Network and Broker Connectivity

- If using streams or notifications, ensure your bridge or client can reach the /rpc endpoint under load—use tools like tcpdump or broker-side logs to detect dropped packets.

By following these steps—capturing the raw exchange, validating structure, confirming method registration, inspecting error codes, and adding targeted logging—you'll systematically pinpoint and resolve any issues in your JSON-RPC request/response flow.

6.2.2 Understanding Error Codes and Handling Exceptions

JSON-RPC defines a standardized set of error codes, and MCP servers add their own range for adapter-specific failures. Properly mapping exceptions to these codes—and returning clear messages—makes it far easier for clients to diagnose and recover from errors.

Error Code	Name	Meaning
-32700	Parse error	Invalid JSON was received by the server.
-32600	Invalid Request	The JSON sent is not a valid JSON-RPC request object.
-32601	Method not found	The method does not exist or is not available.
-32602	Invalid params	Invalid method parameter(s), e.g. missing required field or wrong type according to schema.

-32603	Internal error	Internal JSON-RPC error—something went wrong in the dispatch layer (not adapter code).
$-32000 \cdots -32099$	Server error	Reserved for implementation-defined server errors (e.g., adapter failures, downstream errors).
$>=1000$	Application-specific	Your domain can define custom codes here (e.g., 1001 for "Rate limit exceeded").

A. Mapping Python Exceptions to JSON-RPC Errors

Syntax and Validation Errors
python

```python
from jsonrpcserver import JsonRpcError


@method
async def getUser(context, args):
    user_id = args.get("userId")
    if not isinstance(user_id, str):
        # Map to "Invalid params"
        raise JsonRpcError(-32602, "userId must be a string")
```

```
# ...
```

Downstream Failures
python

```python
@method
async def fetchWeather(context, args):
    try:
        resp = await client.get(url)
        resp.raise_for_status()
    except httpx.HTTPStatusError as e:
        # Map 404 to "Method not found" style, others to server error
        code = -32004 if e.response.status_code == 404 else -32000
        raise JsonRpcError(code, f"Weather API error: {e}") from e
```

1. Unhandled Exceptions

Add a global exception hook around your dispatch to catch anything unexpected:
python

```python
@app.exception_handler(Exception)
async def universal_handler(request, exc):
    # Log the full traceback
    logger.exception("Unhandled exception in RPC dispatch")
    return JSONResponse({
        "jsonrpc": "2.0",
        "id": None,
```

```
    "error": {

      "code": -32603,

      "message": "Internal server error"

    }

  })
```

B. Best Practices for Exception Handling

Practice	Benefit
Validate Early	Catch missing or malformed inputs before any business logic.
Use Specific Codes	Map each failure type to the most appropriate JSON-RPC code.
Include Helpful Messages	Provide clear, concise error descriptions, avoiding internal jargon.
Attach data for Debugging	Optionally include structured fields (e.g., {"retryAfter":5}) to guide clients.
Avoid Leaking Sensitive Info	Don't expose stack traces or PII in error messages returned to clients.
Consistent Logging	Log full exception details server-side, correlated by requestId.

C. Client-Side Error Handling Patterns

Inspect the error.code
js

```js
if (response.error) {

  switch (response.error.code) {

    case -32601:

      alert("Requested method is not available.");

      break;

    case -32029:

      setTimeout(() => retryCall(), response.error.data.retryAfter * 1000);

      break;

    default:

      console.error(response.error);

  }

}
```

1. Partial-Failure Workflows
   - In batch calls, process each result or error independently, so one adapter failure doesn't block the entire operation.
2. Back-Off on Server Errors
   - For codes in the -32000 range, implement exponential back-off before retrying to avoid overwhelming a failing service.

By systematically mapping every failure—whether client misuse, adapter logic error, or infrastructure fault—to a clear JSON-RPC code and message, and by logging full diagnostics on the server, you'll make both debugging and client recovery straightforward and reliable.

6.2.3 Tools and Techniques for Efficient Debugging

1. Structured and Correlated Logging
   - **Correlation IDs**: Inject a unique requestId or trace ID into every JSON-RPC call (via middleware) and include it in each log line. This lets you trace a single request through multiple adapters and external calls.
   - **Structured Logs**: Use a JSON-capable logger (e.g., Loguru, structlog) so logs can be filtered, searched, and aggregated by fields like method, userId, durationMs, or errorCode.
2. Interactive API Exploration
   - **HTTP Clients**: Tools like Postman, Insomnia, or the http CLI let you craft, replay, and parameterize JSON-RPC requests, inspect raw responses, and save collections of test cases.
   - **REPL Clients**: In Python, use jsonrpcclient or a simple httpx script in an interactive shell to invoke methods, catch exceptions, and iterate on request payloads in real time.
3. Live Request/Response Inspection
   - **Middleware Dump**: Add FastAPI middleware that logs the full request and response bodies (respecting PII policies) for a configurable subset of methods or clients.
   - **Network Sniffing**: Use tcpdump or Wireshark to capture and inspect HTTP/TCP frames—helpful when diagnosing TLS handshake issues or proxy misconfiguration.
4. Automated and Exploratory Testing
   - **Unit Tests**: Wrap each adapter in pytest functions, mocking external dependencies. Parametrize tests for both success and failure modes to catch edge cases early.
   - **Integration Tests**: Spin up ephemeral services (e.g., using Docker Compose) to validate full RPC flows against real databases, caches, and HTTP endpoints before deployment.
5. Profiling and Performance Analysis
   - **CPU & Memory Profilers**: Tools like py-spy, pyinstrument, or tracemalloc can pinpoint hot code paths, blocking calls, or memory leaks in long-running servers.
   - **AIOHTTP/Starlette Tracing**: Integrate OpenTelemetry or Zipkin to capture per-request spans, measure downstream call latencies (HTTP, DB), and visualize trace waterfalls.
6. Step-Through Debugging

- IDE Breakpoints: Run the server in debug mode (e.g., VS Code or PyCharm), set breakpoints in adapter code, and inspect variables, call stacks, and exception contexts on the fly.
- Conditional Logging: Wrap suspicious branches in if settings.debug_mode: logger.debug(...) so you can enable detailed traces without flooding production logs.

7. Schema Validation and Contract Testing
- JSON Schema Validators: Use jsonschema at the RPC gateway to validate every params payload, catching invalid or unexpected fields before adapter code runs.
- Contract Tests: Define example requests and responses in a shared manifest (e.g., OpenAPI or custom JSON-RPC spec), then generate tests that assert conformance automatically.

8. Replay and Record-and-Replay
- Request Logging: Persist a history of real RPC requests (sanitized) to a log store. Later, replay them against new code versions to verify backwards compatibility.
- Event-Sourcing: For streaming or notification-driven adapters, store events in an append-only log (Kafka, Redis Streams) and replay consumer behavior in a test harness.

9. Runtime Feature Flags and Hot Swapping
- Toggle verbose debug behavior or alternative adapter implementations via feature flags (e.g., LaunchDarkly, Unleash) without restarting the server.
- Implement a plugin loader that can safely unload and reload adapter modules to iterate on fixes without full redeploys.

10. Observability Dashboards and Alerts
- Metrics: Expose Prometheus counters, histograms, and gauges for RPC QPS, error rates per method, and tail-latencies. Build dashboards to spot anomalies at a glance.
- Alerts: Configure thresholds (e.g., error rate > 5%, 95th-percentile latency > 500 ms) to notify your team immediately when things go awry.

By combining these tools—structured logs, interactive clients, profilers, automated tests, and observability platforms—you'll dramatically reduce mean-time-to-resolution for JSON-RPC issues and keep your MCP server operating smoothly.

6.3 Optimizing Server Performance

6.3.1 Best Practices for Optimizing the MCP Server Performance

To ensure your MCP server remains responsive under heavy load and scales efficiently, apply optimizations at multiple layers—from the application code to the deployment environment. Below are proven strategies:

A. Concurrency and Async I/O

- **End-to-End Async**
  Use only asynchronous libraries (e.g., httpx.AsyncClient, asyncpg, aioredis) so the event loop never blocks on I/O.

Worker Processes
Run multiple Uvicorn/Gunicorn workers to leverage multi-core CPUs:
bash

```
# Pure async

uvicorn main:app --workers 4 --host 0.0.0.0 --port 8000

# Gunicorn + Uvicorn workers for CPU-bound tasks

gunicorn main:app -k uvicorn.workers.UvicornWorker -w 4 --bind 0.0.0.0:8000
```

- **Limit Concurrency**
  Tune --limit-concurrency and --timeout-keep-alive to protect against slow clients consuming all workers.

B. Connection Pooling and Resource Reuse

HTTP Client Pooling
Reuse a single httpx.AsyncClient instance with configured connection limits:
python

```
client = httpx.AsyncClient(

  limits=httpx.Limits(max_connections=100,
max_keepalive_connections=20)
```

)

- **Database Pools**
  Create and share a single asyncpg or motor pool at startup, specifying sensible min_size and max_size.
- **Redis and Cache Pools**
  Use shared Redis connection pools to avoid the overhead of new connections per request.

C. Payload and Serialization Optimizations

Faster JSON Library
Use orjson as FastAPI's JSON backend for significantly faster serialization:
python

```python
from fastapi import FastAPI

from fastapi.responses import ORJSONResponse


app = FastAPI(default_response_class=ORJSONResponse)
```

- **Minimize Response Size**
  Return only the fields clients need; use projection in DB queries and filter out unused data before serializing.

D. Batching and Caching

JSON-RPC Batches
Combine related calls into a single batch to reduce network overhead and context-switching:
python

```python
results = await mcp.batch_call([ ... list of call dicts ... ])
```

- **Result Caching**
  Cache idempotent tool calls (e.g., reference data, weather) in Redis with TTLs to reduce external API and DB load.
- **Adaptive TTLs**
  Align cache expiration to data volatility—shorter TTLs for dynamic data, longer for static.

E. Profiling and Monitoring

- **Profiling Hot Paths**
  Integrate py-spy or pyinstrument in staging to identify slow adapters, serialization bottlenecks, or blocking calls.
- **Metrics Instrumentation**
  Expose Prometheus metrics for:
  - **Request latency** (histogram per method)
  - **Error rate** (counter per method)
  - **Concurrent in-flight calls** (gauge)
- **Alerts and Dashboards**
  Set alerts on tail-latency (95th/99th percentile) and error spikes to trigger automated remediation or scale-out.

F. Code and Deployment Practices

- **Lazy Imports**
  Delay importing heavy libraries until needed in an adapter to reduce startup time and memory footprint.
- **Container Resource Limits**
  In Kubernetes or Docker, set CPU and memory requests/limits to enable proper scheduling and avoid noisy neighbors.
- **Autoscaling**
  Use Horizontal Pod Autoscaler (HPA) on CPU, memory, or custom metrics (e.g., request latency) to match capacity to demand.
- **Readiness/Liveness Probes**
  Configure /health and /metrics endpoints so orchestrators can detect unhealthy instances and restart them cleanly.

By combining these practices—leveraging full async I/O, reusing connections, batching and caching calls, and continuously profiling and scaling—you'll maintain a high-throughput, low-latency MCP server that gracefully handles growing workloads.

6.3.2 Load Testing and Performance Benchmarking

Effective load testing and benchmarking help you understand your MCP server's behavior under realistic and extreme conditions, identify bottlenecks, and validate your scaling strategy. Below is a step-by-step approach, tool recommendations, and example scenarios.

A. Define Your Objectives and Metrics

1. Key Metrics
   - **Throughput**: requests per second (RPS) your server can sustain.
   - **Latency**: percentiles (P50, P95, P99) for each method.
   - **Error Rate**: fraction of requests returning errors.
   - **Resource Utilization**: CPU, memory, event-loop latency, connection pool saturation.
2. Test Goals
   - Verify that steady-state RPS meets your SLA.
   - Discover breaking points under stress (peak RPS, method mix).
   - Validate auto-scaling thresholds and health-probe behavior.

B. Prepare Your Test Environment

1. Isolated Staging Cluster
   - Deploy your MCP server in a production-like environment (same container image, resource limits, network policies).
   - Ensure no noisy neighbors or other apps share the same nodes.
2. Synthetic Data and Mocks
   - Use realistic request payloads with representative context and args.
   - Mock external dependencies (databases, third-party APIs) to isolate the MCP server's capacity.
3. Metric Collection
   - Instrument Prometheus on /metrics.

- Collect system metrics (node_exporter) and application logs.
- Set up a Grafana dashboard for live visualization.

C. Choose Your Load-Testing Tool

Tool	Language	Pros	Cons
Locust	Python	Easy to write user-behavior scenarios; supports distributed load.	Requires Python for custom logic.
k6	JavaScript	Lightweight, great for CI, built-in metrics output.	JS-based, steeper learning for complex flows.
JMeter	Java / GUI	Rich GUI, plugins, protocol support.	Heavy, can be cumbersome to scale.
wrk	C	Very fast, simple HTTP benchmarking.	No built-in JSON-RPC helper, scripting in Lua.
Vegeta	Go	Simple CLI, targets and report.	Basic feature set, no distributed mode.

D. Crafting Test Scenarios

1. Single-Method Spike

- o Target one expensive method (e.g., fetchWeather) to measure its per-call cost.
- o Ramp from 1 RPS up to your expected peak + 20% headroom.
2. Mixed-Method Steady Load
    - o Define a weighted mix (e.g., 50% ping, 30% getUserOrders, 20% fetchWeather).
    - o Run at constant RPS for 30 minutes to observe long-term stability and memory growth.
3. Burst and Recovery
    - o Sudden jump from 10 RPS to 200 RPS for 60 seconds, then back to 10 RPS.
    - o Verify rate limiter behavior, autoscaling, and backlog handling.
4. Batch Calls vs. Individual
    - o Compare throughput for 1000 individual calls versus JSON-RPC batch of 1000 requests.
    - o Measure serialization, dispatch, and adapter performance differences.
5. Streaming Load
    - o For streaming methods, simulate N concurrent clients subscribing to a stream of messages at M messages/sec.
    - o Observe memory and connection churn over time.

E. Example: Locust Scenario

python

```python
# locustfile.py

from locust import HttpUser, task, between

import json


class MCPUser(HttpUser):

    wait_time = between(0.1, 1)
```

```python
    def on_start(self):

        self.headers = {"Content-Type": "application/json"}


    @task(5)

    def ping(self):

        payload =
{"jsonrpc":"2.0","id":1,"method":"ping","params":{"context":{},"args":{}}}

        self.client.post("/rpc", data=json.dumps(payload),
headers=self.headers)


    @task(3)

    def fetch_weather(self):

        payload = {

          "jsonrpc":"2.0","id":2,"method":"fetchWeather",

          "params":{"context":{},"args":{"city":"London,UK"}}

        }

        self.client.post("/rpc", data=json.dumps(payload),
headers=self.headers)


    @task(2)

    def get_orders(self):

        payload = {

          "jsonrpc":"2.0","id":3,"method":"getUserOrders",

          "params":{"context":{},"args":{"user_id":"u42","limit":5}}

        }
```

```
    self.client.post("/rpc", data=json.dumps(payload),
headers=self.headers)
```

Run with:

bash

```
locust -f locustfile.py --host=http://mcp-staging:8000 --users 100 --spawn-
rate 10
```

F. Analyzing Results

1. Throughput vs. Latency
   ○ Plot RPS against P95/P99 latency; identify knee points where latency
     spikes sharply.
2. Error Trends
   ○ Chart error rate over time; correlate with resource metrics (CPU %-util,
     memory usage).
3. Resource Saturation
   ○ Look for connection pool exhaustion, GC pauses, or ulimit exhaustion (too
     many open files).

G. Iterative Tuning

1. **Optimize Hot Adapters**:
   ○ Profile slow methods, refactor blocking calls, add caching or batching.
2. **Scale Horizontally**:
   ○ Increase worker count or replicas, adjust HPA thresholds.
3. **Adjust Rate Limits**:
   ○ Reconfigure per-method quotas to protect downstream services.
4. **Re-Run Tests**:
   ○ Confirm improvements and ensure no regressions.

By following this structured approach—defining clear goals, using the right tools,
simulating realistic loads, and closely monitoring both application and system metrics—
you'll build confidence that your MCP server can meet production demands and scale
gracefully.

6.3.3 Analyzing and Improving Server Response Times

Slow response times undermine user experience and can back up event streams. Tackling latency requires a cycle of **measurement**, **analysis**, and **optimization**. Below are concrete steps and techniques.

A. Measure End-to-End Latency

1. Instrument Per-Method Histograms

Expose Prometheus histograms keyed by method name:
python

```python
from prometheus_client import Histogram


rpc_latency = Histogram(

  "mcp_rpc_latency_seconds",

  "RPC method latency",

  ["method"]
)


@app.post("/rpc")
async def rpc_endpoint(request: Request):
  body = await request.body()
  method = extract_method(body)
  with rpc_latency.labels(method=method).time():
    return await async_dispatch(body.decode())
```

  - Track P50/P95/P99 for each tool.
2. Distributed Tracing

- Use OpenTelemetry or Zipkin to trace request spans through middleware, JSON-RPC dispatch, and adapter calls.
- Correlate traces with downstream HTTP/DB spans to pinpoint slow segments.
3. Synthetic Benchmarks
   - Automate "heartbeat" calls (e.g., every minute ping) from an external service to log real-world latency over time.

B. Profile Hot Paths

1. CPU Profiling
   - Run py-spy top in production-like load to identify functions consuming the most CPU time.
2. Async-Loop Analysis
   - Use asyncio.get_running_loop().slow_callback_duration to log callbacks running longer than a threshold.
3. Allocation Tracking
   - Use tracemalloc to locate unexpected memory allocations that could slow down GC.

C. Common Latency Culprits & Fixes

Culprit	Optimization
Blocking I/O	Convert to async libraries (httpx.AsyncClient, asyncpg).
Cold Starts	Pre-load heavy dependencies at startup (models, DB pools).
Large Payloads	Stream or paginate responses; only return needed fields.

Repeated Context Enrichment	Cache enriched context (e.g., user profile) with TTL.
Synchronous JSON Parsing	Use faster backends (e.g., orjson) for serialization.

D. Caching and Batching

In-Process LRU Cache
python

```python
from functools import lru_cache


@lru_cache(maxsize=1024)

async def fetchReferenceData(key: str):

  # expensive external call
```

1. Batch Database Queries
   - Group multiple lookups into single SQL query or JSON-RPC batch to reduce round-trips.

E. Connection Tuning

- HTTP Keep-Alive
  - Configure httpx.AsyncClient(limits=Limits(...), keepalive_expiry=...).
- DB Pool Sizing
  - Monitor pool utilization; match max_size to concurrent workload without exhausting DB.

F. Asynchronous Concurrency Controls

- Limit Concurrency

Protect the event loop by capping simultaneous tasks with semaphores:
python

```python
semaphore = asyncio.Semaphore(100)

async def limited_call(...):

    async with semaphore:

        return await actual_adapter(...)
```

- Timeouts & Circuit Breakers
  - Fail fast on slow downstream services to avoid head-of-line blocking.

G. Continuous Improvement Workflow

1. **Set Baselines**: Record current P95 latency for key methods.
2. **Implement One Change**: e.g., switch to orjson or add caching.
3. **Re-Benchmark**: Run the same load test and compare metrics.
4. **Iterate**: Focus on the next highest-latency hotspot.

By rigorously measuring, profiling, and applying targeted optimizations—especially around I/O, serialization, and pooling—you'll drive down response times and keep your MCP server snappy under real-world load.

6.4 Interactive Q&A

6.4.1 Common Issues You've Encountered When Setting Up MCP Servers

1. Module Import and Registration
   - Have you ever forgotten to import a new adapter module in main.py, leading to "Method not found" errors?
   - How do you track which adapters are registered versus which are pending deployment?
2. Environment Variable Misconfiguration

- o Which environment variables (DSNs, API keys, file paths) have tripped you up in .env vs. production?
- o What strategies do you use to validate that all required settings are present at startup?
3. Blocking vs. Async Code
    - o Did you inadvertently introduce blocking calls (sync DB queries or file I/O) that stalled the event loop?
    - o How did you detect and refactor those to async equivalents?
4. JSON-RPC Schema Mismatches
    - o Have your clients ever sent parameters that didn't match your tool's JSON Schema, causing -32602 errors?
    - o What tooling or tests do you have in place to catch schema drifts early?
5. CORS or Network Access Issues
    - o When exposing /rpc to browser-based clients, did missing CORS headers block your requests?
    - o How did you configure CORSMiddleware to avoid overly permissive or too-strict settings?
6. Rate-Limiter Overreach
    - o Have you seen legitimate calls fail with 429 errors because your token-bucket thresholds were too low?
    - o What metrics helped you right-size per-method and per-client rate limits?
7. Timeouts and Error Handling
    - o Which methods have you needed to wrap in asyncio.wait_for to prevent head-of-line blocking?
    - o How do you ensure that a timeout in one adapter doesn't cascade into a complete workflow failure?
8. Connection Pool Exhaustion
    - o Did your database or cache start rejecting connections under load?
    - o How did you adjust your pool sizes or introduce back-pressure to stabilize your server?
9. Logging and Observability Gaps
    - o Have you ever struggled to trace a request end-to-end because of missing correlation IDs or sparse logs?
    - o What changes did you make to your logging middleware or metrics instrumentation to fill those gaps?
10. Hot-Reload vs. Production Stability
    - o When using development hot-reload, did you encounter module duplication or stale code running?

- How do you balance rapid iteration in dev with deterministic behavior in prod?

Reflect on these common pain points—what solutions have worked best for you, and which areas still need improvement?

6.4.2 Discussion Points on Performance Optimization Strategies

1. Defining and Validating SLAs
   - What latency percentiles (P95, P99) and throughput (RPS) targets does your MCP deployment need to meet?
   - How do you verify those SLAs under realistic vs. peak loads?
2. Baseline Instrumentation
   - Which key metrics (RPC latency histograms, error rates, connection-pool usage) do you collect by default?
   - How do you ensure your instrumentation has minimal overhead?
3. Identifying Hot Paths
   - How do you profile your server to pinpoint slow adapters or JSON-RPC dispatch bottlenecks?
   - Which tools and workflows (e.g., py-spy, OpenTelemetry tracing) have been most effective?
4. Caching Strategies and TTL Tuning
   - Which RPC calls benefit most from result caching, and how do you choose appropriate TTLs?
   - How do you handle cache invalidation when underlying data changes?
5. Batching vs. Real-Time Calls
   - When should you group multiple JSON-RPC requests into a single batch to reduce overhead?
   - How do you balance batch size against the need for low end-to-end latency?
6. Connection Pool and Resource Reuse
   - How do you size your HTTP, database, and Redis pools to match expected concurrency without over-consuming backend resources?
   - What signals (e.g., pool wait time, queue length) inform you that pools need retuning?
7. Serialization and Payload Minimization
   - Have you measured the impact of different JSON libraries (e.g., orjson vs. the default) on serialization speed?
   - How do you ensure your RPC methods return only the fields clients actually need?
8. Concurrency Tuning

- What combination of event-loop concurrency, thread-pools, and worker processes yields the best throughput on your hardware?
- How do you detect and eliminate blocking calls that starve the event loop?

9. Back-Pressure and Flow Control
- How do your streaming adapters handle bursts of data—drop, buffer, or signal producers to throttle?
- What mechanisms do you use to prevent head-of-line blocking when one method is slow?

10. Autoscaling and Deployment Configuration
- Which metrics (CPU, memory, custom RPC latency) drive your HPA policies in Kubernetes or your cloud autoscaling groups?
- How do you verify that readiness/liveness probes and rollout strategies don't introduce performance regressions?

11. Load-Testing Insights
- Which test scenarios (steady-state mixed load, burst traffic, batch vs. individual calls) have revealed unexpected bottlenecks?
- How do you incorporate those findings into your optimization roadmap?

12. Logging and Observability Trade-Offs
- How much logging verbosity can you afford before it meaningfully impacts latency?
- Where do you draw the line between actionable diagnostics and performance overhead?

Reflecting on these points will help you craft a holistic performance-optimization plan—one that spans code, configuration, and infrastructure—to keep your MCP server both fast and resilient.

Chapter 7: Real-World Applications of MCP Servers

7.1 AI-Assisted Decision-Making Systems
7.1.1 How MCP Enhances AI-Based Decision-Making Tools

1. Unified Access to Heterogeneous Data Sources
   - **Problem**: Decision models often require inputs from databases, external APIs, file stores, and real-time feeds—each with its own SDK, protocol, and auth scheme.
   - **MCP Benefit**: MCP adapters wrap every integration behind a consistent JSON-RPC interface. AI workflows simply "call" methods like getMarketData, fetchCustomerProfile, or readInventoryFile, without embedding service-specific code in the model logic.
2. Automatic Context Propagation
   - **Problem**: Complex decisions depend on metadata—user identity, session parameters, locale, or risk thresholds—that must be threaded through multiple service calls.
   - **MCP Benefit**: Every JSON-RPC request carries a context object. Adapters automatically receive session IDs, user roles, and request timestamps, enabling consistent authorization, auditing, and personalized behavior without manual wiring.
3. Dynamic Capability Discovery
   - **Problem**: In evolving environments, new decision-support tools (e.g., a new compliance checker or pricing engine) come online frequently. Hard-coded client code must be updated to use them.
   - **MCP Benefit**: Clients can call listMethods at runtime to discover available tools and their schemas. Decision orchestrators adapt on the fly—invoking new capabilities when they appear, and gracefully degrading if they vanish.
4. Composable, Branching Workflows
   - **Problem**: Decision logic often follows complex branching: "If credit score < 600, run high-risk flow; else, offer standard loan." Embedding that in monolithic code leads to maintenance headaches.

MCP Benefit: Workflow code inspects context (e.g., creditScore) and conditionally invokes tools:
python

```
if context["creditScore"] < 600:

    result = await mcp.call("runHighRiskAssessment", context, args)

else:

    result = await mcp.call("runStandardAssessment", context, args)
```

- This keeps branching logic simple and decouples decision criteria from tool implementations.
5. Consistent Error Handling and Retry Semantics
    - **Problem**: Each integration may fail in different ways—timeouts, 5xx, malformed data—requiring bespoke retry logic and fallbacks.
    - **MCP Benefit**: MCP enforces uniform error codes and allows adapters to communicate retry hints (retryAfter). Decision engines can implement generic fallback strategies (e.g., use cached data, raise manual review flags) based purely on error codes.
6. Auditability and Explainability
    - **Problem**: Regulated domains (finance, healthcare) require that every decision step be logged with inputs, outputs, and timestamps. Piecing together ad-hoc logs from disparate systems is error-prone.
    - **MCP Benefit**: Since every tool invocation is a discrete JSON-RPC call with a context.requestId, you can capture a complete trace of the decision pipeline. Coupled with structured logging, you can reconstruct why a particular branch was taken.
7. Performance Optimization via Batching and Caching
    - **Problem**: Decision systems often query the same reference data (e.g., exchange rates) multiple times within one workflow, causing redundant network trips.

MCP Benefit: MCP supports JSON-RPC batch calls and adapter-level caching. You can batch related calls:
json

```
[

{ "jsonrpc":"2.0","id":1,"method":"getRate","params":... },

{ "jsonrpc":"2.0","id":2,"method":"getRate","params":... }
```

]

- o and return cached results for idempotent queries, dramatically reducing latency.

8. Real-Time and Streaming Data Integration
   - o **Problem**: Some decisions depend on transient, high-velocity feeds (e.g., market tick data). Polling isn't fast or efficient enough.
   - o **MCP Benefit**: Streaming adapters use JSON-RPC notifications and partial responses to push real-time context into decision engines. Agents subscribe to streams (e.g., streamMarketTicks) and react instantly as events arrive.

9. Separation of Concerns for Maintainability
   - o **Problem**: Mixing decision logic with data-access code makes systems brittle and hard to extend.
   - o **MCP Benefit**: Decision models focus purely on *what* to decide—encoded in workflow orchestrators—while *how* to fetch data, authenticate, parse, and secure it lives entirely in adapters. This modularity accelerates both development and testing.

10. Scalability and Operational Resilience
    - o **Problem**: As decision workloads grow, blending compute, I/O, and context enrichment in a single process can become a bottleneck.
    - o **MCP Benefit**: You can scale MCP server instances horizontally, autoscale specific adapters (e.g., heavy ML scoring services), and apply rate limiting to protect sensitive downstream systems—ensuring decision pipelines remain available under load.

By leveraging MCP's unified, context-aware bridge between AI models and diverse data or service endpoints, organizations can build decision-support systems that are **modular**, **auditable**, **resilient**, and **extensible**—empowering both rapid iteration and robust, compliant operation in real-world environments.

7.1.2 Use Cases in Finance, Healthcare, and E-Commerce

Below are representative scenarios in three major industries where MCP servers add significant value to AI-assisted decision-making workflows.

A. Finance: Real-Time Portfolio Risk Management

1. Context Requirements
   - o **Market Data**: Live price and volume feeds for equities, FX, and derivatives.

- - **Portfolio Holdings**: Customer positions, leverage ratios, margin requirements.
  - **Risk Parameters**: Value-at-Risk (VaR) thresholds, stress-test scenarios, regulatory limits.

MCP Workflow
python

```python
# 1. Fetch live market ticks and portfolio snapshot in parallel
ticks, holdings = await mcp.batch_call([
  {"id":1,"method":"streamMarketTicks","params":...},
  {"id":2,"method":"getPortfolioHoldings","params":...}
])
# 2. Compute risk metrics
risk = await mcp.call("calculateVaR", context, {
  "ticks": ticks["result"], "holdings": holdings["result"]
})
# 3. Branch on risk alert
if risk["value"] > context["userLimits"]["maxVaR"]:
    await mcp.call("sendRiskAlert", context, {"risk": risk})
```

2. Benefits
   - **Low Latency**: Streaming adapters deliver ticks at microsecond granularity.
   - **Regulatory Audit**: Every risk calculation and alert is logged with requestId for compliance.
   - **Dynamic Tooling**: New analytics (e.g., CVaR, Greeks) can be plugged in without client changes.

B. Healthcare: Personalized Treatment Recommendation

1. Context Requirements

- Patient Data: EHR (FHIR) records, lab results, imaging summaries.
- Clinical Guidelines: Latest treatment protocols and drug–interaction databases.
- Patient Preferences: Allergy history, advance directives, insurance coverage.

MCP Workflow
python

```python
# 1. Enrich patient context

patient, labs = await mcp.batch_call([

  {"id":1,"method":"fetchPatientRecord","params":...},

  {"id":2,"method":"fetchLabResults","params":...}

])

# 2. Check drug interactions

interactions = await mcp.call("checkDrugInteractions", context, {

  "currentMeds": patient["meds"], "proposedMeds": args["proposed"]

})

# 3. Get guideline-based recommendations

recs = await mcp.call("fetchGuidelineRecommendations", context, {

  "diagnosis": args["diagnosis"], "comorbidities": patient["conditions"]

})

# 4. Filter recommendations based on interactions

safe = [r for r in recs["result"] if r["drug"] not in interactions["conflicts"]]

return {"recommendations": safe}
```

2. Benefits
   - Safe Defaults: Fallback to standard protocols if any adapter fails.

- ○ **Explainability**: Each step logged, with sources, for clinician review.
- ○ **Elasticity**: Scale out adapters (imaging, lab) independently under load.

C. E-Commerce: Dynamic Pricing and Inventory Allocation

1. Context Requirements
    - ○ **Customer Profile**: Purchase history, loyalty tier, real-time browsing context.
    - ○ **Inventory Data**: Stock levels across warehouses, shipping lead times.
    - ○ **Competitive Intelligence**: Competitor pricing via web scraping or partner APIs.

MCP Workflow
python

```python
# 1. Gather context

profile, stock, competitor = await mcp.batch_call([

  {"id":1,"method":"getCustomerProfile","params":...},

  {"id":2,"method":"getInventoryLevels","params":...},

  {"id":3,"method":"fetchCompetitorPrices","params":...}

])

# 2. Compute optimal price

price = await mcp.call("calculateDynamicPrice", context, {

  "baseCost": args["cost"], "tier": profile["tier"], "competitor":
competitor["result"]

})

# 3. Reserve inventory if price acceptable

if price <= profile["maxPrice"]:

  await mcp.call("reserveStock", context, {

    "productId": args["productId"], "quantity": args["qty"]

  })
```

```
return {"price": price}
```

2. Benefits
   - **Personalization**: Pricing algorithms adapt to loyalty tier and real-time demand.
   - **Efficiency**: Batch calls minimize database and API round-trips.
   - **Fault Tolerance**: If competitor API is down, fallback pricing model applies.

In each industry, MCP's **uniform JSON-RPC interface**, **context propagation**, and **composable adapters** let you assemble complex decision pipelines—integrating real-time streams, batch data, and domain-specific logic—while maintaining modularity, auditability, and scalability.

7.1.3 Building a Recommendation Engine with MCP

A recommendation engine typically blends **user context, item metadata**, and **interaction history** to surface personalized suggestions. With MCP, each piece of that pipeline lives in a discrete JSON-RPC tool, so your orchestration code remains clean and data-source agnostic.

A. Core Components as MCP Tools

Component	MCP Method	Responsibility
User Profile Fetch	getUserProfile	Returns demographics, preferences, past purchases.
Interaction History	getUserHistory	Streams or batches recent clicks, views, and ratings.

Item Metadata	getItemMetadata	Fetches attributes (category, price, embeddings).
Embedding Computation	computeEmbedding	Generates vector for user or item features.
Vector Search	vectorSearch	Queries a vector store for nearest neighbors.
Collaborative Filter	collaborativeFilter	Suggests items based on similar users' history.
Reranking & Filters	applyBusinessRules	Applies stock, geo-eligibility, or promotion constraints.

B. Sample Orchestration Workflow

python

```python
async def recommendItems(mcp, context, args):
    # 1. Gather context in parallel
    calls = [
```

```json
{"id":1,"method":"getUserProfile","params":{"context":context,"args":{"userId":args["userId"]}}},
```

```
{"id":2,"method":"getUserHistory","params":{"context":context,"args":{"userId":args["userId"],"limit":50}}}
]

profile, history = (r["result"] for r in await mcp.batch_call(calls))


# 2. Compute a user embedding from history

user_emb = await mcp.call("computeEmbedding", context, {"texts": history})


# 3. Retrieve candidate items via vector search

candidates = await mcp.call("vectorSearch", context, {
  "embedding": user_emb, "topK": 100
})


# 4. (Optionally) mix in collaborative recommendations

collab = await mcp.call("collaborativeFilter", context, {"userId": args["userId"], "topK":50})


# 5. Merge, dedupe, and rerank

merged = merge_and_score(candidates["result"], collab["result"])

final = await mcp.call("applyBusinessRules", context, {"items": merged, "userTier": profile["tier"]})


return {"recommendations": final["result"]}
```

C. Real-Time Feedback Loop

- **Implicit Feedback:** Wrap streamUserAction as a notification to update history or embeddings on the fly.
- **Adaptive Models:** Expose an updateModel tool to retrain or fine-tune periodically based on new data.

D. Best Practices

- **Cold-Start Handling:** For new users, fallback to popularity or content-based methods (getPopularItems, contentFilter).
- **Caching:** Cache expensive calls (computeEmbedding, vectorSearch) for active sessions with short TTLs.
- **A/B Testing:** Dynamically switch between recommendation strategies by feature flagging which MCP methods get invoked.
- **Explainability:** Log the top contributing factors (e.g., "similar users also bought") with each recommendation for transparency.

By decomposing your recommendation pipeline into MCP tools and orchestrating them with simple JSON-RPC calls, you'll achieve a modular, scalable engine that's easy to extend, test, and maintain.

7.2 Automating Business Workflows with MCP Servers

7.2.1 Integrating MCP into Business Process Automation Tools

Business Process Automation (BPA) platforms—such as Camunda, Apache Airflow, Temporal, or AWS Step Functions—orchestrate human tasks, system calls, and event-driven logic across an organization. By embedding MCP calls into these workflows, you gain the ability to invoke AI-powered services, enforce context propagation, and maintain a clean separation between process definition and integration logic.

A. External Task Pattern (e.g., Camunda)

1. Define Service Task
   - In your BPMN model, add a **Service Task** with type external and a topic (e.g., mcp-invoke).
2. Worker Implementation
   - Run a lightweight worker that polls for tasks on mcp-invoke, extracts variables as context.args, invokes mcp.call(method, context, args), and completes the task with output variables.

python

```python
# Camunda worker pseudocode

task = client.fetch_and_lock(topic="mcp-invoke")

method = task.variables["method"]

args  = task.variables["args"]

result = await mcp.call(method, {"processInstanceId":
task.processInstanceId}, args)

client.complete(task.id, variables={"mcpResult": result})
```

3. Advantages
    - Decouples process engine from adapter code
    - Allows retry, back-off, and dead-letter handling driven by the BPM engine

B. DAG and Operator Integration (e.g., Airflow)

PythonOperator / TaskFlow API
python

```python
from airflow.decorators import task, dag

from datetime import datetime


@dag(start_date=datetime(2025,4,20), schedule_interval="@daily")

def mcp_workflow():

    @task

    def fetch_customer_profile(user_id):

        return mcp.call("getCustomerProfile", {"dagRunId": "{{ run_id }}"},
{"userId": user_id})
```

```python
@task

def score_risk(profile):

    return mcp.call("calculateRiskScore", {"dagRunId": "{{ run_id }}"},
{"profile": profile})



profile = fetch_customer_profile("u123")

score   = score_risk(profile)
```

1. Context in XCom
    - Airflow's XComs carry MCP context across tasks, ensuring traceability of dagRunId and user information.

C. Workflow SDKs (e.g., Temporal)

**Temporal Workflow Code
python**

```python
# In your workflow definition

async def process_order(self, order_id):

    context = {"workflowId": self.workflow_info.workflow_execution.id}

    profile = await mcp.call("fetchOrderDetails", context, {"orderId":
order_id})

    approval = await mcp.call("evaluateOrderApproval", context, profile)

    return approval
```

1. Activity Isolation
    - Encapsulate MCP calls in Temporal Activities to benefit from retries, timeouts, and rate limiting configured by the platform.

D. Serverless Orchestration (e.g., Step Functions + Lambda)

State Machine Definition
jsonc

```jsonc
{

  "StartAt": "GetProfile",

  "States": {

    "GetProfile": {

      "Type": "Task",

      "Resource": "arn:aws:lambda:...:invokeMcpMethod",

      "Parameters": {

        "method": "getProfile",

        "args": { "userId.$": "$.userId" }

      },

      "Next": "CalculateScore"

    },

    ...

  }

}
```

1. Lambda Bridge
   - A generic Lambda function parses the incoming event, calls your MCP server's /rpc endpoint, and returns the result to Step Functions.

E. Best Practices

- **Correlation IDs**: Propagate the process or workflow instance ID in context for end-to-end tracing.
- **Idempotency**: Ensure MCP methods and workflow tasks are idempotent so retries (driven by the BPA tool) do not cause duplicate side effects.

- **Schema Contracts**: Define JSON Schemas in your MCP tool manifest; have your BPA definitions validate inputs before invoking.
- **Error Handling**: Leverage the BPA tool's retry and compensation patterns; map JSON-RPC errors (e.g., -320xx codes) to specific retry or abort conditions.
- **Monitoring and Alerting**: Instrument both the BPA engine and the MCP server, correlating metrics (task durations, failures) to rapidly detect bottlenecks in process pipelines.

Integrating MCP into your enterprise automation stack transforms monolithic, hard-wired service calls into flexible, context-aware tool invocations—accelerating development, improving maintainability, and unlocking AI-driven decisioning throughout your business processes.

7.2.2 Real-World Example: Automating a Supply Chain Management System

In supply chain management (SCM), coordinating inventory levels, purchase orders, demand forecasts, and shipments across multiple partners can be complex and error-prone. By modeling each integration—ERP lookups, demand forecasting, logistics APIs—as MCP tools, you can orchestrate end-to-end workflows that automatically rebalance stock, place orders, and trigger shipping while preserving full audit trails.

A. Key Components as MCP Tools

Component	MCP Method	Description
Inventory Lookup	getInventoryLevels	Query current stock across warehouses.
Demand Forecast	forecastDemand	Run a time-series model to predict future demand.
Purchase Order Creation	createPurchaseOrder	Place an order in the ERP system.

Supplier API	checkSupplierAvailability	Verify supplier lead times and minimum order quantities.
Logistics Scheduling	scheduleShipment	Book carriers and generate shipping labels.
ERP Update	updateERPRecord	Record status updates back into the central ERP.
Alerting and Escalation	sendSCMAlert	Notify operators of exceptions (stockouts, delays).

B. Orchestration Workflow

Below is a Python-style pseudocode for an automated replenishment workflow that runs nightly:

python

```python
async def nightlyReplenishment(mcp, context, args):
    # 1. Fetch current inventory and upcoming demand forecast
    inv_resp, demand_resp = await mcp.batch_call([
        {"id":1, "method":"getInventoryLevels",
"params":{"context":context,"args":{}}},
        {"id":2, "method":"forecastDemand",
"params":{"context":context,"args":{"horizon":14}}}
    ])
```

```python
    inventory = inv_resp["result"]["warehouses"]

    forecast  = demand_resp["result"]["dailyDemand"]


    # 2. Determine reorder needs per SKU
    to_order = []
    for sku, levels in inventory.items():
        on_hand = levels["onHand"]

        safety  = levels["safetyStock"]

        projected = sum(forecast.get(sku, []))

        target = projected + safety

        if on_hand < target:

            qty = target - on_hand

            to_order.append({"sku": sku, "qty": qty, "warehouse":
levels["warehouseId"]})


    # 3. For each SKU below threshold, check supplier and place PO
    for item in to_order:
        avail = await mcp.call("checkSupplierAvailability", context, {

            "sku": item["sku"], "requestedQty": item["qty"]

        })

        if not avail["result"]["canSupply"]:

            # Notify buyer for manual intervention

            await mcp.call("sendSCMAlert", context, {
```

```
        "type":"supplier_unavailable", "sku": item["sku"], "qty":
item["qty"]

    })

    continue


po = await mcp.call("createPurchaseOrder", context, {

    "supplierId": avail["result"]["supplierId"],

    "sku": item["sku"],

    "quantity": avail["result"]["confirmedQty"],

    "deliveryWarehouse": item["warehouse"]

})


# 4. Schedule shipment once PO is confirmed

shipment = await mcp.call("scheduleShipment", context, {

    "purchaseOrderId": po["result"]["poId"],

    "destination": item["warehouse"],

    "date": po["result"]["expectedDeliveryDate"]

})


# 5. Update ERP with PO and shipment details

await mcp.call("updateERPRecord", context, {

    "poId": po["result"]["poId"],

    "status": "Ordered",

    "shipmentId": shipment["result"]["shipmentId"]
```

```
})
```

```
return {"ordersPlaced": len(to_order)}
```

C. Benefits of the MCP-Driven Approach

- **Modularity**: Each external system (ERP, forecasting service, supplier portal, logistics provider) is wrapped in its own adapter—changes to one do not ripple through the orchestration code.
- **Context Propagation**: The same context (containing userId, requestId, runTimestamp) flows through every call, enabling unified logging, auditing, and error tracing across multiple systems.
- **Error Handling**: Standardized JSON-RPC error codes let you implement generic retry logic or fall back to manual alerts without custom error-parsing for each API.
- **Scalability**: You can scale your MCP server horizontally to handle spikes in SKU counts or forecast computations, while rate-limiting protects downstream suppliers from overload.
- **Maintainability**: Business logic—calculating reorder points, safety stock, and PO quantities—remains in clear orchestrator code, separate from integration details.
- **Extensibility**: Future enhancements (e.g., dynamic lead-time adjustments, multi-supplier bidding) can be introduced by adding new MCP tools and minor changes to the orchestration script.

By encapsulating SCM integrations as discrete, context-aware MCP tools and orchestrating them through simple JSON-RPC workflows, you can automate complex replenishment and logistics processes with minimal glue code—improving agility, reducing errors, and providing end-to-end visibility into your supply chain.

7.2.3 How MCP Helps Businesses Scale and Automate Tasks

1. Consistent, Reusable Integration Layer
   - **Uniform Interface**: By encapsulating every external system—ERP, CRM, logistics, payment gateways—in JSON-RPC tools, MCP creates a stable, language-agnostic contract. New workflows simply invoke existing tools; no repeated SDK wiring or bespoke glue code.

- **Centralized Adapters**: Teams develop and maintain each adapter once. As business needs grow—adding new suppliers, markets, or data sources—you onboard them by writing a new tool, not rewriting every downstream process.
2. Rapid Orchestration of Complex Processes
    - **Declarative Workflows**: Orchestrators (in Airflow, Camunda, Lambda Step Functions, etc.) treat MCP calls as atomic actions. You can compose thousands of such calls into intricate pipelines—forecasting, replenishment, billing—without embedding integration details in the process definitions.
    - **Branching & Dynamic Discovery**: Clients can call listMethods to discover capabilities at runtime and branch logic based on available tools (e.g., choose between multiple shipping carriers), enabling feature flags and A/B tests without code redeploy.
3. Elastic Scalability
    - **Stateless RPC Servers**: MCP servers remain stateless between requests; horizontal scaling is trivial. Auto-scale based on CPU, request latency, or queue depth, and MCP instances transparently share load via a load-balancer.
    - **Isolation of Hot Paths**: You can spin up dedicated MCP clusters for high-volume or latency-sensitive services (e.g., streaming sensor data) while keeping lower-throughput adapters on smaller nodes, optimizing resource utilization.
4. Built-in Rate Limiting and Throttling
    - **Protect Downstream Systems**: Per-method and per-client quotas in MCP prevent runaway processes or misbehaving workflows from overwhelming critical services like ERPs or external suppliers.
    - **Graceful Degradation**: When limits are reached, MCP returns structured errors (-32029 Rate limit exceeded) with retryAfter, allowing orchestrators to back off or switch to fallback strategies automatically.
5. End-to-End Context Propagation
    - **Audit and Compliance**: Every MCP call carries the same context (user ID, workflow/run ID, timestamp), so logs and metrics can be correlated end-to-end. This traceability is essential for diagnosing failures and meeting regulatory requirements.
    - **Dynamic Routing & Authorization**: Context metadata (roles, region, account tiers) can be used by adapters to apply business rules—serving different APIs or pricing models based on the caller's identity without changing orchestration logic.
6. Observability and Monitoring

- ○ **Centralized Metrics**: MCP servers emit per-method latency, error rates, and throughput metrics, enabling real-time dashboards of your entire automation landscape.
- ○ **Distributed Tracing**: By propagating a `requestId` `in context, you stitch together`跨 `services—seeing exactly which step of a 20-task workflow caused a slowdown or error.`

7. Modularity and Extensibility
   - ○ **Plugin Architecture**: New capabilities—machine-learning scoring, compliance checks, specialized analytics—are added as MCP plugins. Business workflows pick them up immediately via discovery, accelerating time-to-market.
   - ○ **Versioned Deprecation**: MCP manifests support versioning and deprecation flags. You can roll out new adapters in parallel with old ones, enforce migration windows, and retire legacy integrations without breaking automated processes.

8. Reduced Operational Complexity
   - ○ **Fault Isolation**: If an adapter or downstream system fails, MCP can short-circuit or reroute calls (e.g., to a fallback cache), preventing whole-pipeline crashes.
   - ○ **Automated Remediation**: Coupling MCP's structured error codes with business-process engines allows automatic retries, compensating actions, or human escalation tasks—reducing manual intervention and freeing teams to focus on high-value work.

By providing a **highly modular, discoverable, and context-aware** integration fabric, MCP empowers businesses to **rapidly automate**, **securely scale**, and **dynamically evolve** their processes—turning complex ecosystems of services into a coherent, resilient automation backbone.

7.3 Case Study: Smart City Systems

7.3.1 Design and Implementation of an MCP-Based Smart City System

A smart city platform must integrate real-time telemetry (traffic, air quality, energy usage), batch data (census, zoning), and human workflows (citizen service requests) into cohesive, context-aware applications. MCP provides the scaffolding to build this system with modular adapters and unified orchestration.

A. System Architecture

plaintext

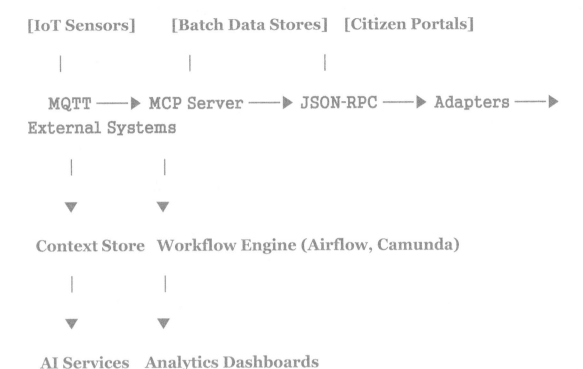

[IoT Sensors]   [Batch Data Stores]   [Citizen Portals]

MQTT ——▶ MCP Server ——▶ JSON-RPC ——▶ Adapters ——▶
External Systems

Context Store Workflow Engine (Airflow, Camunda)

AI Services   Analytics Dashboards

1. **IoT Ingestion**: Traffic cameras, environmental sensors, parking meters publish to MQTT or WebSocket; MCP adapters handle JSON-RPC notifications.
2. **Batch Integrations**: Nightly census and planning data loaded via file and database adapters.
3. **Citizen Interactions**: Mobile/web apps invoke MCP methods (reportPothole, getPermitStatus) through a gateway.
4. **Orchestration**: A workflow engine calls MCP tools to run daily traffic-flow optimization, energy load forecasting, or citizen-service dispatch.
5. **Context Store**: Redis holds latest sensor states keyed by location and timestamp, enabling cross-service context lookups.

B. Core MCP Tools and Adapters

Domain	MCP Method	Purpose
Traffic	streamTrafficData	Ingest live vehicle counts and speeds.

Air Quality	streamAirQuality	Capture $PM_{2.5}$, CO_2 readings from sensors.
Parking	getParkingAvailability	Query real-time space counts via REST API.
Energy Grid	forecastEnergyLoad	Run ML model on historical usage to predict demand.
Citizen Services	createWorkOrder	Submit and track service requests (e.g., potholes).
GIS Data	fetchMapTile	Retrieve map segments for visualization.

Each adapter isolates protocol, auth, and error handling behind a consistent JSON-RPC interface.

C. Example Orchestration: Dynamic Traffic Signal Control

python

```python
async def optimizeSignals(mcp, context, args):
    # 1. Fetch latest traffic counts for all intersections
    intersections = args["intersectionIds"]
    calls = [
      {"id":i, "method":"streamTrafficData", "params":{
        "context":context, "args":{"intersectionId":iid}
```

```
    }} for i,iid in enumerate(intersections)
]
data = await mcp.batch_call(calls)
# 2. Compute optimal signal timings
timings = await mcp.call("calculateSignalTimings", context, {
    "counts": [r["result"]["counts"] for r in data]
})
# 3. Push new timings to signal controllers
for t in timings["result"]:
    await mcp.call("sendSignalConfig", context, {
        "intersectionId": t["intersectionId"],
        "phaseDurations": t["phases"]
    })
return {"updated": len(timings["result"])}
```

- **Context Propagation**: context includes cityZone, timestamp, and requestId for traceability.
- **Batch Calls**: Parallel fetch reduces end-to-end latency.
- **Branching**: Optional fallback to manual control if model fails.

D. Best Practices

- **Geo-Partitioned Context**: Namespace keys by zone (traffic:zoneA:intersection42) to shard Redis and distribute load.
- **Rate Limiting**: Throttle high-frequency streams (10 Hz) to prevent overload; use MQTT QoS.
- **Data Freshness**: Include timestamp in context to reject stale sensor updates.
- **Fallback Mechanisms**: On adapter failure (e.g., sensor offline), use historical averages or adjacent sensor data.

- **Monitoring & Alerts**: Track per-adapter error rates, context-store evictions, and workflow durations; alert on anomalies.

By modeling each sensor feed, historical dataset, and citizen interaction as MCP tools—and orchestrating them via simple JSON-RPC workflows—you can build a scalable, maintainable smart city platform that adapts in real time to evolving urban needs.

7.3.2 Connecting IoT Devices, Data Storage, and External APIs

A cohesive smart-city system meshes real-time IoT streams, durable data stores, and third-party services. MCP lets you encapsulate each integration behind JSON-RPC adapters, so your orchestration logic stays clean and focused on city-wide workflows.

A. IoT Device Ingestion

1. Protocol Adapters

MQTT: Wrap sensor topics as streaming tools:
python

```python
@method
async def streamTrafficFlow(context, args):
    async def gen():
        async with MQTTClient(settings.mqtt_url) as client:
            await client.subscribe(f"traffic/{args['intersectionId']}/flow")
            async for msg in client.unfiltered_messages():
                data = json.loads(msg.payload)
                yield {"count": data["count"], "ts": data["ts"]}
    return stream(gen())
```

- **WebSockets / CoAP**: Similar streaming patterns via JSON-RPC partials.
2. Gateway Bridges

Use lightweight bridges (e.g., Node.js, Python) to forward raw MQTT/WebSocket into your MCP /rpc endpoint as notifications:
bash

```bash
mosquitto_sub -t 'aqi/+/sensor' | \

 xargs -I{} curl -d
'{"jsonrpc":"2.0","method":"streamAirQuality","params":{},"args":{...}}'
```

B. Real-Time and Historical Data Storage

1. Time-Series DBs

Adapter: storeSensorReading writes to InfluxDB or TimescaleDB:
python

```python
@method

async def storeSensorReading(context, args):

 await tsdb.write(args["measurement"], args["tags"], args["fields"],
args["timestamp"])

 return {"status":"ok"}
```

2. Context Cache (Redis)

Keep only current state for low-latency lookups:
python

```python
await redis.hset(f'sensor:{sid}:current', mapping={"value":val,"ts":ts})
```

3. Batch ETL
   ○ Nightly jobs invoke MCP file-I/O and DB tools to archive daily snapshots from cache → long-term store.

C. External API Integrations

Weather & Environmental Data
python

```python
@method

async def fetchWeather(context, args):

    resp = await httpx.get(f"{settings.weather_api}/forecast",
params={"loc":args["zone"]})

    resp.raise_for_status()

    data = resp.json()

    return {"temp":data["temp"], "precip":data["rain"]}
```

GIS and Mapping Services
python

```python
@method

async def getMapTile(context, args):

    url = f"{settings.gis_url}/tiles/{args['z']}/{args['x']}/{args['y']}.png"

    r = await httpx.get(url)

    r.raise_for_status()

    return {"tile": r.content.hex()}
```

D. Orchestrating Hybrid Workflows

python

```python
async def cityDashboardUpdate(mcp, context, args):

    # 1. Pull real-time sensor cache + external weather
```

```
cache, weather = await mcp.batch_call([

{"id":1,"method":"getCachedSensor","params":{"args":{"sensorId":args["sensorId"]}}},

{"id":2,"method":"fetchWeather","params":{"args":{"zone":args["zone"]}}
}

])
    # 2. Compute comfort index
    idx = compute_comfort(cache["result"]["value"],
weather["result"]["temp"])
    # 3. Store index in time-series DB
    await mcp.call("storeSensorReading", context, {
        "measurement":"comfort_index",
        "tags":{"zone":args["zone"]},
        "fields":{"index":idx},
        "timestamp":now_iso()
    })
    return {"index": idx}
```

E. Best Practices

Practice	Why It Matters
Protocol-Specific Libraries	Use battle-tested MQTT, CoAP, or WebSocket clients for reliability.

Stream vs. Store Separation	Keep hot "current" context in Redis; archive to TSDB for analytics.
Batch and Real-Time Hybrid	Combine notifications for live updates with scheduled ETL for history.
Schema Validation	Validate incoming sensor payloads and API responses against JSON Schema.
Rate Limiting	Protect external APIs (weather, GIS) with per-method throttles.
Circuit Breakers & Fallbacks	On API failure, fallback to cached or default values to maintain service.
Secure Transport	Use TLS/mTLS for MQTT, HTTP, and broker connections.
Correlation Context	Propagate requestId and zone in context for end-to-end tracing.

By wrapping each IoT protocol, storage backend, and external service behind MCP adapters—and composing them via JSON-RPC workflows—you create a flexible, scalable fabric for smart-city applications that seamlessly blends live telemetry, historical data, and third-party insights.

7.3.3 Lessons Learned from Real-World Applications

1. Design for Partial Failure
   - **Reality**: Sensors go offline, networks partition, APIs timeout.

- **Takeaway**: Build adapters and workflows to tolerate missing or stale data—use cached defaults, historical fallbacks, and human-in-the-loop escalation rather than letting the entire system fail.
2. Schema Versioning Is Crucial
    - **Reality**: IoT devices and external services evolve independently, leading to unexpected field changes or new message formats.
    - **Takeaway**: Embed a schemaVersion in every payload, validate against JSON Schema, and provide migration logic in adapters so you can roll out sensor firmware or API updates without breaking consumers.
3. Context Namespace Discipline
    - **Reality**: In a city-wide deployment, hundreds of sensors, districts, and subsystems share the same cache and topic namespaces.
    - **Takeaway**: Adopt strict key and topic naming conventions (e.g., zone:<zoneId>:sensor:<sensorId>) and include zone or project labels in your JSON-RPC context to prevent cross-pollination and simplify multi-tenant scaling.
4. Latency Budgets Drive Architecture
    - **Reality**: Some applications (traffic signal control) need sub-100 ms turnarounds; others (daily analytics) are more forgiving.
    - **Takeaway**: Define latency targets up front, and architect separate pipelines—real-time streaming for low-latency-critical paths, batch ETL for heavy analytics—rather than one monolithic flow.
5. Centralized Observability Saves Hours
    - **Reality**: Without unified tracing, diagnosing whether a slow-down came from MQTT ingestion, Redis cache, or the signal-timing adapter can take days.
    - **Takeaway**: Instrument every MCP call with correlation IDs, collect per-method metrics, and tie adapters into a distributed tracing system so you have end-to-end visibility at a glance.
6. Automated Recovery Beats Manual Intervention
    - **Reality**: City control centers can't wait for human operators when a storm floods sensors or carrier outages interrupt data feeds.
    - **Takeaway**: Implement self-healing patterns—auto-reconnect logic in adapters, circuit breakers that switch to fallback computations, and queued notifications that replay once systems recover.
7. Security Can't Be an Afterthought
    - **Reality**: Exposed endpoints and device credentials were targeted within weeks of rollout.

- ○ **Takeaway**: From day one, enforce mTLS for device and server communications, scope every API key to minimal privileges, and audit every JSON-RPC invocation to detect anomalies before they escalate.
8. Stakeholder Alignment Is Key
   - ○ **Reality**: Urban planners, IT, field engineers, and privacy officers often have divergent requirements.
   - ○ **Takeaway**: Model MCP adapters and workflows as shared contracts— document method schemas, error codes, and SLAs in a central manifest and involve all teams in design reviews to surface requirements early.
9. Incremental Rollout Minimizes Disruption
   - ○ **Reality**: Flipping a new adapter or workflow atomically city-wide risked data loss and panic.
   - ○ **Takeaway**: Use feature flags and canary deployments—enable new capabilities for a subset of zones or sensor types first, monitor behavior, then gradually expand to full production.
10. Continuous Improvement Culture
    - ○ **Reality**: Aftergo live, new scenarios (e.g., emergency evacuations, public events) always emerge.
    - ○ **Takeaway**: Treat your MCP server as a living platform—regularly review logs, update adapters to handle novel context, and iterate on workflows in sprints rather than "big bang" projects.

These lessons underscore that building and operating a real-world MCP-based smart city system is as much about robust architectural patterns, operational discipline, and cross-team collaboration as it is about code. Prioritizing resilience, observability, and incremental delivery will keep your platform both reliable and adaptable to evolving urban challenges.

7.4 Interactive Q&A

7.4.1 How Would You Automate Workflows in Your Industry Using MCP?

1. Process Identification
   - ○ Which recurring tasks or decision points in your domain—order fulfillment, claims processing, compliance checks—could be expressed as discrete MCP tools?
2. Context Modeling
   - ○ What contextual data (user identity, transaction IDs, location, time) must accompany each step, and how would you structure your context object to carry it through?
3. Tool Design & Integration

- For each external system you need to talk to (ERP, CRM, databases, IoT feeds), what adapters would you build, and what would their JSON-RPC signatures look like?

4. Orchestration Strategy
   - Would you implement your workflows as streaming pipelines (notifications + partial results), batch RPC calls, or a hybrid? When is each approach most appropriate?

5. Error Handling & Compensation
   - How would you map common failures (timeouts, rate-limits, schema errors) into your business logic—retry, alert, or compensate—and which JSON-RPC error codes would you leverage?

6. Tool Discovery & Dynamic Paths
   - Could your processes benefit from runtime discovery (via listMethods), choosing alternative tools if some integrations are offline or in maintenance?

7. Idempotency & State Management
   - How would you ensure that retries or duplicate notifications don't cause repeated side effects—aligning each tool with idempotent behavior and state versioning?

8. Workflow Automation Platform
   - Which BPA or orchestration engine (Airflow, Camunda, Step Functions, Temporal) would you embed your MCP calls into, and how would you propagate context and correlation IDs through it?

9. Monitoring, Metrics & Alerts
   - What metrics (per-method latency, error rate, throughput) would you track, and how would you tie them back to business KPIs—cycle time, SLA compliance, cost savings?

10. Scalability & Evolution
    - As your volume grows or new systems come online, how will you scale your MCP clusters, version your adapters, and roll out changes with minimal process disruption?

Reflect on these points to sketch out a robust, context-aware automation blueprint tailored to your industry's unique workflows.

7.4.2 Discussion on the Challenges Faced in Smart City Systems

1. Data Heterogeneity and Integration
   - How do you reconcile disparate data formats—from legacy SCADA systems and modern IoT protocols to GIS datasets—into a unified context model?

- What strategies (schema mapping, canonical data models) help you onboard new sensor types or external feeds rapidly?

2. Scalability of Real-Time Processing
   - Can your platform handle spikes in event volume (e.g., major public gatherings, emergencies) without degradation?
   - How do you partition streams—by geographic zone, sensor category, or priority—to balance load and maintain low latency?

3. Network Reliability and Edge Constraints
   - Many city sensors operate over flaky or bandwidth-constrained wireless networks. How do you design for intermittent connectivity, local buffering, and graceful back-off?
   - When and where do you perform edge vs. cloud processing to optimize cost and responsiveness?

4. Security and Privacy
   - With sensors capturing video, location, or personal data, how do you enforce end-to-end encryption, strict access controls, and PII-minimization?
   - What methods ensure that only authorized services can invoke critical control adapters (e.g., traffic signals, street lighting)?

5. Data Quality and Calibration
   - Environmental and traffic sensors drift over time. How do you detect and correct calibration errors, outliers, or "ghost" readings to prevent faulty decisions?
   - What feedback loops (manual audits, cross-validation with adjacent sensors) maintain trust in your data?

6. Interoperability and Vendor Lock-In
   - Cities often deploy heterogeneous devices from multiple vendors, each with proprietary APIs. How do you abstract these differences so your MCP adapters remain maintainable?
   - What governance processes ensure that new vendor solutions comply with your integration standards?

7. Governance, Compliance, and Stakeholder Alignment
   - Smart city projects span IT, public works, law enforcement, and citizen advocacy—each with different priorities. How do you define common success metrics and SLAs?
   - How do you embed audit trails, data retention policies, and transparency mechanisms to satisfy regulatory and public-trust requirements?

8. Cost Management and ROI

- Real-time streaming, large-scale storage, and high-availability infrastructure can be expensive. Which KPIs drive decisions around where to invest vs. rely on batch analytics?
- How do you prove value (reduced congestion, energy savings, improved response times) to secure ongoing funding?

9. Evolution and Future-Proofing
- As technology (5G, edge AI, citizen-generated data) advances, how do you design your MCP toolset and manifest to accommodate new capabilities without massive rewrites?
- What deprecation policies and versioning schemes keep your system agile yet stable?

10. Operational Resilience and Disaster Recovery
- In the event of a natural disaster or major outage, how do you ensure your MCP server, context store, and adapters remain available or fail over gracefully?
- What automated drills (simulated outages, data center failovers) validate your recovery plans?

Reflecting on these challenges—and the patterns you've established for context propagation, modular adapters, and robust orchestration—will help you architect a truly resilient, scalable, and impactful smart city platform.

Chapter 8: Scaling and Deploying MCP Servers

8.1 Horizontal Scaling for High Availability

8.1.1 Configuring MCP Servers for High Availability and Fault Tolerance

Ensuring your MCP deployment stays up under load—and recovers gracefully from failures—requires planning across the application stack. Below are key strategies and configurations.

A. Stateless Application Design

- No Sticky State
    - MCP server instances should be **stateless**: all request-specific state lives in external stores (Redis, databases, message brokers).
    - Allows you to add or remove server nodes without rebalancing session affinity.
- Shared Configuration
    - Load adapter manifests, feature flags, and rate-limit settings from a centralized configuration service (e.g., Consul, etcd) or synchronized environment (ConfigMap).

B. Load Balancing and Traffic Routing

- External Load Balancer
    - Deploy an L4/L7 load balancer (e.g., AWS ALB, GCP LB, NGINX) in front of your MCP instances.
    - Configure health-check endpoints (/healthz, /metrics) so unhealthy pods are removed automatically.
- Session Affinity (Optional)
    - If certain workflows rely on connection-level context (e.g., WebSockets), enable sticky sessions or use a shared message broker instead of HTTP affinity.

C. Service Discovery and Auto-Scaling

- Kubernetes Deployments
    - Use a Deployment or StatefulSet with **Horizontal Pod Autoscaler (HPA)** driven by CPU, memory, or custom metrics (e.g., request latency).
    - Configure **readiness** and **liveness** probes to prevent routing traffic to unready pods during rolling updates.
- Container Auto-Scaling

- In non-K8s environments, integrate with your orchestration layer (ECS, Nomad) to scale instances based on queue length or RPC QPS.

D. Shared Context and Data Stores

- Redis Cluster / Sentinel
  - Run Redis in clustered mode with Sentinel failover so all MCP instances can read/write context state even if a node fails.
  - Ensure your Redis clients are configured with automatic master discovery and reconnection.
- Database High Availability
  - Use a managed database with multi-AZ replicas or a clustered NoSQL store.
  - Configure your ORM/driver for automatic retry on failover and connection pool reinitialization.

E. Leader Election for Single-Writer Tasks

- Avoid Split-Brain
  - For tasks that must run on exactly one node (e.g., scheduled batch jobs, index rebuilds), implement leader election via a distributed lock in Redis or Zookeeper.
  - Only the elected leader runs the job; on failure, another instance takes over.

F. Circuit Breakers and Bulkheads

- Protect Downstream Dependencies
  - Wrap adapter calls with circuit breakers (e.g., using pybreaker) to prevent repeated failures from cascading.
  - Use **bulkheads** (separate thread pools or queues per adapter) so one slow dependency doesn't block all RPCs.

G. Rolling Updates and Blue–Green Deployments

- Zero-Downtime Deployments
  - Use rolling updates in Kubernetes, ensuring new pods pass readiness checks before old ones terminate.
  - For major version changes, consider blue–green or canary deployments, routing a subset of traffic to the new version and monitoring key metrics.

H. Monitoring, Logging, and Alerting

- Health Metrics
  - Expose Prometheus metrics for RPC latencies, error rates, and adapter-specific failures.
  - Alert on elevated P95/P99 latencies or spike in server-side errors.
- Distributed Tracing
  - Propagate a trace ID in each JSON-RPC context and integrate with OpenTelemetry to follow requests across services and detect performance hotspots.

By combining **stateless design**, robust **load balancing, shared high-availability stores**, and operational patterns like **leader election** and **circuit breakers**, you ensure your MCP servers remain resilient, scalable, and continuously available—even in the face of component failures or traffic surges.

8.1.2 Load Balancing Techniques for Distributed Systems

Distributing incoming JSON-RPC requests across multiple MCP server instances ensures high throughput, low latency, and resilience. Below are key load-balancing patterns and their trade-offs, along with practical configuration tips.

A. Layer-4 vs. Layer-7 Load Balancing

Layer	Mechanism	Pros	Cons
L4	TCP-level (round-robin, least-conn)	Very fast, minimal protocol awareness	Can't inspect HTTP paths or headers
L7	HTTP/HTTPS (NGINX, HAProxy, ALB)	Route by URL, header, method; health checks	Slightly higher overhead

- Use **L4** (e.g., AWS Network Load Balancer) when you need ultra-low latency and simple distribution of TCP connections.
- Use **L7** (e.g., NGINX, AWS ALB) for sophisticated routing—sticky sessions for WebSockets, path-based routing (/rpc, /healthz), and per-method rate limits.

B. Common Load-Balancing Algorithms

Algorithm	Description	When to Use
Round-Robin	Evenly cycles through available servers	Uniform capacity, stateless services
Least Connections	Chooses instance with fewest active connections	Varying request durations
IP Hash	Hashes client IP to pick a server (sticky by IP)	Simple session affinity without cookies
Consistent Hash	Hashes on a key (e.g., sessionId) for true affinity	WebSockets, streaming where stickiness is critical
Weighted	Assigns weights to instances based on capacity	Mixed-size VMs or pods, canary vs. stable pools

C. Service Discovery and DNS-Based Balancing

- DNS Round-Robin
  - List multiple A-records for your MCP service—clients pick one at random or in order.
  - **Pitfalls**: DNS caching can lead to uneven distribution; no health-check integration.
- Client-Side Load Balancing
  - Embed a service registry (Consul, etcd) in clients or sidecars.
  - Clients fetch healthy endpoints and apply algorithms (round-robin, least-conn) locally.

D. Health Checks and Failover

- Active Health Probes
  - Configure your load balancer to poll /healthz or a lightweight ping endpoint.

- Mark instances unhealthy on consecutive failures and exclude them from the pool.
- Passive Health Detection
    - Load balancer observes real requests—if an instance returns 5xx too often or times out, it's automatically ejected.
- Graceful Draining
    - When scaling down, mark pods as draining so new connections go elsewhere; allow existing sessions (e.g., WebSocket streams) to finish.

E. Handling WebSockets and Streaming RPC

- Sticky Sessions
    - For long-lived WebSocket or streaming connections, use **consistent-hash** (on sessionId) or **cookie-based** affinity in your L7 load balancer.
- Stateless Streaming
    - Alternatively, decouple sessions via a message broker: clients reconnect to any MCP instance, which subscribes to the same broker topic—no affinity needed.

F. Service Mesh and Advanced Routing

- Envoy / Istio
    - Sidecar proxies handle L7 routing, retries, circuit breaking, and telemetry out of the box.
    - Define **VirtualServices** to split traffic (canary, A/B tests) between two MCP versions.
- Traffic Shadowing
    - Mirror a fraction of real traffic to a new cluster for testing under live load without affecting production behavior.

G. Sample NGINX L7 Configuration

nginx

```
http {

  upstream mcp_servers {
```

```nginx
    least_conn;

    server mcp-1:8000 max_fails=3 fail_timeout=30s;

    server mcp-2:8000 max_fails=3 fail_timeout=30s;

}


server {

  listen 80;

  location /rpc {

    # Route JSON-RPC calls to upstream

    proxy_pass http://mcp_servers;

    proxy_http_version 1.1;

    proxy_set_header Connection "";

    proxy_buffering off;

    # Optional: limit concurrent JSON-RPC requests

    limit_req zone=mcp burst=20 nodelay;

  }


  location /healthz {

    proxy_pass http://mcp_servers/healthz;

  }

 }

}
```

```
# Define a rate-limit zone in same file

limit_req_zone $server_name zone=mcp:10m rate=50r/s;
```

H. Best Practices Checklist

1. **Multiple LB Layers**: Combine a global DNS LB for geo-distribution with local L4/L7 for in-cluster balancing.
2. **Health Check Endpoints**: Implement /healthz and /metrics in MCP servers—distinguish readiness vs. liveness.
3. **Monitor LB Metrics**: Track backend latency, active connections, and error codes at the load balancer level.
4. **Automate Scaling**: Tie LB target group size to your autoscaling group; ensure new instances register automatically.
5. **Secure Ingress**: Terminate TLS at the LB or sidecar; use mTLS in-cluster for service-to-service traffic.

By selecting appropriate algorithms, ensuring robust health checks, and leveraging both L4 and L7 capabilities (or a service mesh), you can distribute MCP workloads evenly, maintain low latency, and achieve fault-tolerant, highly available deployments.

8.1.3 Best Practices for Scaling Out MCP Servers

1. Containerize and Orchestrate
   - Package your MCP server and its adapters as container images (Docker), ensuring all dependencies and configuration are baked in.
   - Deploy via an orchestration platform (Kubernetes, ECS) so pods/tasks can be scaled, scheduled, and managed automatically.
2. Define Clear Resource Requests and Limits
   - In Kubernetes, set requests and limits for CPU and memory on your MCP containers.
   - This prevents noisy-neighbor issues and allows the scheduler to make informed bin-packing decisions.
3. Autoscaling Policies
   - **Horizontal Pod Autoscaler (HPA)**: Scale out based on CPU, memory, or custom Prometheus metrics like RPC QPS or P95 latency.

- **Cluster Autoscaler**: Ensure your cluster can add nodes when pods can't be scheduled due to resource constraints.

4. Separate Hot and Cold Workloads
   - Identify latency-sensitive ("hot") adapters—streaming sensors, real-time inference—and run them on a dedicated pool of high-performance nodes.
   - Batch or less-critical tasks (overnight ETL, large file I/O) can use cheaper, lower-specification nodes.

5. Connection Pool Hygiene
   - Configure shared connection pools (DB, Redis, HTTP) with appropriate maximums for your expected concurrency.
   - Monitor pool saturation metrics—if your MCP pods frequently exhaust their pools, either increase pool size or scale out pods.

6. Graceful Startup and Shutdown
   - Implement readiness probes that only pass once all connection pools and caches are initialized.
   - On shutdown, use preStop hooks to disable new traffic and allow in-flight requests to complete before SIGTERM.

7. Rolling and Canary Deployments
   - Roll out new versions gradually—update a subset of pods (canary), validate key metrics, then proceed with the rest.
   - Use feature flags or "manifestVersion" in context so clients can opt into new capabilities without disruption.

8. Multi-Zone and Multi-Region Redundancy
   - Spread MCP pods across multiple availability zones (or regions) to tolerate data-center failures.
   - Use geo-DNS or global load balancers to route clients to the nearest healthy endpoint.

9. Service Mesh Integration
   - Leverage Istio or Linkerd for built-in retries, circuit breaking, mutual TLS, and fine-grained traffic shifting.
   - Offload rate limiting and observability concerns to the mesh, keeping your MCP code focused on business logic.

10. Centralized Configuration and Feature Flags
    - Store rate limits, pool sizes, and feature toggles in a central config service (Consul, etcd, ConfigMaps) rather than environment variables.
    - Allow real-time adjustments without container restarts.

11. Cache Common or Expensive Results
    - Use Redis or in-process LRU caches for idempotent or slow adapters (reference data, model embeddings).

- Align TTLs with data volatility to maximize cache hit rates without stale results.

12. Monitor and Alert Proactively
    - Track per-method metrics: latency histograms, error rates, request counts.
    - Set alerts on tail-latency regressions, sudden error spikes, or resource saturation (CPU, memory, connection pool waits).

13. Chaos Testing and Resilience Drills
    - Regularly inject failures (pod kills, network partitions) to validate your autoscaling, failover, and circuit-breaking strategies.
    - Practice disaster-recovery scenarios to ensure your system remains highly available under real failure conditions.

14. Cost-Aware Scaling
    - Use spot/preemptible instances for non-critical batch workloads to reduce cloud spend.
    - Adjust scaling thresholds and resource allocations based on cost targets and business priorities.

15. Document Scaling Playbooks
    - Maintain runbooks that describe how to diagnose scaling issues, adjust autoscaler parameters, and perform emergency rollbacks.
    - Keep these playbooks versioned alongside your MCP manifests so on-call teams can respond rapidly.

By adhering to these best practices—combining robust container orchestration, intelligent autoscaling, traffic management via service mesh, and comprehensive observability—you'll ensure your MCP servers can scale elastically, recover from failures automatically, and deliver consistent, low-latency service as your workloads grow.

8.2 Containerization and Deployment with Docker

8.2.1 Dockerizing MCP Servers for Easier Deployment

Packaging your MCP server and its adapters into a Docker container simplifies consistent deployments, dependency management, and environment parity across development, staging, and production.

A. Multi-Stage Dockerfile

Use a multi-stage build to produce a small, production-ready image:

dockerfile

```dockerfile
# Stage 1: Build dependencies and install Python packages
FROM python:3.11-slim AS builder

# Prevent Python from writing .pyc files and buffering stdout/stderr
ENV PYTHONDONTWRITEBYTECODE=1 \
    PYTHONUNBUFFERED=1

# Set working directory
WORKDIR /app

# Install build-time dependencies
RUN apt-get update && \
    apt-get install -y --no-install-recommends gcc build-essential && \
    rm -rf /var/lib/apt/lists/*

# Copy constraints and requirements
COPY requirements.txt .
COPY requirements-dev.txt .

# Install dependencies into a wheelhouse
RUN pip wheel --wheel-dir=/wheels --no-deps -r requirements.txt
RUN pip wheel --wheel-dir=/wheels --no-deps -r requirements-dev.txt
```

```dockerfile
# Stage 2: Create minimal runtime image

FROM python:3.11-slim


# Create non-root user

RUN addgroup --system mcp && adduser --system --ingroup mcp mcp


# Set working directory

WORKDIR /app


# Copy wheels and install only production dependencies

COPY --from=builder /wheels /wheels

RUN pip install --no-index --find-links=/wheels -r /app/requirements.txt && \
    rm -rf /wheels


# Copy application code

COPY . /app


# Use unprivileged user

USER mcp


# Expose RPC and health ports

EXPOSE 8000 8080
```

```
# Health-check probe

HEALTHCHECK --interval=30s --timeout=5s --start-period=10s \
 CMD curl -fs http://localhost:8080/healthz || exit 1


# Entrypoint

CMD ["uvicorn", "main:app", "--host", "0.0.0.0", "--port", "8000", "--workers", "4"]
```

- **Multi-Stage**: Builds dependencies separately to keep the final image lean.
- **Non-Root User**: Runs as mcp user to reduce attack surface.
- **Healthcheck**: Ensures Kubernetes or Docker Swarm can detect unhealthy containers.
- **Workers**: Configured for multi-core utilization.

B. Docker Compose for Local Development

Provide a docker-compose.yml to spin up the MCP server alongside Redis, Postgres, or other dependencies:

yaml

```yaml
version: '3.8'
services:
  mcp-server:
    build: .
    image: myorg/mcp-server:latest
    container_name: mcp-server
    restart: unless-stopped
```

```yaml
    ports:
      - '8000:8000'
      - '8080:8080'
    environment:
      - REDIS_URL=redis://redis:6379/0
      - SQL_DSN=postgresql://user:pass@postgres:5432/mcpdb
      - MONGO_URI=mongodb://mongo:27017/mcpdb
      - FILE_ROOT=/data/files
    volumes:
      - ./files:/data/files
    depends_on:
      - redis
      - postgres
      - mongo

  redis:
    image: redis:7-alpine
    container_name: redis
    restart: unless-stopped
    ports:
      - '6379:6379'

  postgres:
```

```yaml
    image: postgres:15-alpine

    container_name: postgres

    restart: unless-stopped

    environment:

      - POSTGRES_USER=user

      - POSTGRES_PASSWORD=pass

      - POSTGRES_DB=mcpdb

    volumes:

      - pgdata:/var/lib/postgresql/data


  mongo:

    image: mongo:6.0

    container_name: mongo

    restart: unless-stopped

    volumes:

      - mongodata:/data/db


volumes:

  pgdata:

  mongodata:
```

- **Volumes**: Persist data for stateful services.
- **Dependencies**: Ensure dependent services start before the MCP server.

C. Pushing to a Registry and Versioning

Tag by Git SHA or Semantic Version
bash

```
GIT_SHA=$(git rev-parse --short HEAD)

docker build -t myorg/mcp-server:$GIT_SHA .

docker tag myorg/mcp-server:$GIT_SHA myorg/mcp-server:latest

docker push myorg/mcp-server:$GIT_SHA

docker push myorg/mcp-server:latest
```

1. **Immutable Tags**: Deploy by specific SHA tags to ensure reproducibility; latest for development convenience only.

D. Best Practices

Practice	Rationale
Small Base Images	Reduces attack surface and speeds up pulls (use slim or alpine).
Multi-Stage Builds	Keeps final image minimal by excluding build tools.
Non-Root Execution	Limits container privileges for security.
Environment-Specific Config	Pass secrets via environment variables or a secrets manager, not hard-coded.

Health Probes & Readiness Checks	Allows orchestrators to manage pod lifecycle gracefully.
Automated CI/CD Builds	Integrate Docker builds into your pipeline, with vulnerability scanning.
Immutable Artifact Storage	Host images in a secure, access-controlled registry (e.g., ECR, GCR).
Resource Limits in Compose/K8s	Prevent noisy neighbors; define mem_limit and cpus.
Image Scanning	Run container image scanners (Trivy, Clair) to catch vulnerabilities.

By following these Dockerization patterns—clean multi-stage builds, security-focused configuration, and clear CI/CD integration—you'll achieve consistent, repeatable, and secure deployments of your MCP server across all environments.

8.2.2 Setting up Docker Compose for multi-container environments
Below is a sample docker-compose.yml that brings up an MCP server alongside typical dependencies (Redis, PostgreSQL, MongoDB, and a reverse-proxy/load-balancer). It demonstrates networks, volumes, health checks, and environment configuration for a realistic multi-container setup.

yaml

```yaml
version: '3.8'


# Define shared networks for service isolation
```

```yaml
networks:
  backend:
    driver: bridge
  frontend:
    driver: bridge


volumes:
  redis_data:
  pgdata:
  mongo_data:
  mcp_files:


services:
  # ------------------------
  # Reverse proxy / LB
  # ------------------------
  proxy:
    image: nginx:stable-alpine
    container_name: mcp-proxy
    depends_on:
      - mcp-server
    volumes:
      - ./nginx.conf:/etc/nginx/nginx.conf:ro
```

```yaml
    ports:
      - '80:80'      # HTTP
      - '443:443'    # HTTPS
    networks:
      - frontend
      - backend


  # ------------------------
  # MCP JSON-RPC server
  # ------------------------
  mcp-server:
    build:
      context: .
      dockerfile: Dockerfile
    image: myorg/mcp-server:latest
    container_name: mcp-server
    depends_on:
      - redis
      - postgres
      - mongo
    environment:
      # Connection strings
      REDIS_URL: redis://redis:6379/0
```

```yaml
      SQL_DSN: postgresql://user:pass@postgres:5432/mcpdb

      MONGO_URI: mongodb://mongo:27017/mcpdb

      FILE_ROOT: /data/files

      # Optional feature flags or tuning

      RATE_LIMITS_JSON: '{"fetchWeather": 5}'

      BUCKET_SIZES_JSON: '{"fetchWeather": 10}'
    volumes:

      - mcp_files:/data/files
    healthcheck:

      test: ["CMD", "curl", "-f", "http://localhost:8000/healthz"]

      interval: 15s

      timeout: 5s

      retries: 3
    networks:

      - backend



  # ------------------------

  # Redis for context store, caching

  # ------------------------
  redis:

    image: redis:7-alpine

    container_name: redis

    volumes:
```

```yaml
    - redis_data:/data
  command: ["redis-server", "--save", "", "--appendonly", "no"]
  healthcheck:
    test: ["CMD", "redis-cli", "ping"]
    interval: 10s
    timeout: 3s
    retries: 3
  networks:
    - backend


# ------------------------
# PostgreSQL for relational data
# ------------------------
postgres:
  image: postgres:15-alpine
  container_name: postgres
  environment:
    POSTGRES_USER: user
    POSTGRES_PASSWORD: pass
    POSTGRES_DB: mcpdb
  volumes:
    - pgdata:/var/lib/postgresql/data
  healthcheck:
```

```yaml
    test: ["CMD-SHELL", "pg_isready -U user -d mcpdb"]

    interval: 15s

    timeout: 5s

    retries: 5

  networks:

    - backend



  # -----------------------

  # MongoDB for document storage

  # -----------------------

  mongo:

    image: mongo:6.0

    container_name: mongo

    volumes:

      - mongo_data:/data/db

    healthcheck:

      test: ["CMD", "mongo", "--eval", "db.adminCommand('ping')"]

      interval: 15s

      timeout: 5s

      retries: 5

    networks:

      - backend
```

Explanation and Best Practices

- Multiple Networks
  - backend isolates internal services (MCP, Redis, Postgres, Mongo).
  - frontend exposes only the proxy, minimizing attack surface.
- Health Checks
  - Each service defines a healthcheck so orchestrators (Compose, Docker Swarm) can detect and restart unhealthy containers.
- Depends_on
  - Ensures correct startup order, though healthchecks are still needed to wait for full readiness.
- Volumes
  - Persist data (redis_data, pgdata, mongo_data) and shared files (mcp_files).
- Environment Configuration
  - Connection strings refer to service names (e.g., redis, postgres).
  - Feature flags and tuning knobs (rate limits, bucket sizes) can be passed as JSON env vars.
- Reverse Proxy
  - Handles TLS termination, L7 routing (/rpc, /healthz) and can implement rate limiting or authentication before traffic reaches MCP.
- Scaling Out
  - In a production cluster, replace docker-compose with Kubernetes Deployment/StatefulSet manifests; use ConfigMaps/Secrets for environment variables and PersistentVolumeClaims for volumes.

This setup lets you spin up your entire stack locally with a single docker-compose up --build, ensures consistent networking and configuration, and lays the groundwork for production-grade deployments.

8.2.3 Deploying MCP Servers on Cloud Platforms (AWS, GCP, Azure)

When you're ready to move beyond Docker Compose into production-grade infrastructure, the major clouds all offer first-class container and orchestration services. Below are deployment patterns and best practices for AWS, GCP, and Azure.

A. Amazon Web Services (AWS)

1. Container Registry & CI/CD
   - **ECR**: Push your multi-stage images to Elastic Container Registry.
   - **CodePipeline / CodeBuild**: Automate builds, vulnerability scans, and deployments on each git push.

2. Container Orchestration
   - EKS (Kubernetes)
     - Use Helm charts or Kustomize to deploy your MCP server, Redis, Postgres, etc., with Deployment and StatefulSet.
     - Configure **Cluster Autoscaler** and **Vertical Pod Autoscaler** for dynamic scaling.
   - ECS Fargate
     - Run MCP as a Fargate service behind an Application Load Balancer (ALB).
     - Define Task Definitions for each service, specify CPU/memory, and autoscale based on CloudWatch metrics (CPU, request count).
3. Networking & Security
   - **VPC & Subnets**: Place backend tasks in private subnets; expose only the ALB in a public subnet.
   - **Security Groups**: Lock down ports (e.g., 8000 for /rpc, 8080 for /healthz).
   - **IAM Roles**: Grant each task least-privilege access to Secrets Manager, SSM Parameter Store, and AWS-managed databases.
4. Secrets & Configuration
   - Store DB credentials, API keys, and feature-flags in **AWS Secrets Manager** or **SSM Parameter Store**, and mount them as environment variables.
5. Observability
   - Ship logs to **CloudWatch Logs** via the AWS logging driver.
   - Expose Prometheus metrics and ingest them into **CloudWatch Metrics** or a self-managed Prometheus + Grafana stack on EKS.

B. Google Cloud Platform (GCP)

1. Container Registry & Build
   - **Artifact Registry** or **Container Registry** for images.
   - **Cloud Build** triggers that lint, test, and build your Docker image on push.
2. Compute Options
   - GKE (Kubernetes)
     - Use GKE Autopilot or Standard, deploy with Deployment/StatefulSet manifests or Helm.
   - Cloud Run
     - For stateless, HTTP-only workloads: deploy your MCP server container directly to Cloud Run with automatic scaling to zero.
3. Networking & Security

- **VPC-Native Clusters**: Use private GKE clusters with VPC-peering to your databases.
- **Serverless VPC Access**: Let Cloud Run reach private services via a managed connector.
- **IAM & Workload Identity**: Assign GCP service accounts to your pods or Cloud Run services for fine-grained access to Secrets Manager and SQL.

4. Secrets & Config
   - Use **Secret Manager** to store credentials, and mount them into GKE as K8s Secret volumes or into Cloud Run via environment variables.
5. Logging & Monitoring
   - Leverage **Cloud Logging** and **Cloud Monitoring** (formerly Stackdriver) to collect logs, metrics, and traces.
   - Configure uptime checks for /healthz and alerting policies on high P95 latency or error rate.

C. Microsoft Azure

1. Container Registry & Pipelines
   - **Azure Container Registry (ACR)** for your images.
   - **Azure DevOps** or **GitHub Actions** to build, scan, and push images on each merge.
2. Orchestration Services
   - AKS (Kubernetes Service)
     - Deploy with Helm charts, leverage Cluster Autoscaler, and integrate with Azure Monitor for containers.
   - Azure Container Instances (ACI)
     - For simple, stateless workloads: run individual containers on-demand without managing nodes.
   - Azure App Service for Containers
     - Host the MCP HTTP endpoint in a PaaS environment that handles scaling and SSL for you.
3. Networking & Security
   - **Virtual Networks**: Place your ACR, AKS, Azure Database for PostgreSQL/MySQL, and Redis Cache in the same VNet.
   - **Private Endpoints**: Use Private Link to secure database access.
   - **Managed Identities**: Give your pods or app service managed identities to fetch secrets from **Azure Key Vault**.
4. Secrets & Configuration
   - Store DB connection strings and API keys in **Key Vault**; reference them in your Deployment spec via secretsStoreCSI.
5. Observability

- Integrate with **Azure Monitor** for logs and metrics.
- Use Application Insights for distributed tracing of JSON-RPC calls and adapter performance.

D. Cross-Cloud Best Practices

- **Infrastructure as Code**: Define your clusters, networking, and IAM in Terraform or CloudFormation/Deployment Manager.
- **Immutable Deployments**: Bake your configuration into images or use ConfigMaps/Secrets so deployments are reproducible.
- **CI/CD Integration**: Automate canary or blue–green releases with smoke tests before shifting production traffic.
- **Multi-Region Redundancy**: For critical workloads, deploy across regions and use global load balancers (Route 53 latency-based, Cloud Load Balancing, Azure Traffic Manager).
- **Cost Optimization**: Use spot/preemptible instances for non-critical batch tasks; right-size your nodes and autoscaling thresholds.

By aligning with each cloud's container and orchestration services—and externalizing secrets, health checks, and observability—you'll achieve consistent, secure, and scalable MCP server deployments across AWS, GCP, or Azure.

8.3 Continuous Integration and Deployment for MCP Servers

8.3.1 Setting up a CI/CD Pipeline for MCP Projects

A robust CI/CD pipeline ensures that changes to your MCP server code—adapters, orchestration scripts, and infrastructure manifests—are automatically tested, built, and deployed with minimal manual intervention. Below is a blueprint you can adapt to GitHub Actions, GitLab CI, Jenkins, or any modern CI/CD system.

A. Pipeline Stages

1. Lint & Static Analysis
   - **Python linters**: flake8, isort, black for style.
   - **Security scanning**: bandit for Python security; container scanners like Trivy for your Dockerfile.
2. Unit & Integration Tests
   - **Adapter unit tests**: Mock external dependencies to verify logic.
   - **JSON-RPC end-to-end tests**: Spin up a test instance and exercise key methods via HTTP.
3. Build Artifacts

- **Python packages**: Build wheels or a virtualenv.
- **Docker image**: Multi-stage build producing a production image tagged by commit SHA and semantic version.
4. Publish Artifacts
   - **Docker registry**: Push to ECR / GCR / ACR / Docker Hub.
   - **Package index** (optional): Upload wheels to a private PyPI.
5. Deploy to Staging
   - **Infrastructure as Code**: Apply Terraform/Helm manifests to a staging cluster.
   - **Smoke tests**: Run simple RPC calls (ping, listMethods) and health-check endpoints.
6. Approval & Promotion
   - Manual or automated gating based on test results, security scan passes, and stakeholder sign-off.
7. Deploy to Production
   - Rolling or canary update in Kubernetes/ECS/Cloud Run.
   - Post-deploy integration tests and synthetic transactions to verify behavior.

B. Example: GitHub Actions Workflow

yaml

```yaml
name: CI/CD Pipeline


on:

  push:

    branches: [ main ]

  pull_request:


jobs:

  lint:

    runs-on: ubuntu-latest
```

```yaml
steps:

  - uses: actions/checkout@v3

  - name: Install dependencies

    run: pip install flake8 black isort bandit

  - name: Lint with flake8

    run: flake8 .

  - name: Format check

    run: black --check .

  - name: Security scan

    run: bandit -r adapters main.py


test:

  runs-on: ubuntu-latest

  needs: lint

  services:

    redis:

      image: redis:7-alpine

      ports: [6379:6379]

    postgres:

      image: postgres:15-alpine

      env:

        POSTGRES_USER: user

        POSTGRES_PASSWORD: pass
```

```yaml
      POSTGRES_DB: mcpdb
    ports: [5432:5432]
  steps:
    - uses: actions/checkout@v3
    - name: Install test deps
      run: pip install -r requirements.txt -r requirements-dev.txt
    - name: Run unit tests
      run: pytest --maxfail=1 --disable-warnings -q
    - name: Run integration tests
      run: pytest tests/integration


build-and-push:
  runs-on: ubuntu-latest
  needs: test
  if: github.ref == 'refs/heads/main'
  steps:
    - uses: actions/checkout@v3
    - name: Login to registry
      uses: docker/login-action@v2
      with:
        registry: ${{ secrets.REGISTRY_URL }}
        username: ${{ secrets.REGISTRY_USER }}
        password: ${{ secrets.REGISTRY_TOKEN }}
```

```yaml
    - name: Build and push Docker image
      uses: docker/build-push-action@v3
      with:
        push: true
        tags: |
          ${{ secrets.REGISTRY_URL }}/mcp-server:latest
          ${{ secrets.REGISTRY_URL }}/mcp-server:${{ github.sha }}

  deploy-staging:
    runs-on: ubuntu-latest
    needs: build-and-push
    environment: staging
    steps:
      - uses: azure/k8s-actions@v1     # or GCP/GitHub cloud provider action
        with:
          method: apply
          manifests: |
            ./k8s/staging/mcp-deployment.yaml
      - name: Verify deployment
        run: |
          kubectl rollout status deployment/mcp-server -n staging
          curl --fail http://mcp-staging.example.com/healthz
```

```yaml
promote-to-production:
  runs-on: ubuntu-latest
  needs: deploy-staging
  if: github.event.pull_request.merged == true
  environment: production
  steps:
    - uses: azure/k8s-actions@v1
      with:
        method: apply
        manifests: |
          ./k8s/production/mcp-deployment.yaml
    - name: Post-deploy smoke test
      run: |
        curl --fail https://mcp.example.com/healthz
```

C. Best Practices

- **Secrets Management**: Always source credentials (DB, registry tokens) from your CI's secret store.
- **Immutable Tags**: Deploy by SHA or semantic version; avoid latest in production to ensure reproducibility.
- **Parallelism**: Run linting, unit, and integration tests in parallel to speed up feedback.
- **Fail Fast**: Stop the pipeline on lint or unit-test failures—don't waste time building broken artifacts.
- **Environment Parity**: Use the same container image in staging and production to eliminate "works on my machine" issues.
- **Rollback Strategy**: Maintain the last-known-good manifest or image tag so you can revert quickly.

- **Monitoring Pipeline Health**: Alert on pipeline failures; keep the team aware when deployments break.

By codifying these steps into your CI/CD platform, you'll achieve automated, reliable releases of your MCP server—accelerating feature delivery while minimizing risk.

8.3.2 Automating Testing and Deployment Processes

1. Automated Test Environments
   - **Ephemeral Clusters**: Spin up a throwaway Kubernetes namespace or Docker Compose stack in CI for integration and end-to-end tests.
   - **Service Virtualization**: Mock downstream dependencies (third-party APIs, legacy systems) so tests run reliably and quickly.
2. Pipeline-Driven Test Suites
   - **Unit Tests**: Run pytest with coverage thresholds on every PR; fail the build if coverage drops.
   - **Integration Tests**: Execute against the ephemeral environment; exercise key JSON-RPC methods (ping, critical adapters) via HTTP calls.
   - **Contract/Schema Tests**: Validate that your tool manifest and adapter schemas match, using JSON-Schema validators.
   - **Security Scans**: Automate static analysis (Bandit, Snyk) and container image scans (Trivy) after each build.
3. Parallelization and Caching
   - **Test Parallelism**: Split tests into jobs (lint, unit, integration) running in parallel to reduce overall runtime.
   - **Dependency Caching**: Cache Python wheels and Docker layers between runs to speed subsequent pipeline executions.
4. Infrastructure as Code & GitOps
   - **Declarative Manifests**: Keep Kubernetes Helm charts, Terraform modules, or ARM/Bicep files alongside your code.
   - **GitOps Workflows**: Use Argo CD or Flux to automatically reconcile your cluster state to the Git repo. Pushing a manifest change triggers a deploy.
5. Deployment Strategies
   - **Canary Releases**: Gradually shift a small percentage of traffic to the new version, monitor metrics (error rate, latency), then proceed.
   - **Blue/Green**: Stand up a parallel "green" environment, switch the load balancer once smoke tests pass, then decommission the old "blue."
   - **Rolling Updates**: Leverage Kubernetes' maxSurge/maxUnavailable settings to update pods incrementally without downtime.
6. Automated Rollback and Health Checks

- - **Health Probes**: Rely on built-in readiness and liveness checks; if new pods don't become Ready, the deployment halts.
  - **Rollback Hooks**: In CI/CD (GitHub Actions, Jenkins), define a step to revert to the last good image tag or manifest on failure.
7. Post-Deploy Validation
   - **Smoke Tests**: After deployment, run a suite of lightweight RPC calls (e.g., ping, key adapter methods) to verify basic functionality.
   - **Synthetic Monitoring**: Schedule periodic invocations of critical flows (e.g., fetching weather, writing and reading a test file) to catch regressions early.
8. Promotion and Approval Gates
   - **Staging → Production**: Deploy automatically to staging, run full test battery, then require manual approval (or automated quality gates) before production.
   - **Feature Flags**: Wrap new functionality behind flags so you can turn features on/off in production without redeploying.

By weaving these automated testing and deployment practices into your CI/CD pipeline, you'll ensure that every change to your MCP server is thoroughly validated, reliably released, and rapidly recoverable—enabling safe, continuous delivery at scale.

8.3.3 Tools and Services for Automating MCP Server Deployment

To streamline the build, test, and release of your MCP servers—and their adapters—you can leverage a variety of modern tools and services. Below is a categorized list of popular solutions, with notes on how they fit into an end-to-end automation pipeline.

A. Continuous Integration & Delivery (CI/CD) Platforms

Tool/Service	Key Features	When to Use
GitHub Actions	Built-in CI/CD, extensive marketplace, matrix builds	Repos hosted on GitHub; tight Git integration
GitLab CI/CD	Integrated with GitLab, auto-devops, Docker registry	Self-hosted or GitLab SaaS users

Jenkins	Highly extensible via plugins, pipeline as code	Large legacy shops; need on-prem control
CircleCI	Easy YAML setup, fast container caching	Cloud-native teams seeking speed and simplicity
Travis CI	Simple configuration, public repo free tier	Open-source projects or small teams

B. Artifact Registries & Image Scanning

Tool/Service	Key Features
Docker Hub	Public & private repos, automated builds
AWS ECR	Regional, IAM-secured, integrated with EKS
Google Artifact Registry	Multi-format, VPC-secured, integrated with GKE
Azure Container Registry	ACR Tasks builds, Geo-replication
Trivy / Clair / Anchore	Scans images for CVEs and policy violations

C. Infrastructure as Code (IaC)

Tool/Service	Key Features
Terraform	Cloud-agnostic, rich provider ecosystem, state management
Pulumi	Code in Python/TypeScript/Go, integrates with existing code
AWS CloudFormation	Native on AWS, drift detection, Change Sets
Azure Resource Manager	ARM/ Bicep templates for Azure resources
Google Deployment Manager	Declarative GCP resource configs

D. Configuration & Secret Management

Tool/Service	Key Features
HashiCorp Vault	Dynamic secrets, encryption-as-a-service
AWS Secrets Manager	Rotation, IAM-controlled, integrated with Lambda

Azure Key Vault	RBAC, soft delete, Managed Identities
GCP Secret Manager	Versioning, IAM policies, audit logs
Consul	Key-value store with health checks, ACLs

E. Kubernetes-Native Deployment & GitOps

Tool/Service	Key Features
Argo CD	GitOps continuous delivery, declarative sync, multi-cluster
Flux CD	GitOps, Helm/Kustomize support, alert automation
Helm	Package management for Kubernetes, templating
Kustomize	Native Kubernetes customization without templates
Jenkins X	Kubernetes-native CI/CD with preview environments

Spinnaker	Multi-cloud CD, canary deployments, pipeline orchestration

F. Serverless & PaaS Options

Platform	Key Features
AWS Fargate / ECS	Serverless containers, tight AWS integration
AWS Cloud Run	Serverless HTTP containers on GCP
Azure Container Instances	Fast, per-second billing for containers
Azure App Service	PaaS for web APIs with built-in CI/CD workflows
Google App Engine	PaaS for flexible or standard environments

G. Observability & Alerting

Tool/Service	Key Features
Prometheus & Grafana	Metrics scraping, dashboarding, alert rules

OpenTelemetry	Distributed tracing and metrics, vendor-agnostic
Datadog / New Relic	SaaS APM, logs, metrics, alerting
ELK Stack	Log aggregation, search, visualizations
PagerDuty / Opsgenie	Incident management, on-call scheduling, escalation

H. Example End-to-End Flow

1. Code Push to GitHub
   - Triggers **GitHub Actions**
2. Lint + Test
   - Python lint, unit tests, integration tests in ephemeral k8s or Docker Compose
3. Build & Scan
   - Multi-stage Docker build, push to **AWS ECR**, run **Trivy** scan
4. Deploy to Staging
   - **Terraform** applies staging infra, **Argo CD** syncs k8s manifests
5. Smoke Tests & Approvals
   - Automated health checks; manual approval gate in GitHub Environments
6. Canary Release
   - **Spinnaker** or **Argo Rollouts** shifts 10% traffic, monitors metrics
7. Full Production Rollout
   - On success, 100% traffic cutover; auto-rollback on failure
8. Monitor & Alert
   - **Prometheus** alerts on elevated P95 latency or error spikes

By combining these tools—CI/CD platforms, IaC, GitOps, container registries, and observability services—you can fully automate the build, test, and deployment of your MCP servers, ensuring consistent, secure, and reliable releases across environments.

8.4 Interactive Q&A

8.4.1 How Would You Implement CI/CD Pipelines for Your MCP Server?

1. Choosing Your CI/CD Platform
   - Would you use GitHub Actions, GitLab CI, Jenkins, or a managed service like CircleCI or Azure DevOps?
   - What criteria (integration with your repo host, available runners, pricing) drive that choice?
2. Defining Pipeline Stages
   - How do you break your workflow into linting, unit tests, integration tests, security scans, and artifact builds?
   - Which stages run in parallel versus sequentially to balance speed and feedback quality?
3. Test Environment Provisioning
   - Do you spin up ephemeral Docker Compose stacks or throwaway Kubernetes namespaces for integration and end-to-end tests?
   - How do you mock or virtualize downstream systems so tests remain fast and reliable?
4. Artifact Management and Versioning
   - Will you build Python wheels, Docker images, or both—and where will they be stored (ECR, GCR, ACR, private PyPI)?
   - How do you tag artifacts (commit SHA, semantic version) to ensure immutability and reproducibility?
5. Security and Compliance Gates
   - Where do you insert SAST/DAST tools (Bandit, Trivy, Snyk) into the pipeline, and what thresholds trigger a failure?
   - Do you enforce manual approvals or compliance sign-offs before promoting to production?
6. Deployments and Release Strategies
   - How will you handle staging versus production deployments—blue/green, canary, or rolling updates?
   - What automated smoke tests (health endpoints, ping calls) run post-deploy to validate service health?
7. Managing Secrets and Configuration
   - How do you securely inject database credentials, API keys, and feature flags into build and deploy jobs (Vault, Secrets Manager, CI secrets)?
   - Do you use templated manifests (Helm, Kustomize) or environment-specific overrides?
8. Rollback and Resilience

- What conditions (failed healthchecks, error spikes) trigger automatic rollbacks, and how is that configured in your orchestrator?
        - How do you maintain the "last known good" artifact or manifest for quick recovery?
9. Observability and Feedback Loops
        - How do you integrate pipeline status with your team's chatops (Slack, Teams) or incident management (PagerDuty)?
        - Which monitoring metrics (P95 latency, error rate) feed back into auto-scaling or pipeline health dashboards?
10. Continuous Improvement
        - How often do you review and refine your CI/CD pipeline—pruning flakiness, optimizing stage durations, adding new quality gates?
        - Do you version the pipeline definitions alongside your application code to track changes over time?

Reflect on these points to design a CI/CD process that delivers fast, safe, and repeatable MCP server releases at scale.

8.4.2 Discussion on Containerization and Cloud Deployment Strategies

1. **Choice of Container Runtime & Base Image**
        - How do you select a base image (e.g., Debian slim vs. Alpine) to balance image size, security, and compatibility?
        - What patterns do you follow to keep images minimal (multi-stage builds, removing build-time tools)?
2. **Orchestration Platform Selection**
        - Would you standardize on Kubernetes (EKS/GKE/AKS), or prefer serverless container platforms (Fargate, Cloud Run, ACI)?
        - What SLA, scaling behavior, and operational overhead trade-offs influence that decision?
3. **Networking and Service Mesh**
        - How do you architect pod-to-pod and external service connectivity (ingress controllers, VPCs, private clusters)?
        - Would you adopt a service mesh (Envoy/Istio/Linkerd) for mutual TLS, traffic shifting, or observability?
4. **Secret & Configuration Management**
        - Which secret store (Vault, AWS Secrets Manager, Azure Key Vault, Kubernetes Secrets) fits your security requirements?
        - How do you inject configuration—environment variables vs. mounted config maps—while avoiding drift across environments?
5. **Scaling Patterns**

- o What autoscaling triggers do you use—CPU/memory metrics, custom RPC latency thresholds, or queue depth?
- o How do you accommodate bursty loads versus steady-state traffic in your scaling policies?

6. **Deployment Strategies**
   - o Do you employ canary or blue/green deployments for zero-downtime releases, and which tools (Argo Rollouts, Spinnaker) support that?
   - o How do you automate healthchecks and rollbacks when a new version misbehaves?

7. **Cost Optimization**
   - o Which parts of your deployment can leverage spot/preemptible instances or lower-cost preemptible services without compromising availability?
   - o How do you monitor and cap spend on ephemeral vs. persistent workloads?

8. **Observability & Alerting**
   - o How do you collect and correlate container logs, metrics, and traces for your MCP server and adapters?
   - o What SLOs (e.g., 99th-percentile RPC latency) do you track, and how does that feed into your alerting thresholds?

9. **Disaster Recovery & Multi-Region Architecture**
   - o Do you replicate your MCP deployment across regions or zones for failover, and how do you manage global DNS or traffic routing?
   - o How quickly can you recover from a full-region outage, and what automation supports that?

10. **CI/CD Integration**
    - o How tightly do you couple your container builds and deployments into the CI pipeline—are images tagged and promoted through staging to production automatically?
    - o What manual gates or approvals exist, and how do they balance speed of delivery with safety?

Reflecting on these points will help you tailor your containerization and cloud deployment approach to your team's skills, your application's demands, and your organization's operational and security requirements.

Chapter 9: Best Practices for Maintaining and Securing MCP Servers

9.1 Regular Maintenance and Monitoring

9.1.1 Setting Up Monitoring for MCP Servers

Effective monitoring gives you visibility into your MCP servers' health, performance, and reliability. By instrumenting key signals, building dashboards, and configuring alerts, you can detect issues early, diagnose root causes quickly, and maintain SLAs. Below are the essential elements:

A. Define Key Monitoring Signals

Signal Category	Examples	Purpose
RPC Metrics	• Requests per second (RPS) by method • Latency histograms (P50/P95/P99) • Error rates by code or method	Track throughput, performance, and failures of individual tools.
System Metrics	• CPU & memory usage • Event-loop latency • Open file/connection counts	Ensure the host isn't resource-constrained or leaking.
Dependency Metrics	• Redis latency, hit/miss rates • DB connection pool usage and query times • External API call durations and error rates	Detect when downstream services are becoming bottlenecks.

Streaming Health	• Active stream count	Monitor long-running or real-time pipelines for stalls.
	• Back-pressure events	
	• Kafka/MQTT consumer lag	
Custom Business KPIs	• Alerts sent	Tie infrastructure health to business-level outcomes.
	• Batch jobs completed	
	• Workflow success rates	

B. Instrumentation Techniques

1. Prometheus Client Libraries
   - Use a Prometheus client (e.g., prometheus_client for Python) to expose counters, histograms, and gauges directly in your server.
   - Label metrics with method, status, and other dimensions for granular slicing.
2. OpenTelemetry / Distributed Tracing
   - Integrate an OpenTelemetry SDK to capture spans for each JSON-RPC dispatch, downstream HTTP/DB calls, and adapter logic.
   - Export traces to a tracing backend (Jaeger, Zipkin, or a managed service) to visualize request flows and identify latencies.
3. Structured Logging
   - Emit logs in JSON or structured format, including fields like requestId, method, userId, durationMs, and errorCode.
   - Ship logs to a centralized system (ELK, Splunk, Datadog) to enable search, filtering, and correlation with metrics.
4. Health and Readiness Endpoints
   - Expose /healthz for liveness checks (basic RPC dispatch).
   - Expose /readyz for readiness (e.g., confirm connection pools are primed, adapters loaded).
   - Configure your orchestrator (Kubernetes, ECS) to probe these endpoints.

C. Dashboards and Visualization

1. Prometheus + Grafana
   - Build a dashboard showing:
     - RPS and error rates over time (line charts)
     - Latency percentiles (histogram or heatmap panels)
     - Resource usage (CPU, memory, open connections)
   - Group panels by service, environment, and criticality.
2. Distributed Trace Explorer
   - Use a trace UI to:
     - Filter by slowest requests or error traces
     - Zoom into spans for adapter calls, HTTP requests, and DB queries
     - Compare traces across deployments to detect regressions
3. Log Aggregation UI
   - Create saved searches and dashboards for:
     - High-severity errors (`error.code` ≥ -32000)
     - Authentication or authorization failures
     - Circuit breaker activations or rate limit hits

D. Alerting and Notification

1. Prometheus Alertmanager
   - Define alert rules for:
     - Error rate > X% on any method for Y minutes
     - P95 latency exceeds SLA (e.g., 200 ms)
     - High Redis or DB error/timeout rates
   - Route alerts to Slack, email, PagerDuty, or Opsgenie with runbook links.
2. Synthetic Monitoring
   - Schedule periodic "ping" and critical-path tests (e.g., getUserProfile, streamHealthMetrics) from an external location to detect network or DNS issues.
3. On-Call Escalation
   - Implement escalation policies: page primary on urgent outages, notify secondary or email on warnings.

E. Continuous Improvement

- **Metric Reviews**: Regularly review dashboards in on-call handovers and retrospectives to identify trends or capacity issues.
- **Runbook Integration**: Link each alert to a runbook section describing diagnostic steps, common causes, and remediation commands (e.g., check pool size, restart adapter).

- **Drills and Simulations**: Periodically inject failures (circuit-breaker trip, simulated downstream outage) to verify that monitoring and alerting fire correctly, and teams can respond effectively.

By instrumenting your MCP servers across metrics, logs, and traces—building intuitive dashboards and defining clear alerts—you'll gain the visibility needed to keep your context-aware AI platform reliable, performant, and ready to scale.

8.1.2 Automated Health Checks and Failure Detection

Building robust MCP deployments means more than just exposing a /healthz endpoint—it requires automated probes at multiple layers and timely failure detection so your orchestrator or monitoring system can remediate problems before they impact users.

A. Types of Health Checks

Probe Type	Purpose	Frequency/Timeout
Liveness	Detects fatal deadlocks or crashes; triggers restart.	Every 10–30 s, timeout 1–2 s
Readiness	Signals whether the instance can serve traffic.	Every 5–15 s, timeout 1 s
Startup	Gates readiness until app is fully initialized.	Only during container start
Dependency	Verifies critical downstream services (DB, Redis).	Every 30–60 s, timeout 1–2 s

B. Implementing Health Endpoints

Basic Liveness
python

```python
@app.get("/healthz")
```

```python
async def liveness():

    return {"status": "ok"}
```

Readiness with Dependency Checks
python

```python
@app.get("/readyz")

async def readiness():

    errors = []

    try:

        await redis.ping()

    except Exception as e:

        errors.append(f"Redis: {e}")

    try:

        await db.execute("SELECT 1")

    except Exception as e:

        errors.append(f"DB: {e}")

    if errors:

        raise HTTPException(status_code=503, detail=errors)

    return {"status": "ready"}
```

1. Startup Probe
   - Only return success after loading adapters, establishing pools, and warming caches.

C. Kubernetes Integration

Configuration

yaml

```yaml
livenessProbe:

  httpGet: { path: /healthz, port: 8000 }

  initialDelaySeconds: 30

  periodSeconds: 30

  timeoutSeconds: 2


readinessProbe:

  httpGet: { path: /readyz, port: 8000 }

  initialDelaySeconds: 5

  periodSeconds: 15

  timeoutSeconds: 1


startupProbe:

  httpGet: { path: /readyz, port: 8000 }

  failureThreshold: 30

  periodSeconds: 10

  timeoutSeconds: 1
```

- Behavior
  - Failing liveness triggers pod restart.
  - Failing readiness removes pod from service endpoints until healthy.
  - Startup probe prevents premature readiness/failover flapping.

D. Failure Detection Beyond Probes

1. Passive Error Monitoring
    o   Track per-method error rates and circuit-breaker events; alert when thresholds exceeded (e.g., > 5% errors over 1 min).
2. Synthetic or External Checks
    o   Use an external service (Pingdom, UptimeRobot) to call /rpc with a simple ping payload every minute, alert on failures or elevated latency.
3. Dependency Circuit Breakers
    o   Integrate a library (e.g., pybreaker) to open circuits on repeated downstream failures, preventing exhaustion and surfacing clear errors.

E. Alerting and Automated Remediation

*   Alerts
    o   Configure alerts for probe failures, elevated error rates, resource exhaustion, and unhealthy pod counts.
    o   Route to on-call channels (Slack/PagerDuty) with runbook links.
*   Remediation
    o   Kubernetes auto-restarts unhealthy pods.
    o   Auto-scale up additional instances on sustained readiness failures due to overload.
    o   Circuit-breaker fallback path to degrade gracefully (e.g., read-only mode).

F. Best Practices

*   **Keep Probes Lightweight**: Don't run expensive queries in health endpoints; use simple "SELECT 1" or PING.
*   **Separate Concerns**: Distinguish liveness (keep process alive) from readiness (serve traffic safely).
*   **Monitor Probe Metrics**: Scrape probe success/failure counts and latencies in Prometheus.
*   **Test Failures**: Simulate downstream outages to ensure probes detect and orchestrator recovers.
*   **Document Runbooks**: For each alert, include step-by-step remediation in your team's runbook.

By layering fast, reliable health checks with passive error tracking, external synthetics, and automated orchestration responses, you'll maintain a highly available, self-healing MCP server infrastructure.

9.1.3 Scheduled Maintenance for Smooth Operation

Regular, planned maintenance is essential to keep your MCP servers secure, performant, and highly available. Below are the key maintenance activities, cadence recommendations, and communication best practices.

A. Define and Communicate Maintenance Windows

- **Cadence**:
  - **Weekly**: Non-disruptive tasks (log rotation, cache clear).
  - **Monthly**: Dependency updates, security patching.
  - **Quarterly**: Major version upgrades, capacity testing, disaster-recovery drills.
- **Window Timing**: Schedule during off-peak hours, respecting your users' time zones and peak traffic patterns.
- **Notification**:
  - Announce 1 week in advance, with reminders 24 h and 1 h before.
  - Publish planned downtime on status pages and chat channels.

B. Operating System and Dependency Patching

- Security Updates
  - Subscribe to OS and language-runtime CVE feeds (e.g., Ubuntu Security Notices, Python security advisories).
  - Apply critical patches immediately; bundle non-critical updates into your monthly window.
- Dependency Upgrades
  - Automate weekly checks via Dependabot or Renovate; promote updates through your CI pipeline to staging before production.
  - Test compatibility of major library version bumps (e.g., jsonrpcserver, FastAPI, uvicorn).

C. Database and Cache Maintenance

- PostgreSQL / TimescaleDB
  - **VACUUM ANALYZE** weekly to reclaim storage and update optimizer statistics.
  - **Reindex** quarterly on large tables to prevent bloat.
- Redis
  - **Snapshotting/RDB/AOF**: Verify persistence settings; test restore procedures monthly.
  - **Memory Defragmentation**: Run MEMORY PURGE or MEMORY DEFRAGMENT during low-traffic windows.

- MongoDB / Other Stores
  - Rotate journaling files, rebuild secondary indexes, and test replica failover.

D. Backup and Restore Validation

- Backup Frequency
  - **Incremental**: Every 15 min for critical context stores.
  - **Full**: Daily for relational and document databases.
- Automated Restore Tests
  - Quarterly, spin up a sandbox environment, restore backups, run smoke tests (RPC ping, key adapters).
  - Record restore time and identify bottlenecks.

E. Secret and Certificate Rotation

- Secrets
  - Rotate API keys, database credentials, and service-account tokens every 90 days.
  - Automate via Vault dynamic secrets or cloud KMS secret rotation.
- TLS/mTLS Certificates
  - Use ACME or your PKI's automated renewal; test renewal on staging before production cutover.
  - Maintain alerts for certificates nearing expiration (30 days prior).

F. Capacity Planning and Load Testing

- Baseline Review
  - Monthly, review your RPS, P95/P99 latency, and error metrics.
- Scale-Up Drills
  - Execute a simulated traffic ramp (e.g., 2× peak) in staging to validate autoscaling and rate-limiting behavior.
- Resource Audit
  - Check connection-pool saturation, event-loop backlogs, and thread-pool usage; adjust quotas and scaling policies as needed.

G. Chaos Engineering and Disaster-Recovery Drills

- Fault Injection
  - Simulate pod/node failures, Redis or DB outages during quarterly drills to verify liveness/readiness and automated recovery.
- Runbook Validation

- During each drill, follow your documented runbooks, timing each step, and refine procedures based on lessons learned.

H. Documentation and Stakeholder Communication

- Maintenance Runbooks
  - Maintain versioned playbooks for each task: patch OS, upgrade adapters, rotate secrets, restore backups.
- Stakeholder Updates
  - After each maintenance window, publish a brief report: work performed, issues encountered, and action items for next cycle.

Maintenance Checklist

- Announce upcoming window (1 week, 24 h, 1 h reminders)
- Verify staging patches and upgrades before production
- Apply OS and Python/runtime security updates
- Upgrade critical dependencies via CI/CD
- Run database VACUUM/ANALYZE and Redis defragmentation
- Perform backup restore test and log duration
- Rotate secrets and certificates; confirm new credentials work
- Execute a small-scale load test or autoscaling drill
- Inject a controlled fault (pod kill or dependency outage) and observe recovery
- Update runbooks and publish a maintenance report

By following this structured maintenance regimen—combining regular patching, backup verification, capacity testing, and chaos-driven resilience drills—you'll ensure your MCP servers continue to operate securely and smoothly, even as your usage and dependencies evolve.

9.2 Security Best Practices
9.2.1 Securing MCP Servers Against Common Threats

MCP servers—exposing JSON-RPC endpoints, streaming interfaces, and integrations—face a range of threats from injection attacks to denial-of-service. The following practices help you defend against the most prevalent risks.

A. Threat Matrix

Threat Category	Description	Mitigation Strategies

Unauthorized Access	Attackers calling protected methods without credentials	Enforce strong auth (API keys, OAuth2/JWT, mTLS); RBAC/ABAC
JSON-RPC Injection	Malicious payloads exploiting inadequate input validation	Validate params with JSON Schema; reject unknown fields
Man-in-the-Middle (MITM)	Eavesdropping or tampering with RPC traffic	Enforce TLS 1.2+; use HSTS; require certificate validation
Denial-of-Service (DoS)	Flooding RPC endpoint with requests or opening many streams	Rate-limiting; connection quotas; circuit breakers; WAF rules
Data Leakage	Unintended exposure of sensitive context or logs	Redact secrets in logs; field-level encryption; strict CORS
Supply-Chain Compromise	Malicious or outdated dependencies introducing vulnerabilities	Pin dependencies; run SCA (Trivy, Snyk); regular patching
Privilege Escalation	Abuse of overly broad credentials to access high-risk methods	Least-privilege service accounts; per-method scoping; ACLs

| Lateral Movement | Compromised instance used to pivot to backend services | Network segmentation; private subnets; host firewalls |

B. Core Defensive Controls

1. Strong Authentication & Authorization
   - Require all RPC calls carry valid credentials (Authorization header or client cert).

Map identities to roles or scopes; enforce per-method ACLs:
python

```python
@method
async def deleteUser(context, args):
  if "admin" not in context["claims"]["roles"]:
    raise JsonRpcError(-32604, "Forbidden")
  # ...
```

2. Input Validation & Sanitization
   - Define and enforce JSON Schema for each tool's params and result.
   - Reject unknown or extra fields; use libraries like jsonschema to validate before business logic.
3. Encrypted Transport
   - Serve JSON-RPC over HTTPS with TLS 1.2+; disable weak ciphers.
   - For service-to-service or device connections, enable mutual TLS (mTLS) to authenticate both ends.
4. Rate Limiting & Resource Quotas

Apply token-bucket limits per IP, user, or method to prevent flooding:
python

```python
# In your rate-limit middleware, set per-method limits
```

```python
settings.rate_limits = {"fetchWeather": 5.0}    # 5 calls/sec

settings.bucket_sizes = {"fetchWeather": 10}
```

   - Limit concurrent streams and threads to avoid exhaustion.
5. Network Segmentation & Firewalls
   - Place MCP servers in a private subnet; expose only the proxy or load balancer.
   - Whitelist known IP ranges; block all other ingress.
   - Use security groups or NSGs to restrict egress to required backend ports.
6. Secrets Management & Rotation
   - Store credentials in a vault (HashiCorp Vault, AWS Secrets Manager) with automatic rotation.
   - Mount secrets at runtime rather than baking into images or source code.
7. Dependency Security
   - Pin versions for all Python and system libraries in requirements.txt.
   - Integrate SCA tools (Trivy, Clair, Snyk) in CI to catch known CVEs before deployment.
8. Secure Configuration Defaults
   - Disable debug or verbose error modes in production (DEBUG=False).
   - Enforce CORS only for trusted origins; never use * in production.
9. Structured Logging and Auditing
   - Log each RPC call with requestId, method, userId, and outcome—without logging raw secrets or PII.
   - Ship logs to a centralized system with immutable storage (WORM) for forensic analysis.
10. Automated Patching and Hardening
    - Regularly rebuild your container images from updated base images.
    - Apply OS and runtime security patches in your scheduled maintenance windows.

C. Example: FastAPI Security Middleware

python

```python
from fastapi import FastAPI, Request, HTTPException
```

```python
from fastapi.middleware.cors import CORSMiddleware

app = FastAPI()

# Strict CORS policy
app.add_middleware(
    CORSMiddleware,
    allow_origins=["https://your-trusted-client.com"],
    allow_methods=["POST"],
    allow_headers=["Content-Type", "Authorization"],
)


# Security headers
@app.middleware("http")
async def add_security_headers(request: Request, call_next):
    response = await call_next(request)
    response.headers.update({
        "Strict-Transport-Security": "max-age=63072000; includeSubDomains; preload",
        "X-Content-Type-Options": "nosniff",
        "X-Frame-Options": "DENY",
        "Referrer-Policy": "no-referrer",
    })
    return response
```

```python
# Authentication dependency

from fastapi.security import HTTPBearer, HTTPAuthorizationCredentials


auth_scheme = HTTPBearer()

async def authenticate(creds: HTTPAuthorizationCredentials = Depends(auth_scheme)):

    token = creds.credentials

    user = verify_jwt(token)

    if not user:

        raise HTTPException(401, "Invalid token")

    return user
```

D. Continuous Security Practices

- **Threat Modeling**: Regularly review your architecture to identify new attack vectors.
- **Penetration Testing**: Schedule quarterly pentests and remediation cycles.
- **Chaos Security**: Inject network faults and simulate credential compromise to verify your defenses.
- **Security Runbooks**: Document incident response steps—who to notify, how to revoke keys, and how to restore services.

By layering these controls—authentication, validation, encryption, rate limiting, and proactive security processes—you can harden your MCP servers against the majority of common threats and maintain a secure, resilient context-aware AI platform.

9.2.2 Protecting Sensitive Data and User Privacy

Maintaining user trust and legal compliance requires that you treat all personal or sensitive data with care—throughout ingestion, processing, storage, and logging. Below are key practices for data protection and privacy in your MCP deployment.

A. Data Classification and Minimization

- Classify Data
  - Identify which fields in your JSON-RPC context or args contain PII (names, emails), PHI (health records), or other sensitive information.
  - Tag these fields in your tool manifest so adapters can handle them appropriately.
- Minimize Collection
  - Only collect and transmit the data absolutely necessary for each tool's purpose.
  - Avoid storing raw PII in your context store if you can store a hashed or tokenized identifier instead.

B. Encryption in Transit

- TLS Everywhere
  - Enforce HTTPS for all JSON-RPC and streaming endpoints (TLS 1.2+).
  - Disable legacy ciphers and require strong key exchange algorithms (ECDHE).
- mTLS for Internal Services
  - Require mutual TLS between MCP servers and back-end services (Redis, databases) to prevent MITM within your network.

C. Encryption at Rest

- Full-Disk Encryption
  - Enable disk encryption on all hosts (EBS encryption, LUKS) and managed services (RDS, ElastiCache).
- Database-Level Encryption
  - Turn on Transparent Data Encryption (TDE) for relational databases.
  - Use storage-encrypting tiers for NoSQL stores (MongoDB encrypted storage engines, encrypted Redis clusters).

D. Field-Level and Application-Level Encryption

- Field-Level Encryption

Encrypt particularly sensitive fields (SSNs, medical notes) within your JSON payload before storage:

python

```
from cryptography.fernet import Fernet
```

```python
cipher = Fernet(settings.FIELD_ENC_KEY)

encrypted_ssn = cipher.encrypt(user_ssn.encode())
```

- Decrypt only within the adapter that needs cleartext; propagate tokens elsewhere.
- Tokenization
  - Replace raw values with surrogate keys and store the mapping in a secure vault or HSM, preventing exposure in logs or caches.

E. Access Controls and Audit Logging

- Least-Privilege Access
  - Grant each service account or API key only the permissions it needs (e.g., read-only vs. read-write to specific tables).
  - Use IAM roles or database ACLs—never share a single "god" credential across components.
- Fine-Grained Auditing
  - Log every access to sensitive data—who accessed which field, when, and from which IP or service.
  - Store audit logs in a WORM (write-once) or append-only store; regularly review for anomalies.

F. Data Masking and Redaction

- Masking in Logs
  - Automatically redact or obfuscate PII in structured logs before writing (e.g., show only last 4 digits of SSNs).

Implement a logging filter that strips sensitive keys from any JSON-RPC args or result:
python

```python
SENSITIVE_KEYS = {"ssn","creditCard","patientId"}

def redact(payload):
```

```
return {k:("***" if k in SENSITIVE_KEYS else v) for k,v in
payload.items()}
```

- Redaction on Export
  - When exporting dashboards or metric snapshots, ensure any sample payloads have had sensitive fields removed or masked.

G. Data Retention and Deletion Policies

- Retention Limits
  - Define how long you keep context snapshots, logs, and backups—aligned with legal/regulatory requirements (e.g., GDPR's "right to be forgotten").
  - Automate deletion of expired records (e.g., Redis TTLs, database partition drops).
- Automated Deletion Workflows
  - Provide a tool (e.g., an MCP method deleteUserData) that purges all data associated with a given userIdacross stores, ensuring compliance.

H. Compliance and Privacy Frameworks

- GDPR/CCPA
  - Support data subject requests: allow users to view, correct, or delete their personal data.
  - Log consent and record lawful basis for processing where required.
- HIPAA (Healthcare)
  - For PHI, host MCP servers and storage in HIPAA-compliant environments, sign Business Associate Agreements (BAAs), and enforce enhanced auditing and encryption.
- PCI DSS (Payments)
  - Do not transmit or store full cardholder data. If you must, use PCI-certified vaults and never log sensitive payment fields.

I. Regular Privacy Reviews and Penetration Testing

- Privacy Impact Assessments
  - Periodically review new adapters or workflow changes to assess privacy risks and update documentation.

- Security and Penetration Tests
    - Engage third-party auditors to test for data leakage, insecure endpoints, or misconfigurations—remediate findings promptly.

By applying these layered protections—from minimizing data collection and encrypting it in transit and at rest, to enforcing fine-grained access controls, masking in logs, and automating retention policies—you'll safeguard user privacy and ensure your MCP servers comply with the most stringent data-protection standards.

9.2.3 Implementing Secure APIs and Services

Building secure APIs around your MCP server means enforcing multiple layers of protection—from transport to application logic. Here are the key practices and patterns:

A. Strong Authentication and Authorization

1. OAuth 2.0 / JWT
    - Issue short-lived JWTs via an authorization server, embedding sub, aud, exp, and custom claims (roles, scopes).
    - Validate signature, expiration, issuer, and audience in middleware before dispatching JSON-RPC.
2. API Keys and mTLS for Machine-to-Machine
    - Use long, random API keys stored in a vault and rotated regularly.
    - For high-assurance integrations, require mutual TLS: clients present certs signed by your CA.
3. Per-Method Scoping
    - Tag each MCP method with required scopes/roles in your tool manifest.

In your dispatcher, enforce:
python

```python
if required_scope not in context["claims"]["scopes"]:

    raise JsonRpcError(-32604, "Insufficient scope")
```

B. Input Validation and Schema Enforcement

1. JSON Schema Validation
   o Define params and result schemas for every method. Use jsonschema at the gateway to reject invalid payloads (extra properties, wrong types) before reaching adapter logic.
2. Reject Unknown Fields
   o Configure your validator with "additionalProperties": false to prevent injection of unrecognized parameters.

C. Transport-Level Protections

1. TLS Configuration
   o Enforce TLS 1.2+ with strong ciphers (ECDHE + AES GCM). Disable TLS 1.0/1.1 and weak suites.
   o Enable HSTS (strict-transport-security header) to prevent downgrade attacks.
2. HTTP Security Headers
   o Add headers globally:
      - X-Frame-Options: DENY
      - X-Content-Type-Options: nosniff
      - Referrer-Policy: no-referrer
      - Content-Security-Policy for any web UI.

D. Rate Limiting and Throttling

1. Per-Client and Per-Method Limits

Use token-bucket rate limits in middleware to cap calls:
python

```python
rate = settings.rate_limits.get(method, settings.default_rate)

bucket = settings.bucket_sizes.get(method, settings.default_bucket)
```

2. Global Quotas and Burst Controls
   o Protect against global DoS by limiting total RPS across all clients, and allow controlled bursts.

E. Secure Error Handling

1. Consistent Error Codes
   - Avoid returning stack traces or internal messages. Map exceptions to JSON-RPC codes (-32600...-32604, -32000 range).
2. Minimal Data in Responses
   - Do not echo sensitive input back in error messages. Provide only what's necessary (e.g., "Invalid params: missing field 'userId'").

F. Logging, Auditing, and Monitoring

1. Structured Audit Logs
   - Log each request/response with fields: timestamp, requestId, method, userId, statusCode, and sanitized args.
   - Ensure logs cannot be tampered with (WORM storage).
2. Real-Time Alerting
   - Alert on repeated authentication failures, unexpected method calls, or spikes in 403/401 errors.

G. API Gateway and WAF Integration

1. Gateway
   - Place an API gateway (e.g., AWS API Gateway, Kong, Apigee) in front of MCP to centralize auth, throttling, and TLS.
2. Web Application Firewall
   - Deploy a WAF to block common attacks (SQL-injection, XSS) even though JSON-RPC isn't directly susceptible to some web vulnerabilities.

H. Regular Security Reviews and Penetration Testing

- **Code Reviews**: Enforce security-focused reviews for any adapter that handles sensitive data.
- **Pentests**: Quarterly tests against your public endpoints, including fuzzing your JSON-RPC interface.
- **Dependency Audits**: Automated SCA to flag vulnerable library versions.

By combining these layers—robust auth, strict validation, hardened transport, proactive rate limiting, careful error handling, and continuous auditing—you'll ensure your MCP APIs remain resilient to threats and maintain the confidentiality, integrity, and availability of your AI services.

9.3 Versioning and Managing Protocol Changes

9.3.1 How to Handle Protocol Versioning with MCP

Managing changes to your MCP-based JSON-RPC interface—whether adding new features, fixing bugs, or making breaking changes—requires a clear versioning strategy and migration plan to avoid disrupting clients. Below are patterns and best practices for protocol versioning in MCP.

A. Semantic Versioning for Tool Manifests

- Manifest Version
    - Embed a top-level manifestVersion (e.g., "1.2.0") in your tool manifest JSON.
    - Increment **MAJOR** for incompatible changes, **MINOR** for backwards-compatible additions, and **PATCH** for bug fixes.
- Per-Method Versioning
    - In each tool entry, include a "version" field.
    - Clients can inspect toolManifest.tools["myMethod"].version to detect available capabilities.

B. Version Negotiation in Context

- Client-Declared Support

Clients include a clientSupportedVersions array in their context:
jsonc

"context": {

 "requestId": "abc123",

 "clientSupportedVersions": ["1.0.0", "1.1.0"]

}

- Server Selection Logic

- The server picks the highest compatible version ≤ the client's maximum, or returns a -32010 VersionMismatch error with supported versions.

C. Path or Header-Based Versioning

1. URL Path Versioning
   - Run parallel endpoints (/v1/rpc, /v2/rpc)—each binds to a different manifest.
   - During migration, clients switch from /v1 to /v2 at their own pace.
2. Custom Header
   - Clients send X-MCP-API-Version: 2.
   - Middleware routes the request to the appropriate handler or manifest.

D. Deprecation and Sunset Policies

- Deprecation Notices

Mark deprecated methods or fields in the manifest:
jsonc

```jsonc
{

  "name": "oldMethod",

  "deprecated": true,

  "deprecationDate": "2025-07-01",

  "replacement": "newMethod"

}
```

- Client Warnings

For calls to deprecated methods, return a warning in the JSON-RPC response's data block:
json

```json
"error": {

  "code": -32011,
```

```
    "message": "Deprecated method",

    "data": {"replacement": "newMethod"}

}
```

- Sunsetting
  - After the deprecation date, disable the old version and return -32601 Method not found.

E. Backward Compatibility Strategies

1. Non-Breaking Additions
   - Add new optional parameters with defaults; ensure existing clients continue to work without changes.
2. Adapter Layer Transforms
   - Keep a compatibility shim in your server that translates old-version requests to the new internal format.
3. Feature Flags
   - Use flags to toggle new behaviors on or off per-client, allowing staged rollout.

F. Migration Workflow

1. Develop New Version
   - Implement changes in a feature branch; update manifest version; add tests for both old and new behaviors.
2. Publish Beta Manifest
   - Expose a /manifest?version=2 endpoint or tag for clients to test against.
3. Client Integration Period
   - Give clients time (e.g., 4–6 weeks) to update their code to the new version.
4. Deprecation Announcement
   - Communicate end-of-life for the old version—include dates and migration guides.
5. Removal
   - After the sunset date, remove support for old version and clean up deprecation code.

G. Best Practices Checklist

- Adopt **semantic versioning** for your manifest and methods.
- Expose a **manifestVersion** and per-method version in your tool manifest.

- Support **version negotiation** via context or headers.
- Provide clear **deprecation warnings** and **replacement guidance**.
- Maintain **backward compatibility** shims during transition periods.
- Document version lifecycles (release date, deprecation date, removal date).
- Automate **tests** for both legacy and current protocol versions.
- Use **feature flags** to stage new functionality without broad disruption.

By following these guidelines—combining semantic versioning, manifest-driven negotiation, deprecation policies, and compatibility shims—you'll evolve your MCP protocol in a controlled, transparent way that keeps client integrations smooth and predictable.

9.3.2 Backward Compatibility and Future-Proofing MCP Systems

Ensuring that your MCP ecosystem continues to serve existing clients even as you introduce new features or refactor internals is critical to long-term stability. Here are strategies to maintain backward compatibility and keep your system adaptable to future needs.

A. Design for Extensibility from Day One

- Optional Parameters
  - When adding new inputs to a method, make them *optional* and provide sensible defaults so existing clients aren't forced to change.
- Non-Breaking Response Enhancements
  - Only ever append new fields to the JSON-RPC result object; avoid renaming or removing existing fields.

B. Manifest-Driven Versioning

- Parallel Manifests
  - Host multiple versions of your tool manifest (/manifest/v1, /manifest/v2), each describing the contract for that version.
- Version Negotiation
  - Require clients to declare their supported manifest version in context (e.g., context.clientVersion). The server selects the matching manifest and schema for validation.

C. Compatibility Shims and Adapters

- Shim Layer

- Introduce a compatibility shim that intercepts calls to old method signatures and translates them into the new internal format.

python

```python
if context["clientVersion"] == "1.0":

    # translate v1 args to v2 format

    args = upgrade_args_v1_to_v2(args)

return await internal_v2_method(context, args)
```

- Facade Methods
  - Keep legacy method names around as simple wrappers over the new implementation, emitting a deprecation warning in the response metadata.

D. Schema Evolution Practices

- JSON Schema oneOf

Use oneOf in your parameter schema to accept either the old or the new shape during transition periods:

json

```json
"params": {

  "oneOf": [

    { "$ref": "#/definitions/OldParams" },

    { "$ref": "#/definitions/NewParams" }

  ]

}
```

- Schema Version Tags
  - Tag each schema with a version number so you can trace which schema branch was used to validate a given request in your logs.

E. Deprecation and Sunset Policies

- Embedded Deprecation Metadata
    1. In your manifest, mark deprecated methods with <deprecated>: true and include <sunsetDate> and <replacement> fields.
- Grace Periods
    1. Communicate a clear timeline:
    2. **Announcement** (T – 60 days)
    3. **Grace Period** (T – 0 to T + 90 days)
    4. **Sunset** (after T + 90 days, method is disabled)

F. Automated Compatibility Testing

- Regression Suites
    ○ Maintain a suite of tests against every supported manifest version to ensure that changes don't break existing contracts.
- Contract Tests
    ○ Use tools that generate tests from your JSON-RPC schemas—every time a schema changes, tests fail if clients rely on old behavior.

G. Feature Flags and Gradual Roll-Outs

- Per-Client Flags
    ○ Gate new functionality behind flags keyed by clientId. Flip the flag on for internal or beta clients first.
- Canary Clients
    ○ Route a small percentage of real traffic (by IP or client ID) to the new code path, monitor metrics, then widen the roll-out.

H. Monitoring for Compatibility Drift

- Telemetry on Version Usage
    ○ Track the distribution of context.clientVersion values in your metrics to know when it's safe to retire old code paths.
- Error Alerting

- o Alert on spikes in -32602 Invalid params or -32601 Method not found from specific client versions—likely indicates clients hitting new validations early.

By combining manifest-driven versioning, shims for legacy behavior, clear deprecation policies, and rigorous automated testing, you can evolve your MCP server's capabilities without disrupting existing integrations—future-proofing your system as both client and server needs grow.

9.3.3 Managing Updates and Migrations Without Downtime

Evolving your MCP servers—whether rolling out new features, migrating databases, or refactoring adapters—should not interrupt client workflows. The following patterns enable seamless, zero-downtime updates and migrations.

A. Deployment Strategies

1. Rolling Updates
   - o Use your orchestrator's native rolling-upgrade feature (Kubernetes Deployment with maxSurge and maxUnavailable) to replace pods one at a time, ensuring capacity is never fully drained.
   - o Couple with **readiness probes** so new pods only receive traffic when healthy.
2. Blue/Green Deployments
   - o Maintain two identical environments ("blue" and "green"). Deploy the new version to green, run smoke tests, then switch your load balancer to green in one atomic step.
   - o If issues arise, rollback by flipping back to blue instantly.
3. Canary Releases
   - o Route a small percentage (e.g., 5%) of traffic to new MCP instances via service mesh or weighted load-balancer rules. Monitor metrics closely before scaling up to 100%.
4. Traffic Shadowing
   - o Mirror live traffic to a new version without impacting responses. Use mirrored traffic to validate behavior under real load before exposing the new version.

B. Backward-Compatible Schema and Contract Changes

    1. Non-Breaking Database Migrations
- Perform additive schema changes first (e.g., add new columns with defaults).
- Deploy code that writes to both old and new schema.
- Migrate data in the background.
- Remove legacy columns only after all pods are on the new version.

    2. Dual-Write, Dual-Read Patterns
- During a migration, have the MCP adapter write to both old and new stores, and read preferentially from the new store when available. Once all reads are verified, decommission the old store.

    3. Feature Toggles for New Behavior
- Gate new code paths behind feature flags. Flip flags when you know the new code is stable. Allows turning off problematic features instantly.

C. Stateful Migrations

    1. Zero-Downtime ETL
- For large data migrations (e.g., context-store format changes), run an asynchronous ETL that backfills in small batches while the system remains live.
- Use a version marker in each record; new reads detect both versions and transform on the fly.

    2. Rolling Database Migrations
- In Kubernetes, use **Job** or **CronJob** resources to run migrations independently of the MCP pods.
- Ensure schema changes are backward-compatible (e.g., avoid dropping columns until all code is updated).

D. Graceful Shutdown and Connection Draining

    1. PreStop Hooks
- In Kubernetes, use a preStop hook to remove a pod from the load-balancer and wait (sleep) for in-flight requests to complete before SIGTERM.

    2. Connection Draining

o   Configure your load-balancer to allow existing connections to finish with a timeout window before forcibly closing.

E. Version Negotiation and Compatibility Shims

1.   Side-By-Side Manifests
     o   Serve multiple tool manifests (e.g., /manifest/v1, /manifest/v2) and route clients based on a version header or context field.
     o   Run both versions in parallel until all clients have migrated.
2.   Adapter Shims
     o   Keep legacy adapters active alongside updated ones, using conditional logic (based on context.clientVersion) to invoke the correct implementation.

F. Automated Validation

1.   Pre- and Post-Deploy Smoke Tests
     o   Script critical JSON-RPC calls (ping, key workflows) to run automatically against both old and new versions before traffic is shifted.
2.   Synthetic Monitoring During Rollouts
     o   Increase the frequency of synthetic transactions during deployments to catch regressions immediately.

G. Observability and Rollback Triggers

1.   Real-Time Metrics
     o   Monitor error rates, latency percentiles, and resource utilization on both versions.
2.   Automated Rollback
     o   Configure your deployment tool or service mesh (e.g., Argo Rollouts) to automatically rollback if key metrics exceed thresholds (e.g., error rate > 1%, P95 latency spike).

By combining **incremental deployments**, **backward-compatible migrations**, **feature flags**, and **automated validations**, you can iterate on your MCP servers rapidly and confidently—ensuring uninterrupted service even as your system evolves.

9.4 Interactive Q&A

9.4.1 What Steps Would You Take to Secure Your MCP Implementation?

1. Authentication Strategy
   - Which mechanism will you adopt—API keys, OAuth2/JWT, or mutual TLS—and how will you manage token issuance, rotation, and revocation?
2. Authorization Model
   - Will you use RBAC, ABAC, or scope-based permissions? How will you enforce per-method ACLs in your JSON-RPC dispatcher?
3. Transport Security
   - How will you enforce TLS 1.2+ (and ideally TLS 1.3) on all endpoints, and where will you terminate or pass through mutual TLS for internal service calls?
4. Input Validation
   - Which JSON Schemas will you define for each method's params and result, and how will you reject unexpected or extra fields before business logic runs?
5. Rate Limiting & Throttling
   - What per-client, per-method quotas will you configure to guard against abusive or accidental overload, and how will you surface retry hints to well-behaved clients?
6. Secrets and Configuration
   - Where will you store sensitive credentials (vault, Secrets Manager, Key Vault), how will you inject them securely into your containers, and what is your rotation policy?
7. Network Segmentation
   - How will you isolate your MCP servers—using private subnets, security groups/NSGs, and firewalls—and expose only the necessary ingress via a hardened proxy or load balancer?
8. Logging & Auditing
   - What structured audit logs will you emit for each RPC call (including requestId, userId, method, and outcome), and how will you ensure logs are immutable and monitored for anomalies?
9. Dependency Security

- How will you pin and scan all Python and OS libraries for vulnerabilities (using tools like Trivy or Snyk), and what is your process for applying patches and upgrades?

10. Error Handling & Leak Prevention
    - How will you avoid exposing stack traces or sensitive data in error responses, and what sanitation filters will you apply to redact PII from logs?

11. Health Checks & Incident Response
    - Which security-focused health probes (e.g., authentication failures, high 403 rates) will trigger alerts, which channels will you use, and what runbooks will operators follow?

12. Regular Security Reviews
    - How often will you conduct threat modeling, penetration tests, and privacy impact assessments to adapt your controls to new threats?

Reflect on each of these areas to build a multilayered defense that keeps your MCP servers—and the sensitive AI workflows they support—safe and compliant.

9.4.2 Discussion on Maintaining Server Uptime and Reliability

1. **Service Level Objectives (SLOs) & Error Budgets**
    - What availability target (e.g., 99.9%, 99.99%) will you commit to, and how do you allocate your error budget across features?
    - How do you track SLA compliance over time and correlate outages to specific causes?

2. **Redundancy & Fault Domains**
    - How do you distribute MCP instances across zones or regions to tolerate datacenter failures?
    - What components (load balancer, context store, database) require active-active vs. active-passive setups?

3. **Autoscaling & Capacity Planning**
    - Which metrics (CPU, memory, custom RPC latency) drive your horizontal autoscaling policies?
    - How do you ensure you have headroom for traffic spikes without overprovisioning?

4. **Health Probes & Connection Draining**
    - How are your liveness, readiness, and startup probes configured to detect unhealthy pods without false positives?
    - What process ensures in-flight requests are drained gracefully before a pod is terminated?

5. **Circuit Breakers & Bulkheads**

- How do you partition critical adapters or downstream calls into isolated pools to prevent a failure in one component from cascading?
- Which thresholds trigger a circuit breaker, and how do you handle fallback logic?

6. **Automated Recovery & Self-Healing**
   - What automation (e.g., Kubernetes restarts, cluster auto-recovery, process supervisors) is in place to restore failed instances?
   - How do you detect "crash loops" or repeated readiness failures and escalate for manual intervention?

7. **Observability & Alerting**
   - Which key metrics and logs are essential for early detection of performance degradation or resource starvation?
   - How do you configure alert thresholds and routing (Slack, PagerDuty) to minimize noise and ensure actionable incidents?

8. **Disaster Recovery & Backups**
   - What is your RTO/RPO for critical state (context store, database), and how frequently do you test restores?
   - Do you maintain warm standbys or cold backups in a separate region?

9. **Maintenance Windows & Change Management**
   - How do you schedule routine maintenance (patches, migrations) to minimize impact, and how are stakeholders notified?
   - What rollback mechanisms exist if an update introduces instability?

10. **Chaos Engineering & Resilience Testing**
    - How often do you inject failures (pod kills, network partitions, latency spikes) to validate your failover paths and autoscaling?
    - What have been your biggest learnings from these resilience drills?

Reflecting on these points will help you build and operate an MCP infrastructure that remains available, performant, and resilient—even under unexpected failure scenarios.

Chapter 10: The Future of MCP and AI Systems

10.1 Emerging Trends in MCP and AI Development

10.1.1 The Future of Context-Aware Systems in AI

As AI continues its rapid evolution, context-awareness will shift from a nice-to-have feature into a core pillar of intelligent systems. Here are key directions shaping the next generation of context-aware AI:

A. Persistent, Multi-Scale Memory

- **Long-Term Context Stores**: Systems will maintain both short-lived session context (current conversation or task) and longer-term user or system histories—spanning days, weeks, or months. This layered memory will enable truly personalized experiences that evolve over time, from adaptive tutoring systems to health monitoring agents that learn a patient's rhythms.
- **Hierarchical Context Models**: AI agents will manage context at multiple granularities—momentary sensor readings, episodic event logs, and overarching project or life-goal frameworks—allowing them to shift seamlessly between immediate actions and strategic planning.

B. Federated and Privacy-Preserving Context Sharing

- **Edge-First Context Processing**: With privacy concerns paramount, context evaluation will increasingly occur on-device or at the network edge, passing only distilled insights or anonymized embeddings to centralized servers. This hybrid approach balances the need for rich context with regulatory and ethical constraints.
- **Federated Learning of Context Patterns**: Devices and clients will collectively learn abstracted context-patterns (e.g., typical activity sequences or anomaly signatures) without sharing raw personal data, enabling AI services to generalize insights while preserving user privacy.

C. Real-Time, Multi-Modal Context Fusion

- **Converging Sensor Streams**: Future AI systems will ingest tightly synchronized audio, video, text, physiological, and environmental sensor feeds, fusing them into a coherent context model. For example, a mobile AI assistant might combine gait analysis, voice tone, calendar events, and location data to proactively suggest contextually relevant actions.

- **Dynamic Context Weighting**: Advances in continual learning will allow AI agents to automatically weigh different context channels—giving more credence to the most predictive modalities in a given scenario, such as favoring visual cues in a driving safety system or physiological signals in a health alert.

D. Intent-Driven and Goal-Oriented Context Frameworks

- **Declarative Intent Layers**: Rather than hard-coding workflows, systems will accept high-level intents ("plan my travel," "optimize energy usage"), then dynamically assemble context-aware pipelines by discovering and composing tools at runtime.
- **Adaptive Goal Management**: AI agents will negotiate objectives—prioritizing, deferring, or delegating sub-goals based on evolving context and resource constraints, enabling more resilient and flexible autonomous workflows.

E. Standardization and Interoperability

- **Evolving Protocols**: As context-awareness becomes ubiquitous, standards like MCP will evolve to accommodate richer data types—graph structures, temporal logic, and semantic ontologies—enabling seamless handoffs between disparate AI services and platforms.
- **Context Manifests and Discovery**: Future manifests will include machine-readable capabilities regarding supported context domains (e.g., "temporal reasoning," "emotion detection"), allowing clients to negotiate context richness and quality of service dynamically.

F. Challenges and Research Frontiers

- **Context Drift and Consistency**: Maintaining coherent context as environments change—sensor failures, user behavior shifts, or concept drift—will demand robust versioning, reconciliation, and uncertainty modeling.
- **Scalable Context Storage**: Balancing the performance of real-time context lookups with the cost of storing vast histories will drive innovations in

hierarchical caches, summarization algorithms, and hybrid in-memory/distributed stores.

By integrating these trends—persistent multi-scale memory, federated privacy-preserving processing, real-time multi-modal fusion, intent-driven frameworks, and evolving interoperability standards—context-aware AI systems will advance from reactive assistants to proactive, adaptive partners that understand not just what we say, but why and how it fits into our larger goals and environments.

10.1.2 Trends in Protocol Development and Open Standards

As context-aware AI systems proliferate, the protocols that glue together models, tools, and data sources are evolving rapidly. Key trends and emerging standards include:

A. Convergence on Declarative API Specifications

- OpenAPI for RPC
  - While OpenAPI has long focused on REST, extensions and community drivers (e.g., OpenRPC) are adapting its schema-first style to JSON-RPC and other RPC frameworks.
  - Tool manifests can be published in OpenAPI/OpenRPC format, driving automatic client generation, documentation, and validation.
- JSON Schema 2020-12 Adoption
  - The newest JSON Schema draft brings unevaluatedProperties, $defs, and rich conditional validation—ideal for versioned RPC payloads and strict contract enforcement in MCP adapters.

B. Movement Toward Binary and HTTP/2-Based Protocols

- gRPC and Protobuf
  - High-performance environments are shifting from text-based JSON-RPC to gRPC over HTTP/2 with Protobuf-defined services.
  - Emerging tool chains generate both JSON-RPC and gRPC interfaces from a shared interface definition, letting you choose human-readable or low-latency transports.

- WASM and CBOR
  - In constrained or edge deployments, compact binary formats (CBOR) and WebAssembly-embedded context processors promise smaller footprints and faster parse times.

C. Event-Driven and Streaming Standards

- AsyncAPI
  - AsyncAPI formalizes event-stream definitions (Kafka, MQTT, WebSockets) in a way analogous to OpenAPI for HTTP; it's increasingly used to describe MCP notification and streaming adapters.
  - Tool manifests may include both RPC and AsyncAPI sections, giving clients a unified interface for request-response and pub/sub patterns.
- W3C Web of Things (WoT)
  - The WoT Thing Description spec provides a standardized way to describe device capabilities and data models; mapping these to MCP tool definitions enables plug-and-play IoT integration.

D. Standardized Function-Calling and Plugin Protocols

- LLM Plugin Manifests
  - Formats pioneered by the OpenAI Plugin spec—self-describing JSON manifests that declare endpoints, authentication, and parameters—are converging on a generalized "function-calling" approach across LLM platforms.
  - MCP servers are beginning to publish plugin-style manifests, allowing LLMs to autodiscover and invoke context-aware tools seamlessly.
- OAuth2 and OpenID Connect Integration
  - Embedding authorization metadata directly into protocol manifests (e.g., supported OAuth2 flows, token request URLs) ensures that tool discovery and secure invocation happen in a single handshake.

E. Semantic and Linked-Data Extensions

- JSON-LD and Hydra
  - For domains requiring semantic interoperability (healthcare, finance), JSON-LD enables annotation of RPC payloads with linked-data contexts, and Hydra provides hypermedia controls for discoverable APIs.
  - MCP manifests may include JSON-LD contexts to describe the meaning of parameters, aiding cross-system integration and regulatory compliance.

F. Community-Driven Governance and Interop

- OpenRPC Initiative
  - The OpenRPC community is building tooling and best practices around JSON-RPC 2.0, including manifest validation, SDK generation, and a public registry of RPC specifications.
- W3C and IETF Working Groups
  - Broader web standards bodies are considering profiles for real-time data APIs, schema evolution, and OAuth profiles for machine-to-machine interactions—areas directly relevant to the future of MCP.

By embracing these converging trends—declarative specifications, high-performance transports, unified event/RPC descriptions, standardized plugin manifests, and semantic annotations—MCP and its successor protocols will become more interoperable, secure, and capable of powering the next generation of context-aware AI ecosystems.

10.1.3 Predictions for the Integration of MCP with Next-Gen AI Technologies

1. Native LLM Function-Calling and Tool Synthesis
   - Future large language models will come with built-in support for JSON-RPC-style "function calls." MCP manifests will be discoverable by LLMs at runtime, enabling dynamic synthesis of adapter invocations (e.g., selecting which data sources or analytic tools to call based on the user's query).
   - LLMs will generate and refine MCP workflows autonomously—gluing together available tools into ad-hoc pipelines without hand-coded orchestration.
2. Tighter Memory and Knowledge Graph Integration
   - Context stores will evolve into full graph-based memory backends, with adapters exposing Knowledge Graph query primitives (queryKG, updateKG) alongside traditional JSON-RPC methods. AI agents will traverse and augment knowledge graphs in real time, enabling explainable, multi-hop reasoning across diverse data domains.
3. On-Device and Edge-Native MCP Runtimes
   - Lightweight MCP server implementations compiled to WebAssembly (WASM) will run directly on edge devices—smartphones, IoT gateways, or even browsers—allowing low-latency, privacy-preserving context handling and model invocations without a round-trip to the cloud.

4. Self-Optimizing Pipelines via Reinforcement Learning
   - MCP workflows will be instrumented for continuous performance feedback. Reinforcement Learning controllers will tune adapter selection, batching strategies, and rate limits automatically—optimizing for latency, cost, or accuracy objectives based on historical telemetry.
5. Neuro-Symbolic and Hybrid AI Workflows
   - Adapters will not only wrap conventional services but also hybrid AI components—combining neural LLMs with symbolic solvers, constraint engines, or domain-specific rule systems. MCP call graphs will interleave probabilistic LLM responses with deterministic symbolic computations in a unified execution flow.
6. AutoML and Model-Driven Adapter Generation
   - Given a high-level specification (e.g., "classify invoices," "forecast demand"), AutoML systems will generate both the underlying model and the corresponding MCP adapter code—publishing a new JSON-RPC tool without manual implementation, complete with schema, validation, and monitoring hooks.
7. Secure, Verifiable Compute with Trusted Execution Environments
   - MCP adapters that handle highly sensitive tasks (cryptographic operations, private data analytics) will execute inside hardware-backed enclaves (SGX, TPM). The MCP manifest will include enclave attestation data, allowing clients to verify that calls ran in a trusted context.
8. Composable Agent Architectures and Orchestration Fabrics
   - Projects like AutoGPT and BabyAGI will mature into standardized agent frameworks built on MCP. Agents will declare capabilities (tools they can call) via manifest, spawn sub-agents for parallel exploration, and coordinate through a shared MCP server acting as the "control plane."
9. Blockchain-Anchored Audit Trails and Incentive Layers
   - Critical workflow steps and context mutations will be hashed and recorded on a permissioned blockchain, providing immutable, verifiable audit trails. Adapters may optionally offer token-based incentives or micropayments for third-party data providers, integrated directly into MCP call semantics.
10. Context-Driven Personalization at Planetary Scale
    - By federating MCP servers across edge, cloud, and partner networks, context-aware services will personalize interactions in real time for billions of users—tuning language style, recommendation logic, and privacy levels based on continuous consented feedback loops and global context trends.

Together, these advancements point toward an MCP ecosystem where **AI agents**, **tools**, and **infrastructure** co-evolve—enabling **autonomous**, **explainable**, and **secure** context-aware systems that learn, adapt, and optimize themselves in production, across every scale from edge devices to global data fabrics.

10.2 Innovations in AI and Data Integration
10.2.1 How AI Will Evolve in Terms of Data Integration and Context

1. Unified Data Fabrics with Embedded Context
   - Future AI systems will sit atop "data fabrics" that unify disparate sources—databases, data lakes, streaming platforms—into a single logical layer. Contextual metadata (lineage, quality scores, timestamp semantics) will be managed alongside the data, allowing models and agents to query not just raw values but richly annotated context ("this sensor reading was taken under heavy rain at 3 m altitude").
2. Semantic Data Integration via Knowledge Graphs
   - AI-driven integration will increasingly leverage knowledge graphs to encode relationships between entities, domains, and processes. Rather than brittle point-to-point connectors, adapters will map data into a shared graph model, enabling semantic joins (e.g., linking customer profiles to purchase histories and support interactions) and simplifying downstream context assembly.
3. Self-Service, AI-Powered ETL Pipelines
   - Low-code/no-code platforms will embed AI agents that can auto-discover schema patterns, infer transformations, and generate integration workflows on the fly. A data steward might simply ask, "Combine last quarter's sales with marketing spend by region," and the system will synthesize the necessary MCP adapters and pipelines.
4. Real-Time Context Enrichment and Event-Driven Flows
   - As event streaming platforms mature, AI models will process and enrich context in motion: filtering, aggregating, and embedding live data—then making that enriched context available to downstream tools via standardized JSON-RPC streams. This "context MES" (Manufacturing Execution System) approach will power everything from predictive maintenance to live personalization.
5. Federated and Privacy-Preserving Integration
   - With privacy regulations proliferating, AI systems will adopt federated integration patterns: local context preprocessing at the edge or in customer-owned enclaves, sharing only aggregated or de-identified insights to the central fabric. Differential privacy and homomorphic

encryption will ensure that rich context can be leveraged without exposing raw PII.

6. Automated Schema Evolution and Resilience
   o AI will monitor integration pipelines for schema drift—new fields, deprecated formats, missing values—and automatically adjust adapters or alert engineers. Versioned context snapshots and schema registries will allow seamless incremental upgrades, maintaining compatibility while evolving data contracts.

7. Context-Aware Knowledge Discovery
   o Beyond simple data delivery, integrated AI will surface contextual insights—anomalies, trends, causal links—directly to users or automated workflows. For instance, a context-aware dashboard might highlight that a spike in customer support calls correlates with a recent UI change, based on integrated logs, telemetry, and sentiment analysis.

8. Composable, On-Demand Data Services
   o Data sources and context enrichers will be exposed as composable MCP tools. AI agents will synthesize end-to-end workflows—combining real-time feeds, batch pulls, and model inferences—into ad-hoc "data functions" that can be invoked on demand, unlocking dynamic, context-driven applications without manual pipeline coding.

By weaving these capabilities together, the next generation of AI systems will treat data and context not as static inputs, but as first-class, evolving assets—automatically integrated, semantically rich, and orchestrated in real time to power deeply intelligent, context-aware applications.

10.2.2 The Role of MCP in Integrating with Machine Learning Models and Deep Learning Frameworks

Model Context Protocol (MCP) provides a structured, context-aware bridge between AI orchestration layers and the diverse landscape of machine learning (ML) and deep learning (DL) systems. Here's how MCP streamlines and strengthens these integrations:

A. Unified Inference Interface

- Adapter Wrappers for Model Serving
  o Each model (TensorFlow SavedModel, PyTorch TorchScript, ONNX runtime, etc.) is exposed as an MCP "tool" implementing a standard JSON-RPC method (e.g., runModelInference).

- Clients need only invoke mcp.call("runModelInference", context, { "modelName": ..., "inputs": ... }) regardless of underlying serving technology.
- Parameter and Metadata Passing
  - The context object carries user/session metadata (e.g., userId, traceId, performance SLAs), while argsconvey model inputs.
  - Adapters enrich context with model-specific metadata—version, batch size, GPU device—so downstream logging and auditing capture full inference provenance.

B. Batch vs. Streaming Inference

- Synchronous (Batch) Calls
  - For tasks like image classification or tabular predictions, clients use standard RPC calls. MCP adapters handle input serialization (e.g., base64 images) and output deserialization (e.g., label probabilities), abstracting away REST vs. gRPC serving endpoints.
- Asynchronous Streaming
  - For real-time video analytics or audio processing, MCP supports JSON-RPC notifications and streaming partial results.
  - An adapter might implement streamInferenceResults that yields inference outputs frame by frame, ideal for low-latency DL pipelines.

C. Contextual Pre- and Post-Processing

- Pre-Inference Pipelines
  - Common preprocessing steps (normalization, tokenization, feature engineering) are factored into separate MCP tools (preprocessText, normalizeImage), allowing reuse across models and ensuring consistency.
- Post-Inference Actions
  - After inference, adapters can chain follow-on actions—thresholding, result filtering, logging to a metrics store, or calling downstream tools (e.g., storePrediction, triggerAlert)—all within the same MCP call graph.

D. Model Lifecycle Management

- Dynamic Model Discovery
  - By calling listModels or listMethods, clients discover which models are currently deployed and their versions. This enables runtime selection of the best-performing model for a given context.
- Hot-Swap and Blue/Green Serving

- MCP manifests can declare multiple versions of a model; feature flags in context route calls to "v2" vs. "v1" implementations, supporting canary rollouts and instant rollback without touching client code.

E. Performance and Resource Optimization

- Batching Requests
  - MCP adapters can internally batch multiple JSON-RPC calls arriving within a short window into a single model inference call—reducing overhead and improving GPU utilization.
- Hardware Affinity and Auto-Scaling
  - Context flags (e.g., "useGPU": true) guide adapters to route heavy DL workloads to GPU-enabled inference clusters, while lighter models remain on CPU nodes.
  - Metrics exported by adapters (latency histograms, throughput counters) feed into autoscaling policies to spin up more GPU pods under load.

F. Monitoring, Explainability, and Auditing

- Per-Inference Metrics
  - Each adapter emits standardized metrics—batch size, execution time, memory usage—for Prometheus/Grafana dashboards, enabling deep performance analysis across models.
- Explainability Hooks
  - For interpretable AI, adapters expose additional methods (getFeatureAttributions, explainPrediction) that clients can call with the same JSON-RPC interface, integrating LIME, SHAP, or attention-map generators into pipelines.
- Immutable Audit Trails
  - By logging every inference invocation—inputs (hashed for privacy), model version, outputs, and associated context—you build a full audit trail critical for regulated domains (finance, healthcare).

G. Integration with ML Platforms

- MLFlow, Kubeflow, Sagemaker
  - MCP adapters wrap platform-specific SDKs or REST APIs, providing a uniform RPC interface. Whether retrieving model artifacts from MLFlow's registry or invoking an Amazon SageMaker endpoint, the calling pattern remains the same.
- Custom Training and Serving

- Beyond inference, MCP can orchestrate training workflows via methods like startTrainingJob, getTrainingStatus, and fetchModelMetrics, embedding end-to-end model lifecycle into the MCP ecosystem.

By abstracting away the heterogeneity of ML/DL frameworks and embedding rich context propagation, batching, monitoring, and lifecycle controls, MCP becomes the **de facto integration layer** for AI-driven pipelines—enabling teams to mix and match models, optimize resource use, and maintain governance without bespoke glue code.

10.3 Closing Thoughts: Continuous Learning and Contributions

10.3.1 How to Stay Up-to-Date with Developments in MCP

1. Watch the Official Repositories and Releases
   - **GitHub**: ⋆ Star and "Watch" the MCP and related adapter project repos to get notifications on new releases, issues, and pull requests.
   - **Release Notes**: Read each new release's changelog to catch breaking changes, deprecations, and new features.
2. Subscribe to Community Channels
   - **Mailing Lists / Forums**: Join any MCP or OpenRPC mailing lists or discussion forums to see RFCs, design proposals, and peer questions.
   - **Slack / Discord**: Participate in relevant channels (e.g., OpenRPC Slack, LLM-developer Discords) where maintainers and users share best practices and announce updates.
3. Follow Specification and Ecosystem Working Groups
   - Keep an eye on **OpenRPC** or JSON-RPC working group repos/issue trackers to learn about emerging protocol enhancements, JSON Schema versions, and interoperability guidelines.
4. Read Blogs, Newsletters, and Thought-Leader Posts
   - Subscribe to newsletters like **API Specification Weekly, AI Infrastructure Digest**, or **OpenAPI Weekly**for curated updates.
   - Follow blog posts and technical deep dives from companies building on MCP (OpenAI, major AI tooling vendors).
5. Attend Conferences and Meetups
   - Look for sessions at **API Days, KubeCon/CloudNativeCon, AI and ML Conferences**, and **JSON Schema or OpenAPI Summits** where MCP-style integration patterns are discussed.
   - Join local or virtual **developer meetups** to hear case studies and live demos.
6. Track Standards and Related Protocols

- Monitor progress in adjacent standards—**OpenRPC**, **AsyncAPI**, **JSON Schema**—since advances there often feed into MCP's evolution.
- Review draft proposals on the W3C or IETF mailing lists for real-time data APIs and RPC extensions.

7. Engage in Hands-On Projects and Hackathons
   - Build side projects or contribute to open-source adapters; real-world experimentation surfaces gaps and inspires feature requests.
   - Participate in hackathons focused on LLM plugins or API integration— often the birthplace of novel MCP use cases.

8. Subscribe to Academic and Industry Research
   - Keep an eye on arXiv, O'Reilly reports, and industry whitepapers exploring context-aware AI, model orchestration, and hybrid tool-LLM systems— these often drive new protocol requirements.

9. Set Up Alerts and Dashboards
   - Create GitHub "Topic" or RSS alerts for keywords like #MCP, #ModelContextProtocol, #JSONRPC to surface blog posts, talks, and issue discussions.
   - Maintain a simple dashboard of relevant repos, specification sites, and conference agendas to review periodically.

By combining proactive watching of code and spec repos, active participation in community forums and events, and ongoing hands-on experimentation, you'll ensure you're at the forefront of MCP advancements and best practices.

10.3.2 Contributing to the MCP Ecosystem and Community

Becoming an active participant in the MCP community not only accelerates your own learning but helps grow the protocol, tooling, and best-practices that everyone relies on. Here are concrete ways you can make valuable contributions:

A. Participate in Specification and Design

- Issue Reporting & Feature Requests
  - Open clear, well-scoped issues on the MCP (or OpenRPC) GitHub repos when you encounter bugs, inconsistencies, or missing capabilities.
  - Provide minimal repro steps or sample payloads to help maintainers diagnose problems quickly.
- RFCs and Design Proposals
  - Draft a short proposal (Markdown) for new protocol features, versioning strategies, or schema enhancements.

- Engage in review discussions—offer constructive feedback, cite real-world use cases, and iterate on proposals with the community.
- Schema Contributions
  - Submit additions or corrections to the official JSON Schema definitions for MCP manifests and method payloads.
  - Help migrate examples to the latest JSON Schema draft, ensuring broad interoperability.

B. Build and Share Adapters, Tools, and SDKs

- Open-Source Adapters
  - Contribute adapters for popular services (e.g., Databricks, Salesforce, custom IoT platforms) by wrapping their APIs behind MCP-compatible JSON-RPC methods.
  - Host your adapter on GitHub with clear README, manifest snippet, and quickstart examples.
- CLI and Developer Tooling
  - Create or extend CLI utilities (e.g., mcpctl) to generate new tool templates, validate manifests, or spin up local dev servers.
  - Publish your tools on npm/PyPI so others can install them easily.
- SDK Generators and Samples
  - Contribute to or build SDK generators that turn MCP manifests into strongly-typed client libraries (TypeScript, Python, Go).
  - Provide sample applications illustrating common patterns—batch calls, streaming adapters, context enrichment pipelines.

C. Enhance Documentation and Learning Resources

- Tutorials and Cookbooks
  - Write step-by-step guides on topics like "Building Your First MCP Adapter," "Automating Deployments with Docker," or "Securing Your MCP Server."
  - Package these as blog posts, GitHub Pages sites, or MDX-powered doc sections in the main repo.
- Interactive Examples
  - Publish minimal example projects (with Docker Compose) that newcomers can clone and run in seconds—showcasing core features like tool discovery, JSON-RPC batching, and streaming.
- Webinars and Workshops
  - Offer short screencasts or live coding sessions to walk through setup, deployment, or advanced scenarios (e.g., canary releases, feature flags).

- Collaborate with community meetups or conferences to deliver hands-on workshops.

D. Engage in Community Support and Mentorship

- Forum and Chat Participation
  - Answer questions on community forums (OpenRPC Discussions, StackOverflow) and real-time channels (Slack, Discord).
  - Share your lessons learned and troubleshoot newcomers' integration challenges.
- Code Reviews and Pair-Programming
  - Volunteer to review PRs in the MCP repos—help improve test coverage, ensure consistent style, and validate edge cases.
  - Mentor new contributors via pair-programming sessions, guiding them through your first contributions.

E. Advocate and Evangelize

- Case Studies and Conference Talks
  - Present your real-world MCP implementations—smart city, healthcare AI, robotics integration—at user group meetings or industry events.
  - Highlight how context-awareness and protocol discipline improved your system's resilience and agility.
- Cross-Project Collaboration
  - Work with adjacent communities (OpenAI Plugin authors, AsyncAPI contributors, OpenAPI spec leads) to align best practices, share schema extensions, and ensure interoperability across ecosystems.

F. Sustain and Grow the Community

- Organize Meetups and Hackathons
  - Host virtual or in-person events where practitioners can demo their MCP projects, discuss patterns, and collaboratively solve common challenges.
- Stewardship and Governance
  - Step into maintainer or reviewer roles—help shape roadmaps, prioritize issues, and ensure the project's long-term health.

By investing your time—whether through code, documentation, mentorship, or advocacy—you'll help the MCP ecosystem mature into a vibrant, diverse community. Your contributions will not only refine the protocol itself but also lower the barrier for others to build cutting-edge, context-aware AI systems.

Official Specifications & Repositories

- MCP / OpenRPC GitHub: The canonical source for the Model Context Protocol and related tooling. Watch for new releases, issue discussions, and community PRs.
  https://www.open-rpc.org
- **JSON-RPC 2.0 Spec**: Foundation for RPC semantics—essential for understanding request/response patterns and error codes.
  https://www.jsonrpc.org/specification
- API & Protocol Standards
  - **OpenRPC**: A schema-first approach to JSON-RPC, with tooling for manifest validation and SDK generation.
    https://www.open-rpc.org
  - **AsyncAPI**: Standard for describing event-driven, streaming interfaces; complements MCP's notification and streaming patterns.
    https://www.asyncapi.com
- Books & Publications
  - **"Designing APIs with Swagger and OpenAPI"** (O'Reilly) by Joshua S. Ponelat & Lukas Rosenstock—while focused on REST, its principles apply to RPC design and versioning.
  - **"Building Event-Driven Microservices"** (O'Reilly) by Adam Bellemare—for deep dives on streaming, back-pressure, and event-based architectures.
  - **"Fundamentals of Stream Processing"** by Chris Riccomini & Michael Noll—covers high-throughput, low-latency data pipelines that MCP streaming adapters can leverage.
- Online Courses & Tutorials
  - **"API Design and Fundamentals of Google Cloud's Apigee API Platform"** (Coursera) — covers API design, versioning, and security patterns.
  - **"gRPC: Up and Running"** (Pluralsight) — if you're exploring high-performance RPC transports alongside JSON-RPC.
  - **"Kafka Streams and ksqlDB"** (Confluent) — for real-time context pipelines complementary to MCP notifications.
- Newsletters & Blogs
  - **API Specification Weekly** (by Kin Lane) — curated digest of API-related tooling and standards news.
  - **ProgrammableWeb** — frequent articles on API trends, protocol developments, and case studies.

- - **CNCF Newsletter** — for updates on cloud-native frameworks, service meshes (Envoy, Istio) that often integrate with MCP services.
- Community Forums & Chat
  - **OpenRPC Discussion Forum**: Pose questions about MCP tooling, manifest design, or error-handling best practices. https://github.com/open-rpc/open-rpc/discussions
  - **#api-specifications Slack** (via the API Evangelist community) — real-time chat with spec authors, early adopters, and tool maintainers.
  - **Stack Overflow** (tag: [json-rpc]) — for troubleshooting adapter implementations and client-side usage.
- Conferences & Meetups
  - **API Days** (global) — sessions on API design, security, and governance; often feature workshops on OpenRPC and related specs.
  - **KubeCon + CloudNativeCon** — see talks on service meshes, distributed tracing, and micro-gateway patterns that underpin MCP deployments.
  - **Data Streaming & Real-Time Analytics Summits** — practical strategies for integrating MCP streams in analytics pipelines.
- Research & Whitepapers
  - **arXiv preprints** on "contextual AI" and "knowledge graph integration" — to stay abreast of academic advances in multi-modal context modeling.
  - **O'Reilly Radar** — periodic reports on emerging AI and data-integration technologies (e.g., federated learning, edge AI).
- Hands-On Labs & Sandboxes
  - **Postman Workspaces** for OpenRPC: interactive playgrounds to experiment with JSON-RPC manifests and mocks.
  - **Katacoda / Play with Kubernetes**: spin up ephemeral clusters to test MCP deployments, service meshes, and blue/green rollouts in your browser.

By regularly engaging with these resources—specifications, books, courses, communities, and hands-on labs—you'll deepen your mastery of MCP, JSON-RPC, and the broader ecosystem of context-aware AI and protocol development.

10.4 Interactive Q&A

10.4.1 Discussion on Future Advancements in MCP and AI

1. Autonomous Workflow Synthesis

- How might LLMs automatically generate and optimize MCP call graphs at runtime, selecting the best combination of tools based on high-level user intents?

2. Edge-Native Context Processing
   - What challenges and opportunities arise when running MCP adapters and lightweight JSON-RPC servers on IoT devices or mobile phones for ultra-low-latency context handling?

3. Federated and Privacy-First Context Sharing
   - How can MCP evolve to support federated queries—where raw data stays on-device or in customer-owned enclaves and only aggregated insights are shared?

4. Dynamic Schema and Contract Evolution
   - In an environment of rapidly advancing AI components, how should MCP tool manifests handle on-the-fly schema changes—perhaps via runtime schema negotiation or AI-assisted migrations?

5. Adaptive Performance Tuning
   - Could reinforcement-learning controllers tune batching strategies, rate limits, and adapter selection dynamically, optimizing for cost, latency, or accuracy based on live telemetry?

6. Neuro-Symbolic and Hybrid AI Integration
   - As symbolic solvers and neural models converge, how might MCP orchestrate pipelines that blend deterministic logic with probabilistic LLM outputs for explainable reasoning?

7. Blockchain and Verifiable Audit Trails
   - What are the use cases and implications of anchoring critical MCP context mutations or inference results on a distributed ledger for immutability and compliance?

8. Standards Unification and Interop
   - With JSON-RPC, gRPC, OpenAPI, and AsyncAPI all evolving, how could MCP serve as a nexus—bridging these protocols into a cohesive, multi-transport specification?

9. AutoML-Driven Adapter Generation
   - How soon might we see tools that, given a dataset or API definition, automatically generate both the ML model and its corresponding MCP adapter, complete with schemas and tests?

10. Explainability and Human-Agent Collaboration
    - As AI systems take on more autonomous tasks, how will MCP integrate explainability tools (SHAP, LIME, attention maps) so that every decision can be audited and understood by humans?

11. Resilience Through Chaos and Self-Healing
    ○ How can MCP servers incorporate chaos-engineering principles—automatically detecting, isolating, and recovering from failures without human intervention?
12. Multi-Agent Coordination
    ○ In scenarios where multiple AI agents collaborate, how might MCP evolve to coordinate complex multi-agent workflows, negotiate shared context, and resolve conflicting actions?

Reflect on these questions to envision how MCP and AI will co-evolve—driving more autonomous, adaptive, and trustworthy context-aware systems.

10.4.2 What excites you most about the potential of MCP in the coming years?
What excites me most about MCP's trajectory is how it transforms the way we architect, extend, and operationalize AI systems—making them more flexible, adaptive, and future-proof. A few highlights:

1. **LLM-Driven Workflow Synthesis**
   Imagine an LLM that, given a high-level goal, can introspect the MCP manifest, discover the right tools, and dynamically assemble a call graph—automatically wiring together data fetchers, pre-/post-processors, and inference models into a cohesive pipeline.

2. **Edge-Native Context Servers**
   Running lightweight MCP runtimes on IoT devices or mobile platforms to handle real-time sensor fusion, on-device inference, and privacy-first context enrichment without a round-trip to the cloud—unlocking ultra-low-latency applications in AR, robotics, and beyond.

3. **Federated, Privacy-Preserving Context Sharing**
   As regulations tighten and user expectations grow, MCP will enable hybrid context architectures: sensitive data stays on-device or on-premise, while only distilled insights or embeddings flow upstream. This federated model keeps personal information private yet powers rich, cross-domain AI experiences.

4. **Autonomous Performance Tuning**
   Embedding reinforcement-learning controllers that observe real-world metrics—latency, throughput, cost—and automatically retune batching windows, rate limits, and autoscaling policies, so your MCP servers literally optimize themselves over time.

5. **Neuro-Symbolic Pipelines**
   Bridging probabilistic LLMs with deterministic solvers, rule engines, and

knowledge graphs via MCP calls—so you get the best of both worlds: the flexibility of neural reasoning and the rigor of symbolic logic, orchestrated transparently in one protocol.

6. **Seamless Protocol Interop**

   Converging JSON-RPC, gRPC, OpenAPI, and AsyncAPI under a unified manifest and negotiation layer—letting you choose human-readable JSON or high-performance binary transports without rewriting your integration code.

7. **Immutable, Blockchain-Anchored Audit Trails**

   For regulated industries—finance, healthcare, supply chain—anchoring critical context mutations or inference results on a permissioned ledger, ensuring every decision is verifiable, timestamped, and tamper-proof.

8. **Plugin-First AI Ecosystems**

   Publishing MCP manifests as "plugins" that LLMs and agents can auto-discover— so third-party services (data providers, custom analytics, domain-specific models) become drop-in capabilities, dramatically accelerating innovation and lowering integration overhead.

9. **Introspective Self-Healing Servers**

   Enabling chaos-engineering and self-diagnosis built into the MCP core: servers that detect anomalies (e.g., drift in context schemas, cascading errors), automatically roll back problematic adapters, and spin up healthy instances without human intervention.

10. **Planet-Scale, Contextual Personalization**

    Federating MCP clusters across edge, on-prem, and cloud, so billions of users get AI experiences tuned to their locale, device, and long-term preferences—while still benefiting from shared learnings and global context trends.

Together, these advancements will elevate MCP from a powerful integration layer to the very **nervous system** of next-generation AI—where context, tools, and intelligence co-evolve in real time, delivering experiences we haven't yet imagined.

Appendices

A.1 MCP Commands, Formats, and Structures

This quick reference summarizes the core JSON-RPC commands, message envelopes, tool manifest entries, and common patterns you'll use when building or consuming MCP servers.

A.1.1 JSON-RPC Envelope

All MCP calls conform to JSON-RPC 2.0. Every request and response follows this structure:

jsonc

```jsonc
// Request

{

  "jsonrpc": "2.0",

  "id": 42,            // integer or string; echoes in response

  "method": "methodName",

  "params": {

    "context": { ... },    // metadata for auth, tracing, user info

    "args": { ... }        // tool-specific arguments

  }

}


// Successful Response

{
```

```
  "jsonrpc": "2.0",

  "id": 42,

  "result": { ... }          // tool-specific return data

}


// Error Response

{

  "jsonrpc": "2.0",

  "id": 42,              // same id; null if parse error

  "error": {

    "code": -32602,        // see Error Codes below

    "message": "Invalid params",

    "data": { ... }        // optional extra info (retryAfter, schema errors)

  }

}
```

A.1.2 Context Object

The context carries cross-cutting metadata. Common fields:

Field	Type	Description
requestId	string	Unique ID for tracing the call end-to-end

clientVersion	string		Client's supported manifest version for negotiation
userId	string		Authenticated user or service identity
roles	array		List of roles/scopes for authorization checks
locale	string		Locale or timezone hints for adapters
traceId	string		Distributed-trace identifier for observability
custom fields	any		Adapter-specific metadata (e.g., tenantId, zone)

A.1.3 Tool Arguments (args)

Each method defines its own schema for args. Example for a weather fetcher:

jsonc

```jsonc
"args": {

  "location": "London,UK",  // required string

  "units": "metric"        // optional enum ["metric","imperial"]

}
```

Schemas are declared in the manifest (see below) and validated on each request.

A.1.4 Batch Calls

Combine multiple requests into one HTTP POST to reduce overhead:

jsonc

```jsonc
[
  {
    "jsonrpc":"2.0","id":1,"method":"getUser","params":{...}
  },
  {
    "jsonrpc":"2.0","id":2,"method":"fetchWeather","params":{...}
  }
]
```

Response is an array of corresponding results/errors.

A.1.5 Streaming and Notifications

Server-Push Streams: Return a stream(generator()) from your adapter:
python

```python
@method
async def streamSensorData(context, args):
    async def gen(): ...
    return stream(gen())
```

Client subscribes by calling the method; server sends a sequence of JSON-RPC **notifications** (no id):
jsonc

```jsonc
// Notification format

{

  "jsonrpc":"2.0",

  "method":"streamSensorData",

  "params": { "context":..., "args": { ... } },

  "result": { ... }  // each chunk

}
```

A.1.6 Error Codes

Code	Name	Meaning
−32700	Parse error	Invalid JSON
−32600	Invalid Request	Not a valid JSON-RPC request
−32601	Method not found	Unknown method name
−32602	Invalid params	Args don't match schema
−32603	Internal error	JSON-RPC dispatch failure
−32000⋯−32099	Server error	Adapter or infrastructure error

| ≥ 1000 | Application-specific | Custom domain-level codes (e.g., 1001 = rate limit) |

A.1.7 Tool Manifest Snippet

Every MCP server publishes a manifest describing its tools:

yaml

```yaml
manifestVersion: "1.2.0"
info:
  title: "My MCP Server"
  version: "v1.2.0"
tools:
  - name: "fetchWeather"
    version: "1.0.0"
    description: "Retrieve weather forecast"
    paramsSchema:
      type: object
      required: ["location"]
      properties:
        location: { type: "string" }
        units: { type: "string", enum: ["metric","imperial"], default: "metric" }
    resultSchema:
```

```yaml
    type: object

    properties:

      temp: { type: "number" }

      condition: { type: "string" }

    auth:

      requiredScopes: ["weather:read"]

    rateLimit:

      rate: 5      # calls per second

      burst: 10

    deprecated: false
```

Clients fetch this via GET /manifest or listMethods to discover available RPC methods, schemas, and policies.

A.1.8 Authentication and Authorization

- **Bearer Tokens / JWT**: Include Authorization: Bearer <token> header; middleware validates issuer, audience, and signature, then populates context.claims.
- **mTLS**: Clients present a certificate; server verifies CN against allowed identities.
- **API Keys**: Simple header x-api-key: <key> mapped to service accounts/roles.

Enforce per-method scopes/roles inside each adapter or via a global guard.

A.1.9 Transport and Security

- **HTTPS Only**: TLS 1.2+ with strong ciphers; HSTS header.
- **CORS**: Use Access-Control-Allow-Origin headers to restrict browser-based clients.
- **Rate Limiting**: Implement in middleware or API gateway to prevent DoS.

A.1.10 Common Patterns

- **Preprocessing Tools**: preprocessText, normalizeData
- **Composite Workflows**: batch_call([...]) + conditional logic
- **Error Wrapping**: Catch exceptions, map to JsonRpcError(code, message)
- **Context Enrichment**: Tools like fetchUserProfile run at the start of workflows to populate context.

Keep this appendix handy as your go-to reference when designing, debugging, or extending your MCP servers and clients. It ensures consistency in message formats, error handling, and integration patterns—hallmarks of a robust, context-aware AI ecosystem.

A.2 JSON-RPC 2.0 Cheat Sheet

A.2.1 Quick Reference for JSON-RPC Syntax and Usage

1. Core Message Structures

Message Type	Structure

Request	jsonc
	{
	 "jsonrpc": "2.0",
	 "id": 1, // string, number, or null
	 "method": "foo",
	 "params": { ... }
	}

Response	jsonc
	{
	 "jsonrpc": "2.0",
	 "id": 1, // must match the request
	 "result": ... // on success
	}

Error	jsonc
	{
	 "jsonrpc": "2.0",
	 "id": 1, // same as request or null if parse error
	 "error": {
	 "code": -32602,
	 "message": "Invalid params",
	 "data": ... // optional
	}
	}

Notification	Like a Request but **no** "id" field—server must not reply.

| Batch | An array of Requests and/or Notifications. The response is an array of matching Responses. |

2. Parameter Styles

By-Name (Object)
json

"params": { "x": 10, "y": 20 }

By-Position (Array)
json

"params": [10, 20]

- **No params**
  Omit entirely if the method takes no arguments.

3. Standard Error Codes

Code	Name	Meaning
−32700	Parse error	Invalid JSON received.
−32600	Invalid Request	Not a valid JSON-RPC request object.
−32601	Method not found	Requested method does not exist.

−32602	Invalid params	Parameters do not match the method's schema.
−32603	Internal error	Error in JSON-RPC dispatch layer.
−32000...	Server error	Reserved for implementation-defined errors.

Tip: Use custom codes ≥ 1000 for domain-specific errors.

4. Examples

Simple Call
http

POST /rpc HTTP/1.1

Content-Type: application/json

```
{

 "jsonrpc":"2.0",

 "id":42,

 "method":"add",

 "params":[3,7]

}
```

Response:
json

```json
{

 "jsonrpc":"2.0",

 "id":42,

 "result":10

}
```

Named Params
json

```json
{

 "jsonrpc":"2.0",

 "id":"abc",

 "method":"concat",

 "params": { "a":"Hello", "b":"World" }

}
```

Response:
json

```json
{

 "jsonrpc":"2.0",

 "id":"abc",

 "result":"HelloWorld"

}
```

Batch Request
json

```json
[

 { "jsonrpc":"2.0","id":1,"method":"ping" },

 { "jsonrpc":"2.0","id":2,"method":"sum","params":[1,2,3] }

]
```

Batch Response:
json

```json
[

 { "jsonrpc":"2.0","id":1,"result":"pong" },

 { "jsonrpc":"2.0","id":2,"result":6 }

]
```

Notification
json

```json
{

 "jsonrpc":"2.0",

 "method":"logEvent",

 "params": { "event":"user_signup", "userId":"u123" }

}
```

1. (No response is sent.)

5. Best Practices

- Always include `"jsonrpc": "2.0"`.
- Use consistent, meaningful id values and log them for traceability.
- Validate params against a JSON Schema before executing business logic.
- Wrap all exceptions in structured error objects—avoid leaking stack traces.
- Keep batch sizes reasonable to prevent overload.
- Log both request and response (with id) to aid debugging and monitoring.

Reference: JSON-RPC 2.0 Specification — https://www.jsonrpc.org/specification

A.3 GitHub Repository and Project Templates
A.3.1 Code Samples, Starter Templates, and Community Resources

Below is a curated list of GitHub repositories, cookie-cutter templates, and sample projects to jump-start your MCP development. Clone or fork any of these to get working examples of servers, adapters, client SDKs, and deployment setups.

Repository / Template	Description	Link
Official MCP Server Reference	Minimal FastAPI-based MCP server with JSON-RPC dispatch, manifest endpoint, and basic auth middleware.	https://github.com/open-rpc/mcp-server-reference
Python Adapter Example	Demonstrates building an MCP tool adapter for a REST API, including JSON-Schema validation and tests.	https://github.com/open-rpc/mcp-python-adapter-example
TypeScript Client SDK Generator	Generates a typed TS client library from an MCP/OpenRPC manifest,	https://github.com/open-rpc/open-rpc-ts-sdk-generator

	with helper functions and docs.	
Cookiecutter MCP Server	Cookiecutter template for a new MCP server (Python + FastAPI + Uvicorn + Prometheus metrics).	https://github.com/userna me/cookiecutter-mcp-serve r
Yeoman Generator for MCP	Yeoman generator that scaffolds out a Node.js MCP server, adapters, and Dockerfile.	https://github.com/userna me/generator-mcp
Docker Compose Starter	Complete Docker Compose setup for MCP server + Redis + Postgres + MongoDB + proxy.	https://github.com/open-rpc/mcp-docker-compose-s tarter
Kubernetes Helm Chart	Helm chart and Kustomize overlays for deploying MCP in Kubernetes (with HPA, probes, and RBAC).	https://github.com/open-rpc/helm-mcp
AsyncAPI + MCP Streaming	Example of combining AsyncAPI definitions and MCP streaming adapters for MQTT/WebSocket flows.	https://github.com/open-rpc/mcp-asyncapi-streami ng
End-to-End Demo: Smart City	Opinionated reference implementation of the smart-city use case—IoT ingestion, workflows, and UI.	https://github.com/youror g/mcp-smart-city-demo

| Sample LLM Plugin Manifest | Shows how to publish an MCP manifest as an LLM plugin (OpenAI style), complete with auth examples. | https://github.com/open-rpc/mcp-plugin-example |

How to Use These Resources

Clone and Inspect
bash

```
git clone https://github.com/open-rpc/mcp-server-reference.git

cd mcp-server-reference
```

Install Dependencies
bash

```
pip install -r requirements.txt
```

or, for Node.js projects:
bash

```
npm install
```

Run Locally
bash

```
uvicorn main:app --reload
```

or with Docker Compose:
bash

```
docker-compose up --build
```

1. **Explore the Manifest**
   Visit http://localhost:8000/manifest (or /openrpc.json) to see available methods, schemas, and metadata.

Generate a Client
bash

```bash
openrpc-cli ts-sdk --input http://localhost:8000/manifest --output ./client-sdk
```

Deploy to Kubernetes
bash

```bash
helm repo add mcp https://open-rpc.github.io/helm-mcp

helm install my-mcp mcp/mcp --namespace production
```

Community and Further Samples

- **OpenRPC Examples**: https://github.com/open-rpc/examples (many JSON-RPC patterns you can adapt to MCP).
- **MCP Topic on GitHub**: Browse repos tagged topic:mcp-protocol to discover community projects.
- **Awesome MCP** (Community-Maintained List): https://github.com/yourorg/awesome-mcp

Use these templates and examples as a springboard—customize them for your language, framework, or cloud environment, and contribute back any improvements to help grow the MCP ecosystem.

A.4 Glossary of Key Terms
A.4.1 Definitions of Important Terms Related to MCP and AI Systems

Term	Definition

Adapter	A modular component that "wraps" an external service, API, or data source—exposing it as a JSON-RPC method in the MCP server. Adapters handle serialization, authentication, retries, and error mapping.
AI Agent	An autonomous or semi-autonomous software entity that perceives context, formulates goals, and invokes tools (via MCP) to accomplish tasks—often powered by LLMs or rule engines.
Asynchronous I/O (Async)	Non-blocking execution model where I/O operations (HTTP, database, file) yield control until data is ready. Enables high concurrency in MCP servers using single-threaded event loops (e.g., Python's asyncio).
Batch Call	A single JSON-RPC request containing an array of multiple calls—reducing HTTP overhead by sending/receiving many requests in one payload.
Circuit Breaker	A resilience pattern that "opens" to block calls to a failing adapter after a threshold of errors—preventing downstream overload and allowing recovery before retrying.
Client Version	The version(s) of the MCP manifest that a client supports, declared in the context for protocol negotiation and backward-compatibility handling.

Context	A JSON object carrying metadata (user ID, requestId, locale, roles, trace ID) alongside each MCP call—used for auth, routing, auditing, and personalized behavior.
Context Store	A persistent or in-memory database (Redis, database, file) that holds the latest or historical context snapshots—enabling stateful interactions across multiple calls.
Deployment	The process of packaging (Docker images), configuring (Kubernetes/Compose), and releasing MCP servers and adapters into runtime environments (cloud or on-premise).
Error Code	A numeric identifier in a JSON-RPC error object (e.g., −32602 for "Invalid params"), standardized by the JSON-RPC spec and extended for application-specific errors (codes ≥ 1000).
JSON-RPC	A lightweight, transport-agnostic remote procedure call protocol over JSON. Defines message envelopes (jsonrpc, id, method, params, result/error) and standard error codes.
Knowledge Graph	A graph-structured database representing entities and their relationships. MCP adapters may expose graph queries or update methods, enabling semantic context integration.

Latency	The time between sending a JSON-RPC request and receiving its response—often measured at P50, P95, or P99 percentiles to gauge typical and tail-latency performance.
LLM (Large Language Model)	Deep neural networks trained on vast text corpora (e.g., GPT-4) that can generate, interpret, and transform language. Integrated via MCP adapters into broader AI workflows.
Manifest	A machine-readable document (JSON or YAML) published by an MCP server, listing available methods, schemas, auth requirements, rate limits, and version information.
Microservices	Independent, loosely coupled services (e.g., adapters, context store, orchestration engine) that communicate via protocols like JSON-RPC—enabling modular, scalable AI architectures.
Model Context Protocol (MCP)	A standardized JSON-RPC–based protocol and tooling to build context-aware AI systems, defining how clients discover, invoke, and manage tool integrations with rich metadata.
Orchestration	The coordination logic—often in Python, workflows, or LLM-driven code—that invokes MCP methods in sequence or parallel, applies branching, and

aggregates results to fulfill high-level tasks.

Plugin
A self-describing MCP manifest (often in OpenRPC/OpenAI-plugin format) that allows third-party services or tools to be dynamically discovered and invoked by AI agents.

Rate Limiting
Controlling the frequency of MCP method invocations (e.g., token-bucket algorithm) to protect downstream systems and ensure fair usage.

Streaming
A pattern where MCP adapters yield a sequence of partial results as JSON-RPC notifications—used for real-time data feeds (sensor streams, live logs, continuous inference).

Semantic Versioning
A versioning scheme (MAJOR.MINOR.PATCH) applied to MCP manifests and adapters—indicating backward-incompatible changes (MAJOR), backward-compatible additions (MINOR), and bug fixes (PATCH).

Tool
A generic term for any MCP-exposed capability—each method defined in the manifest, implemented by an adapter, and discoverable via listMethods.

Trace ID
A unique identifier propagated through context (and often through distributed

tracing systems) to correlate logs, metrics, and spans for end-to-end observability.

Webhook / Notification	A one-way JSON-RPC message (without id) sent by the MCP server or adapter to inform clients of events—used for callbacks, alerts, or asynchronous notifications.
Workload Isolation	Deploying hot (latency-sensitive) and cold (batch) adapters on separate nodes or pools—preventing heavy tasks from impacting real-time performance.

Use this glossary as a quick lookup for the key concepts, components, and patterns that underpin MCP and context-aware AI systems. It will help ensure shared understanding and consistency across design, development, and operations.

A.5 Troubleshooting Guide
A.5.1 Solutions for Common Issues Encountered While Working with MCP Servers

Issue	Symptoms	Common Causes	Solution
Connection Refused / Timeout	HTTP 502/504, TCP resets, long hangs	Server down, wrong host/port, firewall or network block	1. Verify MCP server is running and listening on configured port. 2. Check REDIS_URL/SQL_DSN env vars. 3. Ensure load-balancer or

			proxy forwards to correct endpoint.
			4. Inspect firewall/security-group rules.
"Method not found" (−32601)	JSON-RPC error code −32601	Typo in method name; adapter not registered; wrong manifest	1. Confirm client is calling exact method name from /manifest.
			2. Ensure adapter's @method decorator matches manifest entry.
			3. Reload server to pick up new adapters.
Invalid params (−32602)	JSON-RPC error −32602, schema validation messages	Payload doesn't conform to JSON Schema	1. Compare request params to the method's paramsSchema in manifest.
			2. Use JSON-Schema validator logs to pinpoint mismatches.
			3. Fix data types, required fields, or remove extra properties.

Authentication / Authorization Errors	401 Unauthorized, 403 Forbidden	Missing/invalid token; insufficient scopes or roles	1. Ensure Authorization: Bearer <token> header is present and valid. 2. Verify token claims include required roles/scopes. 3. Check clock skew for JWT expiry.
High Error Rate on Downstream Calls	Frequent adapter errors (-320xx), cascading failures	Downstream API failures, expired creds, network glitches	1. Inspect adapter logs for HTTP status codes or exception traces. 2. Rotate or refresh credentials stored in vault. 3. Add retry logic with exponential back-off or circuit breakers.
Rate Limit Exceeded (−32029)	JSON-RPC error −32029	Client exceeded token-bucket rate; burst too high	1. Review your rate-limit settings in manifest (rate & burst). 2. Throttle client requests or increase limits if safe for downstream.

			3. Implement client-side back-off using retryAfter hint.
Slow RPC Latencies / Timeouts	P95/P99 latency spikes, 504 Gateway Timeout	Blocking sync calls, cold starts, insufficient workers	1. Convert any blocking I/O to async equivalents (e.g., asyncpg, httpx.AsyncClient). 2. Pre-warm pools and caches on startup. 3. Increase worker count or horizontal scale.
Context Inconsistency	Missing or stale context fields across calls	Improper propagation, clearing of context store, TTL expiry	1. Ensure you always pass the same context object in batch or chained calls. 2. Check Redis TTLs and eviction policies. 3. Log requestId at each step to verify lineage.
Streaming Disconnects or Data Loss	Partial or missing notifications, abrupt stream end	Network interruptions, no keep-alive, client unsubscribed	1. Enable HTTP/WebSocket keep-alive or use a message broker

			(MQTT) for resilience.
			2. Catch and log exceptions in stream generators.
			3. Implement reconnection logic on the client.
Healthcheck Failures	Orchestrator constantly restarting pods	Probe too strict or slow, dependency unavailability	1. Differentiate liveness vs. readiness endpoints.
			2. Simplify readiness check to light queries (PING, SELECT 1).
			3. Adjust initialDelaySeconds and timeouts in probe configs.
Schema Drift in Production	Sudden −32602 errors after third-party API upgrade	Third-party changed response format	1. Lock adapters to specific API versions.
			2. Add schema-migration shim: detect and transform new fields.
			3. Update manifest and notify clients of changes.

Unexpected Crashes (OOM, segfault)	Pod/container restarts, OOMKilled logs	Memory leaks, unbounded caches, large batch sizes	1. Profile memory usage and fix leaks (e.g., large in-memory buffers).
			2. Add resource limits and LRU caches instead of unbounded.
			3. Break large batches into smaller chunks.

Troubleshooting Workflow

1. **Reproduce Locally**: Use Docker Compose or a staging cluster with the same versions and configs.
2. **Enable Verbose Logging**: Temporarily increase log level to DEBUG; include requestId, method, and adapter tracebacks.
3. **Check Metrics**: Examine Prometheus dashboards for spikes in latencies, error counts, or resource exhaustion.
4. **Inspect Dependencies**: Validate health and connectivity of Redis, databases, and external APIs.
5. **Iterate and Test**: Apply one fix at a time, rerun targeted integration tests, and confirm resolution before moving to the next issue.

Keep this guide at hand as you build and operate your MCP servers—resolving issues swiftly and maintaining a reliable, context-aware AI platform.

A.6 Further Reading and Resources
A.6.1 Recommended Books, Courses, and Online Resources for Expanding Knowledge

Books

- *Designing Data-Intensive Applications* by Martin Kleppmann
  Deep dive into reliable, scalable data architectures (message queues, stream processing, storage engines).

- *Building Microservices* by Sam Newman
  Best practices for decomposing systems into independent services, including API design and versioning.
- *Fundamentals of Stream Processing* by Chris Riccomini & Michael Noll
  Covers low-latency, high-throughput pipelines—key for real-time MCP streaming adapters.
- *Architecting for Scale* by Lee Atchison
  Patterns for high availability, resilience, and operational maturity in distributed systems.
- *Deep Learning* by Ian Goodfellow, Yoshua Bengio, Aaron Courville
  Foundational text on neural networks—helps you understand and integrate LLM or model-serving adapters.
- *Machine Learning Engineering* by Andriy Burkov
  Holistic guide to productionizing ML, from data pipelines to monitoring and governance.

Online Courses & Specializations

- **Coursera – Machine Learning Engineering for Production (MLOps)** (Andrew Ng)
  End-to-end ML lifecycle, including model deployment, monitoring, and scaling.
- **edX – Distributed Systems** (MITx or similar)
  Core concepts: consensus, fault tolerance, replication—critical for designing MCP clusters and context stores.
- **Pluralsight – Designing and Building APIs**
  Hands-on API design, security, and versioning workshops applicable to MCP/JSON-RPC interfaces.
- **Confluent Academy – Apache Kafka Streams & ksqlDB**
  Real-time event streaming foundations you can leverage alongside MCP's streaming adapters.
- **Udacity – Cloud DevOps Engineer Nanodegree**
  Covers CI/CD pipelines, container orchestration (Kubernetes), and observability—a perfect complement to MCP deployment chapters.

Online Documentation & Community Resources

- **JSON-RPC 2.0 Specification**
  The authoritative guide to request/response structures and error codes.
- **OpenRPC** (https://www.open-rpc.org)
  Schema-first tooling, manifest formats, SDK generators, and a community forum for JSON-RPC best practices.

- **AsyncAPI** (https://www.asyncapi.com)
  Standard for defining and documenting event-driven, streaming interfaces
  (MQTT, WebSockets) alongside MCP.
- **CNCF Cloud Native Landscape**
  Catalog of service meshes (Envoy, Istio), observability stacks (Prometheus,
  Grafana), and deployment tools (Argo CD, Flux).
- **Stack Overflow ([json-rpc] tag)**
  Community Q&A for troubleshooting JSON-RPC and MCP integration
  challenges.
- **GitHub Topics:** mcp-protocol & open-rpc
  Discover open-source adapter projects, sample repos, and community
  contributions.

Use these resources to deepen your understanding of distributed systems, API design,
real-time processing, and AI/ML productionization—skills that will make your work
with MCP and context-aware AI systems even more effective.

Conclusion: Recap of Key Points

As we've journeyed through **Mastering MCP Servers**, several core themes have
emerged—each building on the last to form a comprehensive guide for designing,
deploying, and evolving context-aware AI systems.

1. **Fundamentals & Architecture** (Chapters 1–2)
   – We introduced the **Model Context Protocol** (MCP) as a JSON-RPC
   2.0-based standard for unifying tools and data sources behind a consistent
   interface.
   – You learned how to structure the **JSON-RPC envelope**, propagate a rich
   context object, and publish a discoverable **tool manifest**.
   – Practical setup steps—installing dependencies, configuring local servers, and
   spinning up your first MCP instance—prepared you to build real services.
2. **Building Context-Aware AI Workflows** (Chapters 3–4)
   – We explored how MCP enables **context enrichment**, **dynamic workflows**,
   and **real-time state management**, with deep dives into streaming adapters
   and batch calls.
   – Case studies (healthcare diagnosis, supply-chain automation) illustrated how
   adapters for databases, APIs, file systems, and IoT feeds slot into your pipelines,
   all while preserving traceability and auditability.
3. **Advanced Implementations & Troubleshooting** (Chapters 5–6)
   – You gained techniques for **custom tool development**, **rate-limiting**,

security hardening, and **performance tuning** (profiling, caching, batching).
– A structured troubleshooting guide and interactive Q&As armed you with diagnostics—from parsing JSON errors to debugging streaming disconnects—so you can resolve issues rapidly in production.

4. **Real-World Applications** (Chapter 7)
   – From **AI-powered decision-support** in finance and e-commerce to **smart-city orchestration**, you saw how MCP's modular adapters and context propagation deliver scalable, maintainable, and resilient systems.
   – Examples showed how to integrate with BPM platforms (Camunda, Airflow), serverless workflows (AWS Step Functions), and robotics pipelines, highlighting the protocol's versatility.

5. **Scaling, Deployment & Maintenance** (Chapters 8–9)
   – Best practices for **horizontal scaling**, **load balancing**, **containerization** (Docker, Kubernetes, cloud-native services), and **CI/CD** ensure zero-downtime rollouts and rapid iteration.
   – Regular maintenance tasks—security patching, backup validation, schema migrations—and robust observability (metrics, tracing, alerts) keep your MCP servers healthy and compliant.

6. **Future Trends & Community Engagement** (Chapter 10 & Appendices)
   – We peered into emerging directions: **edge-native MCP runtimes**, **LLM-driven workflow synthesis**, **federated privacy**, and **neuro-symbolic pipelines**—all pointing toward ever more adaptive, autonomous AI ecosystems.
   – Appendices offered quick references (JSON-RPC cheat sheet, troubleshooting), templates (GitHub starter kits), and resources for continuous learning and community contribution.

By applying the patterns and practices in this book, you'll be equipped to build **context-aware, extensible**, and **secure** AI systems—harnessing MCP as the integration backbone that lets models, tools, and data work in harmony. As you implement, iterate, and contribute back, you'll help drive the evolution of context-driven AI into its next exciting chapter.

Building and maintaining context-aware AI systems with MCP is ultimately about **modularity, observability**, and **resilience**. By clearly separating your business logic (the "what") from integration details (the "how"), MCP adapters make it easy to plug in new data sources, algorithms, or services without rewriting your core workflows.

Propagation of a rich, structured **context**—from user identity and session metadata to locale and trace IDs—ensures that every decision, inference, or tool call carries the information needed for personalized behavior, robust auditing, and seamless error handling. Instrumenting your MCP servers with metrics, traces, and health probes gives you the visibility to detect regressions early, tune performance continuously, and recover automatically from failures.

Security and reliability are non-negotiable: enforce strong auth/authz, validate all inputs against JSON Schema, encrypt data at rest and in transit, and bake in rate limits, circuit breakers, and rolling deployment strategies to keep your services safe and available. Regular maintenance—dependency patching, backup restores, capacity testing, and chaos drills—keeps your platform healthy as usage grows.

Finally, MCP thrives on community and evolution. Stay engaged with spec repositories, contribute adapters and templates, share case studies, and experiment with edge-native runtimes or LLM-driven orchestration. As context-aware AI moves from reactive assistants to proactive, adaptive partners, your mastery of MCP will be the foundation for truly intelligent, scalable, and future-proof systems.

Table of Contents

Introduction

Chapter 1: Fundamentals of MCP

- 1.3.1 Simplifying integrations with databases, file systems, and APIs

- 1.3.2 Use cases in AI systems and automation pipelines

- 1.3.3 MCP's role in creating a universal framework for tool integrations

- **1.4 Interactive Q&A**

  - 1.4.1 Review questions to test comprehension of MCP fundamentals

  - 1.4.2 Discussion points on how MCP can be applied to various industries

---

Chapter 2: Setting Up and Configuring MCP Servers

- **2.1 Preparing the Development Environment**

  - 2.1.1 Software requirements: Tools, frameworks, and dependencies

  - 2.1.2 Setting up your local environment for MCP development

  - 2.1.3 Configuring your first MCP server

- **2.2 Creating a Basic MCP Server**

  - 2.2.1 Step-by-step guide to building a simple MCP server

  - 2.2.2 Connecting your server to external data sources (e.g., APIs, databases)

  - 2.2.3 Testing and validating the server setup

- **2.3 Advanced MCP Server Configurations**

  - 2.3.1 Setting up multiple servers for scalability

  - 2.3.2 Load balancing and fault tolerance in MCP

  - 2.3.3 Optimizing server performance for large-scale applications

- **3.5 Interactive Q&A**

  - 3.5.1 How would you apply context in an AI-driven healthcare system?

  - 3.5.2 Discussion on real-time context updates in AI workflows

---

Chapter 4: Data Integration and External System Connectivity

- **4.1 Connecting to Databases and File Systems**

  - 4.1.1 How to configure MCP servers to access databases (SQL, NoSQL)

  - 4.1.2 Reading and writing to file systems using MCP

  - 4.1.3 Best practices for secure data handling

- **4.2 Integrating Web APIs and Services**

  - 4.2.1 Using MCP to connect AI systems to third-party APIs

  - 4.2.2 Examples: Integrating with RESTful APIs, GraphQL APIs, and WebSockets

  - 4.2.3 API authentication and security considerations

- **4.3 Extending MCP with Custom Data Sources**

  - 4.3.1 How to build custom tools for data integration

  - 4.3.2 Connecting to IoT devices, sensors, and other external data sources

  - 4.3.3 Case study: Building a real-time data pipeline using MCP

- **4.4 Interactive Q&A**

  - 4.4.1 How do you handle authentication in API integrations?

  - 4.4.2 Discussion points on data integration challenges

Chapter 5: Advanced MCP Server Implementations

- **5.1 Dynamic Capabilities and Custom Tool Development**

  - 5.1.1 Extending MCP functionality with custom tools

  - 5.1.2 Writing and registering new tools for integration

  - 5.1.3 Managing dynamic capabilities for flexible AI systems

- **5.2 Managing Streaming Data with MCP**

  - 5.2.1,Real-time data processing and stream handling

  - 5.2.2 MCP's role in handling event-driven architectures

  - 5.2.3 Best practices for managing streaming data in AI workflows

- **5.3 Security and Rate-Limiting in MCP Servers**

  - 5.3.1 Implementing rate-limiting to prevent abuse

  - 5.3.2 Authentication and authorization strategies for MCP

  - 5.3.3 Encrypting data transmission and securing sensitive data

- **5.4 Industry Case Study: Robotics**

  - 5.4.1 Using MCP to integrate real-time data from robots

  - 5.4.2 Context-aware systems in autonomous robots

- **5.5 Interactive Q&A**

  - 5.5.1 What security measures would you implement for a robotics application?

  - 5.5.2 Discussion on real-time data processing in autonomous systems

Chapter 6: Troubleshooting and Debugging MCP Servers

- **6.1 Common MCP Server Issues and Their Solutions**

  - 6.1.1 Connectivity problems and how to fix them

  - 6.1.2 Debugging server crashes and timeouts

  - 6.1.3 Handling inconsistent data and failed requests

- **6.2 Debugging JSON-RPC Requests and Responses**

  - 6.2.1 Step-by-step guide to debugging JSON-RPC calls

  - 6.2.2 Understanding error codes and handling exceptions

  - 6.2.3 Tools and techniques for efficient debugging

- **6.3 Optimizing Server Performance**

  - 6.3.1 Best practices for optimizing the MCP server performance

  - 6.3.2 Load testing and performance benchmarking

  - 6.3.3 Analyzing and improving server response times

- **6.4 Interactive Q&A**

  - 6.4.1 Common issues you've encountered when setting up MCP servers

  - 6.4.2 Discussion points on performance optimization strategies

Chapter 7: Real-World Applications of MCP Servers

- **7.1 AI-Assisted Decision-Making Systems**

- 7.1.1 How MCP enhances AI-based decision-making tools

- 7.1.2 Use cases in finance, healthcare, and e-commerce

- 7.1.3 Building a recommendation engine with MCP

- **7.2 Automating Business Workflows with MCP**

  - 7.2.1 Integrating MCP into business process automation tools

  - 7.2.2 Real-world example: Automating a supply chain management system

  - 7.2.3 How MCP helps businesses scale and automate tasks

- **7.3 Case Study: Smart City Systems**

  - 7.3.1 Design and implementation of an MCP-based smart city system

  - 7.3.2 Connecting IoT devices, data storage, and external APIs

  - 7.3.3 Lessons learned from real-world applications

- **7.4 Interactive Q&A**

  - 7.4.1 How would you automate workflows in your industry using MCP?

  - 7.4.2 Discussion on the challenges faced in smart city systems

---

Chapter 8: Scaling and Deploying MCP Servers

- **8.1 Horizontal Scaling for High Availability**

  - 8.1.1 Configuring MCP servers for high availability and fault tolerance

  - 8.1.2 Load balancing techniques for distributed systems

  - 8.1.3 Best practices for scaling out MCP servers

- **8.2 Containerization and Deployment with Docker**

  - 8.2.1 Dockerizing MCP servers for easier deployment

  - 8.2.2 Setting up Docker Compose for multi-container environments

  - 8.2.3 Deploying MCP servers on cloud platforms (AWS, GCP, Azure)

- **8.3 Continuous Integration and Deployment for MCP Servers**

  - 8.3.1 Setting up a CI/CD pipeline for MCP projects

  - 8.3.2 Automating testing and deployment processes

  - 8.3.3 Tools and services for automating MCP server deployment

- **8.4 Interactive Q&A**

  - 8.4.1 How would you implement CI/CD pipelines for your MCP server?

  - 8.4.2 Discussion on containerization and cloud deployment strategies

Chapter 9: Best Practices for Maintaining and Securing MCP Servers

- **9.1 Regular Maintenance and Monitoring**

  - 9.1.1 Setting up monitoring for MCP servers

  - 8.1.2 Automated health checks and failure detection

  - 9.1.3 Scheduled maintenance for smooth operation

- **9.2 Security Best Practices**

  - 9.2.1 Securing MCP servers against common threats

  - 9.2.2 Protecting sensitive data and user privacy

Appendices

- A.6.1 Recommended books, courses, and online resources for expanding knowledge

Conclusion

- Recap of key points

- Final thoughts on building and maintaining context-aware AI systems with MCP